Cambridge Studies in Oral and Literate Culture 8

LET YOUR WORDS BE FEW

Cambridge Studies in Oral and Literate Culture

Edited by PETER BURKE and RUTH FINNEGAN

This series is designed to address the question of the significance of literacy in human societies; it will assess its importance for political, economic, social, and cultural development and will examine how what we take to be the common functions of writing are carried out in oral cultures.

The series will be interdisciplinary, but with particular emphasis on social anthropology and social history, and will encourage cross-fertilization between these disciplines; it will also be of interest to readers in allied fields, such as sociology, folklore, and literature. Although it will include some monographs, the focus of the series will be on theoretical and comparative aspects rather than detailed description, and the books will be presented in a form accessible to nonspecialist readers interested in the general subject of literacy and orality.

Books in the series

LET YOUR WORDS BE FEW
Symbolism of
Speaking and Silence among
Seventeenth-Century Quakers

RICHARD BAUMAN

University of Texas at Austin

CAMBRIDGE UNIVERSITY PRESS

CAMBRIDGE

LONDON   NEW YORK   NEW ROCHELLE

MELBOURNE   SYDNEY

Published by the Press Syndicate of the University of Cambridge
The Pitt Building, Trumpington Street, Cambridge CB2 1RP
32 East 57th Street, New York, NY 10022, USA
296 Beaconsfield Parade, Middle Park, Melbourne 3206, Australia

First published 1983

Printed in the United States of America

Library of Congress Cataloging in Publication Data
Bauman, Richard.
Let your words be few.
(Cambridge studies in oral and literate culture; 8)
Includes bibliographical references and index.
1. Languages – Religious aspects – Society of Friends.
2. Pastoral theology – Society of Friends. 3. Society of
Friends – Doctrinal and controversial works. I. Title.
II. Series.
BX7748.L3B38   1983   289.6   83–1982
ISBN 0 521 25506 6 hard covers
ISBN 0 521 27514 8 paperback

CONTENTS

ACKNOWLEDGMENTS

During the long course of my work on the language of the early Quakers, I have benefited from the aid and support of several institutions and many individuals, and I am pleased to have this opportunity to offer them my thanks. For the financial support of my research and writing I am grateful to the American Philosophical Society for a research grant (1972), to the National Endowment for the Humanities for a fellowship for Independent Study and Research (1978–9), and to the University Research Institute of the University of Texas for a Faculty Research Grant (1978–9). And once again, I would like to acknowledge the unfailing courtesy and willing cooperation over the years of the staff of the Quaker Collection, Haverford College Library, with special thanks to the curator, Professor Edwin Bronner, and to Barbara Curtis and Milton Ream. Thanks also to the staff of Friends House, London, for assistance during my visit there in June 1974.

John Szwed and Erving Goffman offered valuable comments on earlier papers of mine that have been incorporated into this book, and Michael Graves has greatly stimulated my thinking about Quaker sermons in the course of our recent discussions. Several people – Peter Burke, Dell Hymes, Hugh Ormsby-Lennon, and Joel Sherzer – did me the great service of reading and commenting on earlier drafts of the book, for which I owe them all a special debt of gratitude. The comments of Hugh Ormsby-Lennon were especially extensive and provocative, and I consider myself fortunate to have had the benefit of his penetrating understanding of language in seventeenth-century England. To Dell Hymes, my debt began far earlier and extends much deeper. He is the one who first kindled my interest in the ethnography of speaking and schooled me in its principles; my earliest ventures into Quaker socio-linguistics were launched under his direction, and the inspiration of his scholarship has guided most of my work ever since. Likewise, I owe Joel Sherzer far more than thanks for reading my manuscript; in the idiom of the early Quakers we have been yokemates in plowing and cultivating the field of the ethnography of speaking for more than a decade now, and I have learned much from him.

No one has contributed more to the realization of this book than Frances Terry, through her skillful and meticulous work in the preparation and typing of several versions of the manuscript. Once again, I offer her my heartfelt thanks.

Finally, and above all, my thanks to my wife and colleague, Beverly Stoeltje, for the stimulating discussions of ideas and the strong moral support she has offered me over the years, contributing some much-needed color to temper the Quaker gray.

1

INTRODUCTION: THEY SAY NONE SPEAK LIKE US

Through the efforts of literary critics and historians of religion, science, and linguistics, the seventeenth century in England is coming to be understood as a period of extraordinary intellectual preoccupation with language, marked by a complex array of attempts to reconceptualize, reform, and reconstitute language as an instrument in the service of the mind, the spirit, and the social order. Most scholarly efforts to comprehend the seventeenth-century fascination with language center on the twin influences of religion and science as the sources of the intellectual energy devoted to linguistic speculation. Notwithstanding our modern tendency to view religion and science as fundamentally at odds, within the intellectual context of seventeenth-century England religious and scientific truth were closely related spheres of interest, complementary "forms of the will to truth" (Foucault 1972:218) founded on new conceptions of the order of the universe and the ways in which that order might be apprehended and comprehended by mankind.

What is remarkable about the mid-seventeenth century, however, is just how numerous and diverse those conceptions of order were, giving rise to a "Babelish confusion" of contending voices (Ormsby-Lennon 1977:305) in which disorder, rather than order, seemed to rule the day. Indeed, as Hugh Ormsby-Lennon has observed (personal communication), "the Tower of Babel is the key linguistic metaphor of the period," both for those who wished to regain or construct a substitute for the pure Adamic language lost on the plain of Shinar and for those who deplored the apparent worsening of the confusion of languages in their own day, paradoxically brought about by the proliferation of schemes to repair the ruin of Babel.

Seventeenth-century science and religion came in many guises – mystical and rational, radical and respectable – and programs for language reform varied accordingly. Mainstream Puritan religion, in the Calvinist tradition, drew strong direction from Paul's epistles; with regard to communicative ideology and practice in particular, the first Epistle to the Corinthians was a major source of guidance (Fisch 1952:232):

> And I, brethren, when I came unto you, came not with excellency
> of speech or of wisdom, declaring unto you the testimony of God
> . . . And my speech and my preaching was not enticing words or
> man's wisdom, but in demonstration of the Spirit and of power that

1

your faith should not stand in the wisdom of man, but in the Power of God. (1 Corinthians 2.1, 4–5)

Consistent with its denial of the traditional legitimacy of priestly religion and the worldly wisdom of the "natural man," the Puritan movement adopted a self-denying, unadorned communicative style, aptly called the "plain" style. Puritan language reform was also founded on a profound suspicion of Latin and the ornate latinate rhetoric of the Renaissance (Jones 1953:312–315). Latin was, after all, the language of Roman Catholicism – "the language of the beast" – and a cornerstone of the traditional authority of the priests. The reliance of the established clergy on "the wisdom of man" as a key to the understanding of religious truth and their appeal to the esthetic pleasure of the natural man in their artfully crafted sermons were both anathema to the Puritans. In the Puritan view, human capacities were by their very nature insufficient to grasp the infinite being of God (Clark 1978:78), and it was spiritual degeneracy of the worst kind to allow fleshly style or corrupt language to obscure the truth of God's Word still further.

For their part, the learned proponents of the new science faced a related problem. The universe they sought to understand was God's creation, his expression – his Word – and natural languages were inadequate to render it intelligible or to explain it. Latin, the language of the old science, as well as all other natural languages were riddled with defects that tended to obscure the reality of creation rather than to make it more accessible to human understanding. These defects lay in the imprecise meaning of words, the ambiguities of polysemy and figurative language, the superfluity of synonyms, and the proliferation, irregularity, and inconsistency of grammatical rules (Jones 1951:156). Frustrated by these linguistic obstacles to clear scientific expression and communication across languages, the scientists of the Royal Society and their brethren, like the Puritan theologians, pursued an ideal of semiotic simplicity in which language might be reduced to its purest referential terms. The often-quoted passage from Sprat's *History of the Royal Society* (1667, quoted in Clark 1978:65) expresses well the communicative strategies and goals of the new scientific movement: simplicity, economy, and plainness. Their impulse was

> to reject all the amplifications, digressions, and swellings of style, to return back to the primitive purity and shortness when men delivered so many things almost in an equal number of words. They have exacted from all their members a close, naked, natural way of speaking, positive expressions, clear senses, a native easiness, bringing all things as near the mathematical plainness as they can, and preferring the language of artisans, countrymen, and merchants before that of wits or scholars.

Although the linguistic reforms of the new scientists of the Royal Society tended for the most part to be guided by rational principles, there were many parallel efforts, similarly motivated, that were heavily mystical and occult. These were attempts to unlock through language the secret of creation in the service of healing, alchemy, astrology, magic, or other arcane pursuits. Most commonly, the quest was framed as an attempt to regain an Adamic language, lost after Babel (or after the Fall), in which the names assigned to natural things by Adam were at least in some way representative of the true essence of those things (Fraser 1977; Knowlson 1975:12). If such a language could be recovered – the "originating experience" of true discourse regained (Foucault 1972:228) – it "would not only be a means of acquiring knowledge; it would itself *be* knowledge, since each 'word' would provide an accurate description of the things signified" (Knowlson 1975:8, italics in the original). The methods employed in these pursuits, however, by contrast with the rational efforts of the proponents of the new science, were in the mystical tradition of the hermetic philosophers and Jacob Boehme, informed by cabalistic, Rosicrucian doctrines, and resorting to wildly speculative cryptological, numerological, etymological, and allegorical attempts to reconstruct the language of Adam (Aarsleff 1976; Ormsby-Lennon 1977).

Like the new science, this mystical science and its linguistic speculations had close ties to religious thought – not to mainstream Puritanism, but to the more radical sects and religious movements spawned by the religious turbulence of the period. To cite only a single example, but the one most relevant to this book on the early Quakers (for others, see Hill 1975; Ormsby-Lennon 1977), we may consider the following vivid spiritual experience undergone by George Fox in 1648, before a recognizable Quaker movement took shape around him:

> Now was I come up in spirit through the flaming sword into the paradise of God. All things were new, and all the creation gave another smell unto me than before, beyond what words can utter. I knew nothing but pureness, and innocency, and righteousness, being renewed up into the image of God by Christ Jesus, so that I say I was come up to the state of Adam which he was in before he fell. The creation was opened to me, and it was showed me how all things had their names given them according to their nature and virtue. And I was at a stand in my mind whether I should practise physic for the good of mankind, seeing the nature and virtues of the creatures were so opened to me by the Lord . . . And the Lord showed me that such as were faithful to him in the power and light of Christ, should come up into that state in which Adam was before he fell, in which the admirable works of the creation, and the virtues thereof, may be known, through the openings of that divine Word of wisdom and

power by which they were made . . . Thus travelled I on in the
Lord's service, as the Lord led me. (Fox 1952:27–28)

Here, in terms very reminiscent of Jacob Boehme's experience of having
"the nature and virtues of things opened" to him in the year 1600 (Aarsleff
1970:223; Jones 1971[1914]:222), Fox expresses his joy at attaining the Adamic insight of "how all things had their names given them according to their
nature and virtue," at decoding, in effect, the Adamic language. We should
note especially, in the light of Fox's lifelong religious mission, that this
spiritual breakthrough led him for a time to consider the practice of physic
before he decided, once more, to continue on in the Lord's service.

We have no clear evidence that Fox drew his ideas directly from Boehme;
his own insistence on personal revelation and validation of spiritual truth
predisposed him against any acknowledgment of a spiritual or intellectual
debt to any authority. But several scholars have pointed out significant connections and correspondences between Quaker doctrine and the ideas of
Boehme, hermetic philosophy, and other occult lines of religioscientific thought
(Aarsleff 1970:223; Barbour 1964:193; Braithwaite 1955:40–42; Hill 1975:176,
290, 373; Jones 1971[1914]:220–227; Nuttall 1947; Ormsby-Lennon
1977:306). The connections are fascinating and complex, deserving fuller
exploration than they have hitherto received. More relevant to my present
purpose, however, is the fact that this preoccupation with language, whatever
its antecedents, was extended throughout the linguistic and sociolinguistic
usages of the Quakers, making for a distinctive, symbolically resonant Quaker
communicative style. Nor were the Quakers alone in this regard, I should
add, for the proliferation of sectarian speech styles was a prominent component
of the Babelistic confusion of tongues that gave revolutionary England its
characteristic din.

For all the historical importance of this semiotic explosion, and notwithstanding the scholarly attention it has begun to receive, I would suggest that
there is a critical dimension missing from current explorations of the seventeenth-century preoccupation with language insofar as they tend to focus
overwhelmingly upon the elucidation of *ideas* about language, not upon its
social use. The question is this: How was all the intellectual and spiritual
concern with language reform that we have observed paralleled by changes
in the ways ordinary people actually *used* language to communicate with each
other in the conduct of social life? To frame the question in more general
terms: What was the relationship between language as theorized about and
language as used, between linguistic ideology and linguistic practice? The
theological and scientific currents that gave direction to seventeenth-century
speculations about language were themselves impelled by sweeping changes
in the structure of society at large: political revolution, the shaping of modern
capitalism, the concomitant rise of new economic classes, the toleration of

religious dissent. We want to know whether the resultant new ways of dealing with political authority, doing business, negotiating social hierarchy, or conducting religious worship demanded new ways of using language in social life. To answer such questions calls for attention not only to ideas about language, but to *functions* of language, to the role of language as structured by and giving structure to ideology, social relations, groups, and institutions. This is not only language as thought about, but language as *used* by society at large to enact or negotiate social identities and to accomplish social goals.

The perspective I am advocating here is that of the ethnography of speaking; indeed, the present work continues an exploration in the ethnography of speaking in which I have been engaged for more than a decade (Bauman 1970, 1972a,b, 1974a,b). The ethnography of speaking is a branch of linguistic anthropology rooted in the traditional anthropological concern with the interrelationships among language, culture, and society (Bauman and Sherzer 1974, 1975; Hymes 1962, 1974a,b). Its focus, however, is upon aspects of interrelationships that are missing from both grammars and ethnographies taken separately or analytically combined. Grammars deal essentially with the structure of languages as abstract, self-contained codes; ethnographies, with the patterns and structures of sociocultural life. Although there is much to be learned through correlation or conflation of these differentially focused products of linguistic and anthropological inquiry, the ethnography of speaking centers its attention upon a new order of information; its subject matter is *speaking*, the situated *use* of language in the conduct of social life. By focusing on speaking as a cultural system (or as part of cultural systems organized in other terms), the ethnography of speaking seeks to elucidate the interrelationships among language, culture, and society at their source, in the culturally patterned use of language as an element and instrument of social life.

The orientation of the ethnography of speaking requires, among other things, a new way of conceiving of language: not, once again, as an abstract communicative code seen as a collective representation (as *langue* in Saussurean terms), but rather as a complex set of communicative resources available to members of particular speech communities for the communication of social and expressive as well as referential meaning. We are interested not simply in grammar in the traditional sense, but in "means of speech" (Hymes 1974b), which may include linguistic variables (speech styles associated with particular social groups or categories), registers (speech styles associated with particular social contexts), genres, and the like. These means of speech are organized into systems of social use and cultural meaning, what might be called the "speech economy" of a community (Hymes 1974b). The ethnographer of speaking would want to explore such factors as the situated, contextualized use and exploitation of the means of speech in discourse and in social interaction; the patterned interrelationships and organization of these various types of discourse and social interaction in the community; the complex of attitudes, values, and beliefs current in the community concerning the means of speech and their use; and the relationships of these patterns of speaking to other aspects and domains of the culture – social organization, religion, economics, politics, ideology, and so forth (Sherzer 1977:44–45).

The comprehensive presentation of the rationale and program of the ethnography of speaking is beyond the scope of this introduction; for a fuller understanding of the goals and methods of the ethnography of speaking, the reader may wish to turn to the works just cited. My immediate purpose is to suggest the productiveness of exploring language in seventeenth-century England from the perspective the ethnography of speaking provides. From the vantage point of the ethnography of speaking, seventeenth-century England appears not only as a fit subject for the study of the intellectual history of ideas about language but as an especially promising historical and sociolinguistic laboratory in which to examine the dynamics of language in society, the "external conditions of existence" of social discourse (Foucault 1972:229), in a cultural milieu marked by an extraordinarily high degree of self-conscious concern with the spoken word. To undertake such an investigation for all of seventeenth-century England, however, would be at this stage a task of unmanageable scope. I have chosen, therefore, to concentrate my attention in this work on one segment of seventeenth-century English society: the religious society of Quakers, who first emerged as a charismatic movement in the early 1650s. I do so not because I wish to claim that the Quakers were representative or typical; much of what I will discuss in the chapters to follow was in some way or other unique to Quaker doctrine and practice. But I have introduced my study of Quaker language in these more general terms because I am convinced of the general productiveness of a speaking-centered investigation of seventeenth-century English society and culture. Quaker belief and practice were part of a spectrum of configurations in regard to the patterning of spoken communication in English society at large. An analytical perspective that illuminates their ways of speaking penetrates to the very center of their social and cultural life, and I would maintain that like investigations of other sectors of the complex society of which they were a part would be equally revealing.

*   *   *   *

The middle decades of the seventeenth century witnessed the most intense religious ferment of any period in modern English history. During the decade of the Commonwealth especially, ushered in by the revolutionary act of regicide in 1649, there was a great burgeoning of religious excitement energized by the prevailing spirit of radical puritanism and encouraged by the relative openness of the Cromwellian regime to new definitions of religious experience. Few of the sects and movements that were active during that heady period have survived to the present day, to the point that only specialists now recall such groups as the Diggers, Ranters, Muggletonians, Grindletonians, or Fifth Monarchy Men. One of those charismatic movements that did survive was Quakerism,[1] which had its birth during the early years of the Commonwealth.

The dominant Quaker figure of the seventeenth century and perhaps of all time was George Fox (1624–1691), a leader of great charismatic power and influence. Some authorities have credited the emergence of the Quaker movement to his vision and energy. Other scholars have qualified this assessment by tracing the spiritual antecedents of Quakerism in earlier phases of the Reformation, noting the affinities between the Quakers and other contemporary sects, such as the Seekers, Baptists, or Familists, or identifying other Quaker leaders, such as James Nayler, Richard Farnsworth, Edward Burrough, and William Dewsbury (some of whom apparently arrived at a faith much like Quakerism independent of Fox's teachings), who exercised a degree of influence in the early years that approached Fox's own. In any event, an identifiable Quaker movement appears to have coalesced around Fox on his epoch-making journey to carry his faith to Yorkshire and Westmoreland in the north of England, beginning late in the year 1651. By the summer of 1654, when the "Valiant Sixty" (Vipont 1975) moved out on their first great ministerial mission from the north to spread the Truth to the rest of England, the Quaker movement had gained sufficient strength and clarity of purpose to have a significant impact upon the religious life of the country.

This is not the place to recapitulate the history of the seventeenth-century Quakers or to present a comprehensive exposition of their belief and practice. Those tasks have been carried out with great thoroughness by others.[2] Rather, I intend this work as an exploration of one vital central element of Quakerism during the first formative decades of its existence: the role of speaking and silence in Quaker ideology and action.

From the very beginning, Quaker ways of speaking were among the most visible and distinctive aspects of Quakerism, an identifying feature of the Quaker movement. The early Quakers themselves used speaking as a symbolic classifier, distinguishing themselves from all others as speakers of the "pure" or the "plain" language, thereby identifying themselves as the remnant of Israel singled out by the Lord as the people of the "pure language," as foretold by the prophet Zephaniah (Fox 1657:6–7; Payne 1655:17; Zephaniah 3.9–13). Richard Farnsworth, for example, wrote in 1653:

---

[1] Seventeenth-century Quakers preferred the label "Friends" for their fellowship, "Quaker" being a term applied to them in derision. Time has removed the negative connotation from "Quaker," and it has become the most common appellation. I have employed "Friends" and "Quakers" interchangeably in this work. On the origins of the term "Quaker," see Braithwaite 1955:57–58, 131–132, 550.

[2] I have relied most heavily in my research on Barbour 1964; Barbour and Roberts 1973; Braithwaite 1955, 1961; Carroll 1971, 1978; Lloyd 1950; Reay 1980a,b,c; Vann 1969.

> The people in this generation profess themselves to be the people of God, and the scriptures to be their rule . . . but are as the heathen, all their language is corrupt, and if any speak to them in plainness of speech, they are so scornful, that they cannot bear it . . . those that speak in plainness of speech, them they hate. (1653:29)

Non-Quakers too saw Quaker speech as especially distinctive; as Francis Howgill noted in 1654, "they say none speak like us" (Barclay 1841:19).

Well into the 1670s, non-Quakers singled out the Quakers' distinctive speech for notice and censure, rightly identifying it as central to Quakerism, if misapprehending its essential foundation. One anti-Quaker pamphleteer charged in 1672, "his religion is, not to speak like his neighbours" (R. H. 1672a:2), adding later, "his religion is nothing but phrases, being a superstitious observer of new minted modes of speaking" (1672b:3). Another writer, criticizing the Quakers for "laying so much stress of religion upon words and phrases," extended his censure to "the affected use of their distinguishing phrases, tones and gestures" (Fowler 1678:69; see also Faldo 1673:61). Clearly, speaking was viewed as central to Quakerism by Quakers and non-Quakers alike.

As important as it was during those formative years and thereafter, Quaker speech could not fail to attract the attention of scholars from a range of disciplines. Historians of Quakerism have outlined the special speech testimonies of Friends with varying degrees of thoroughness (Harvey 1923, 1928; Walker 1952); students of language have examined their distinctive pronominal usage and other aspects of the plain language and worship (Brown and Gilman 1960; Darnell 1970, 1972b; Estrich and Sperber 1952; Finkenstaedt 1963; Irvine 1979a); and rhetoricians have carried out studies of Quaker rhetorical forms and expressions (Cope 1956; Creasey 1962; Graves 1972). This research notwithstanding, there has been no fully integrated study of the role of speaking and silence in the early development of Quakerism, and we do not have a comprehensive understanding of the patterns, functions, and processes involved. That is what I have undertaken in the pages that follow.

William C. Braithwaite, in his monumental history of the early Quakers, suggests somewhat defensively that

> the witness of Friends on points of speech . . . touched some of the greatest issues of life, and is not to be treated as an excrescence on their main message. We ought rather to feel that the main message, under the conditions of that age, could not have been uttered in its purity and force if Friends had shrunk from giving it fearless application to these parts of life. (1955:495)

Sensing that speech was of more than peripheral importance, Braithwaite could nevertheless go no further than to assign it a supporting role, a kind of objective correlative to "the main message," and so it has continued to be treated, even as Quaker historiography has moved from the detailed documentation of the external history of Friends to the careful social history of more recent scholarship, tracing the social origins of Quakerism, the development of organizational structures within the emergent Society of Friends, and the place of Quakerism within the larger social milieu of the seventeenth century. What I hope to demonstrate in this work, going beyond the efforts of my predecessors, is the true centrality of speaking and its associated principle of silence to seventeenth-century Quakerism, to show that rather than merely supporting the main message they jointly represented one of its major foci, providing a symbolic vocabulary for conceptualizing that message and an instrument for carrying it into action in ways that were in no small part determinative of the course of Quaker development in the formative period of Quaker history.

It may be well to emphasize again here that my frame of reference is ethnographic, rooted in the anthropological tradition of close analysis of cultural systems in particular societies. From this perspective, what matters most is how cultural forms – in this case relating to speaking and silence – fit together and shape the social life of a particular group at a particular time or in a particular period, not so much the sources or analogs of those forms in earlier periods or in other groups, which might be of more importance to historians. I know very well that some of the Quaker beliefs and usages I treat in these pages may have stemmed from earlier experience among or familiarity with the practices of other groups, including Seekers, Familists, Anabaptists, Independents, and Diggers, and that others were shared by sects that were active opponents of Quakerism, including Ranters, Baptists, and Muggletonians.[3] From an ethnographic point of view, however, knowledge of these possible relationships adds little to our understanding of the patterns and functions of speaking and silence among the Quakers themselves, for it was a fundamental tenet of Quakerism that their belief and practice should be inspired and validated by direct revelation from God speaking within. Thus, the early Friends had a built-in unwillingness – if not a doctrinally based incapacity – to acknowledge a cultural debt to other contemporary religious groups or traditional precedents. Where such connections did make a difference to the Quakers and influenced their dealings with others, I will take account of them in my discussion.

---

[3] Useful summaries of possible sources and analogs of Quaker beliefs and practices treated in the chapters to follow may be found in Braithwaite 1955, Chap. 1; Nuttall 1967:171, and Watts 1978:185–193. Ormsby-Lennon's (1977) sociolinguistically informed study of the connections between sixteenth- and seventeenth-century English speech communities and styles and literature contains a wealth of information on religiously based ways of speaking with parallels among the Quakers. A sampling of other relevant references might include Brailsford 1961:46; Cohn 1957:354; Descamps 1972:104; Hayes 1979:143; and Williams 1962:789.

The seventeenth-century Quakers are of special interest to the ethnography of speaking on several grounds. As already noted, distinctive ways of speaking were among the principal factors that established the social identity of the Quakers within the complex society of mid-seventeenth-century England. Not surprisingly, then, speaking represented a cultural focus for the early Quakers, an "area of activity or belief where the greatest awareness of form exists, the most discussion of values is heard, the widest difference in structure is to be discerned" (Herskovits 1963:485). Societies such as the Quakers, in which speaking is the subject of a high degree of interest and evaluation, tend, for understandable reasons, to dominate the literature of the ethnography of speaking. The Quaker case is of special comparative interest, however, for unlike most of the other societies that have been studied from this perspective, in which speaking is positively regarded and highly valued, the Quakers viewed speaking in essentially negative terms and disvalued it. Insofar as one of the larger goals of the ethnography of speaking is the construction of typologies of the role of speaking in culture and society, of the way in which people come to give different meanings to their means of speech (Darnell 1972a), an examination of this contrastive case should be a valuable addition to the literature.

The concept of cultural focus is useful as a means of identifying certain central organizing principles within a culture and providing a focus for ethnographic description. If we consider that a cultural focus is a cultural domain in which meanings, forms, and values are especially heavily elaborated, we may expect to find in such spheres some of the richest and most powerful symbols of a given culture. As the chapters to follow will demonstrate, speaking and silence were indeed key symbols for the seventeenth-century Quakers in all the senses outlined by Sherry Ortner (1973:1339). I would stress that I am not referring here simply to the nature of language as a symbolic code, but to the status of speaking and silence themselves as elaborating symbols, which "extensively and systematically formulate relationships . . . between a wide range of diverse cultural elements" (Ortner 1973:1343). This work, then, is also intended as a contribution to the anthropological study of cultural symbols from the perspective Victor Turner (1975) has labeled "processual symbology" and that he has correctly identified as resonant with the ethnography of speaking in its concern with the social use of symbols in the conduct of social life. Consistent with the program outlined by Turner, the chapters that follow trace the symbols of speaking and silence as they operate in isolable, changing fields of social actions, relationships, and meanings (Turner 1975:145).

The explication of the symbolic meanings of silence among the Quakers should be of particular interest within the context of the growing interest among sociolinguists and linguistic anthropologists in silence as a communicative phenomenon (e.g., Basso 1970; Sacks, Schegloff, and Jefferson

1974:715; Samarin 1965; Tedlock 1972:127). The logocentrism of our culture in general and of the linguistic disciplines in particular fosters a tendency to view silence as merely an abstention from speaking or as an empty interval between utterances, but the Quaker case not only helps to suggest how richly textured and multidimensional the kinds of meanings of silence can be, but also underscores the need to examine the patterns, functions, and meanings of silence, like speaking, in ethnographic, culture-specific terms.

The ethnography of speaking, like all ethnography, is founded in an anthropological tradition of fieldwork, but need not be confined exclusively to field-based research in small-scale societies. The essence of the ethnographic perspective, I would maintain, lies in the premise that sociocultural patterns and processes are *to be discovered* through the systematic examination and analysis of empirical data. Indeed, the extension of the ethnography of speaking to historical cases and complex societies, as in this study of the seventeenth-century Quakers, offers the significant advantage of allowing the investigation of large-scale processes of development and change over extended spans of time that cannot be encompassed by field ethnography. Moreover, the diversity and abundance of the documentary record bearing on speaking and silence among the seventeenth-century Quakers make it possible to comprehend the role of these symbolic and communicative phenomena within the context of certain larger, more general processes bearing on the historical sociology of religion. From its inception, the ethnography of speaking has found language in religious practice to be an especially fruitful focus of attention (see, e.g., Samarin 1976). My study is intended, in part, to demonstrate the productiveness of this research for the elucidation of basic problems in the sociology of religion more broadly conceived.

With the advantages of a reliance upon documentary historical sources, however, come certain disadvantages that should be made explicit. The first and most obvious is that my investigation has had to be limited to those aspects of speaking and silence that the Quakers and other contemporary observers chose to put on record, either by addressing them directly or by recording evidence from which it was possible to reconstruct a pattern. Inevitably, there are gaps in the record – elements that were out of consciousness, or not considered worthy of record, or left deliberately unrecorded for ideological reasons. Notably lacking for the seventeenth-century Quakers, for example, are the *texts* of prayers, sermons, and other religious utterances. Quaker religious speaking was all spontaneous, for reasons discussed later in the work, and there were also principled reasons for not taking down these utterances in writing. Accordingly, I can only envy my colleagues who can go out and record such texts with relative ease. Nevertheless, I hope to show that the richness of the record in other respects compensates for the ways in which this work cannot claim to be a fully comprehensive ethnography of speaking.

A second way in which the record may appear to be skewed is in terms of what might be called informant competence. The Quaker authors of the doctrinal, polemical, and personal documents on which this study is based were in many cases cultural specialists, more sophisticated and articulate concerning matters of doctrine and ideology than the mass of their co-religionists. Ethnographers commonly rely upon cultural specialists, however, and as long as it is understood that not all Quakers – certainly not all the authors of the works I have used – attained this high level of cultural understanding concerning the doctrinal basis of their faith and practice, there should be no special problem. As regards the level of action, the documentary record is so filled with mutually consistent accounts of experiences and events, thanks to the remarkable Quaker penchant for documenting their activities for posterity, that one can rely upon the representativeness of the data with some degree of confidence.

I have situated my study thus far within the context of the ethnography of speaking because that is the primary frame of reference from which I have undertaken it. The bulk of the analysis in the chapters to follow is developed in terms drawn from, and intended initially as a contribution to, that subfield of linguistic anthropology. Because this is, however, a study of a historical case, I anticipate that it may be of some interest to historians as well, especially social historians, concerned, as I am, with the experiential world of past eras. Consequently, it may be appropriate to say something about the potential relevance of this work to related efforts on the part of social historians.

Although it would be unwarranted, especially for an outsider, to characterize the current state of social history – like mid-seventeenth-century England – as a Babelish confusion, there are certainly many contending voices now being heard among social historians proclaiming the demise of old orthodoxies and seeking new keys to truth (e.g., Fox-Genovese and Genovese 1976; Judt 1979; Stone 1979). And like many seekers after truth in that earlier period, the historians are turning in increasing numbers to language as a means of gaining access to new understandings.

Though rooted in part in earlier ideas (e.g., Febvre 1973:10), the current appeal to language is still largely in a programmatic phase, seeking language-centered analytical perspectives developed in other disciplines that may prove productive in the attempts of social historians to gain access to the experiential world of the common people of bygone eras. At this early stage, one may distinguish two principal lines of inquiry in language-centered social history, one focusing on language as a cognitive element in the making of thought, the other on language as a behavioral constituent of social action (History Workshop 1980).

The first of these, more widely pursued than the second, comprehends a variety of concerns, though closely related, arising out of a desire to give fuller dimension to the social patterns and structures discovered through the largely quantitative methods of the "new social history" and the configurations of great ideas discovered in the "paper chase" (Stone 1979:14) of conventional intellectual history. The new goal is to reconstruct the frameworks of thought, perception, and meaning by which ordinary people comprehended their world and the ideologies that guided their actions. Whether framed in relatively neutral terms such as "mental landscape," "mental universe," or "categories of thought" (Samuel 1980:172; Sewell 1980:10; History Workshop 1980:2), or in more Marxist-oriented terms such as "consciousness" and "ideology" (History Workshop 1980:2; Sewell 1980), the focus of such investigations is essentially cognitive, "trying to discover what was going on inside people's heads in the past" (Stone 1979:13). Like the language-based "new ethnography" of the mid to late 1960s (see Tyler 1969), though far less methodologically sophisticated, this approach seeks to uncover cognitive categories through the words that label them.

Bouwsma identifies the concern in these terms: "Through language man orders the chaos of data impinging on his sensorium from . . . 'out there,' organizing them into categories and so making them intelligible for himself, manageable, communicable, and therefore socially useful as well as essential to his private adaptation to the world" (1981:289). For guidance in such investigations, Bouwsma appeals to linguistics, though such trust is sadly misplaced, as that discipline has aggressively eschewed precisely those dimensions of experience of central concern to him, with little – in most quarters no – concern for language either as an index of culturally variable cognitive categories or as an instrument of social life.

Still, Bouwsma's suggestions are preliminary, brief, and programmatic. If we turn to an actual attempt to implement this approach in a substantive study, we may get a better sense of what kind of work is being produced in this developing line of social history. William H. Sewell, in his *Work and Revolution in France: The Language of Labor from the Old Regime to 1848*, places himself among those who have realized that although the largely quantitative and closely focused investigations of the new social history "have succeeded in making much firmer and more complex connections between political or ideological events and social and economic processes . . . it is by no means clear that they have adequately explained – or even adequately grasped – the ideological transformations that these events embodied and brought about" (1980:7). In his study of nineteenth-century French workers and the Revolution of 1848, Sewell was puzzled by the "seemingly paradoxical flowering of the old regime's language in the midst of a radical revolution" (1980:2). Ultimately, the study of the corporate idiom in question – the currency and use of such terms as *société, association, état, corps d'état, fraternité* – and their changing referents became a centerpiece of his investigation as a key to "the mental or ideational aspects of working class social experience" (1980:8).

With a gesture in the direction of the hermeneutic anthropology of Clifford Geertz, Sewell hopes to understand French workers by searching out "the symbolic forms [not confined to verbal language] through which they experienced their world. In part this means reconstructing the meaning of words, metaphors, and rhetorical conventions that they used to talk about and think about their experience" (1980:11). Methodologically, though, with regard to language, his approach is a mixture of old-fashioned historical semantics – the "history of particularly meaningful words" as a means of "writing precise chapters on the history of ideas" suggested by Febvre (1973:10) – and a kind of ad hoc semiotics, probing the shifting relationships between signifier and signified in key linguistic signs.

How much of an advance Sewell's study represents in our understanding of French workers must be left to historians to evaluate. By anthropological standards, however, his approach must be judged as rather primitive. Although the terms he investigates are indisputably socially significant, naming as they do principles or forms of corporate association, he does not subject them to rigorous structural semantic analysis as a part of a unified semantic domain, but rather deals with them as a loose aggregate of individual, though related, terms. He gives us a list of key words and their changing meanings, postulates a connection between these terms and "mental or ideational aspects of working class social experience," and devotes the bulk of his effort to delineating the social structures labeled at various times by the words in question. This does not begin to exploit the full potential of a language-centered social history. And though Sewell professes interest in the symbolic forms by which workers "talk about . . . their experiences," the talk is never more than implicit; nowhere in his work do we see or hear workers' actual talk.

Far better in that regard is the second of our two emergent approaches, which is more closely attuned, at least potentially, to language as a form of behavior, an instrument for the conduct of social life. The chief proponent of this second line of inquiry is Peter Burke, who has turned for guidance not to linguistics per se but more appropriately to sociolinguistics. Burke's interest in sociolinguistics stems from his desire to identify a productive and systematic framework for establishing at a more rigorous level than simply "reflection" the "links between art and ideas and society," primarily in early modern Italy. To this end, Burke has suggested in a brief programmatic statement (1979) a focus on communication, viewing works of art as forms of communication, products of communicative events, and extending his purview outward to encompass entire cultural systems of communication.

The framing questions Burke puts forward, drawn from sociolinguistics, are: "Who says what to whom, for what purposes, in what situations, through what channels, and in what codes?" "How were the messages interpreted by their recipients?" The important historical question is: "How did channels, codes, situations, and so on change during different periods of time?" (1979:36).

These questions direct Burke's attention primarily to communicative genres, roles, repertoires, and functions, as well as to norms of interpretation – "collective mentalities" – which link his concerns to those of his colleagues discussed earlier.

In a subsequent brief essay, "Languages and Anti-Languages in Early Modern Italy" (1981), Burke has begun to implement the program sketched out earlier by identifying in broad terms some of the specific elements of the communicative economy of Italy in the sixteenth and seventeenth centuries. Consistent with the chief concerns of his earlier piece, Burke's emphasis is not on mental structures, but on sociolinguistic ones. Specifically, he outlines the various languages, varieties, and registers that made up the linguistic repertoire of the heterogeneous speech community; some of the social meanings carried by those codes as well as by certain speech forms (e.g., forms of address), genres, and speech acts (e.g., swearing); various communicative functions for which they were used (such as signaling social relationships or hierarchies); and some of the communicative situations in which they were employed. He closes by suggesting a few of the major dimensions of change undergone by those aspects of the speech economy he has outlined.

Burke's work, though again brief and preliminary, is far more systematic by the standards of linguistic anthropology than that of Sewell, solidly informed by sociolinguistics and the ethnography of speaking. Still, his concerns as expressed in this essay – one suspects on the basis of his guiding framework that they will be expanded in subsequent work – are best seen as complementary to those of Sewell; an understanding of the structures of thought and meaning to which language gives us access is fully as important as a knowledge of the social means, patterns, and functions of language in communication.

What I am suggesting, for the full potential of language-centered social history to be reached, is a unified approach that comprehends both the cultural and the social, both the mental and the behavioral, as inextricably interrelated elements in the construction and experience of a world of meaning. To confine our investigation only to the semantics of elements of the linguistic code, however culturally salient the referents of those words or phrases or linguistic forms may be, is to limit ourselves to abstractions at a far remove from the realities of social or cognitive experience. People in the conduct of their social lives do not merely "think" words and abstractly link them to referents "out there" in the construction of systems of meaning. Nor do they go around "behaving" languages or rules for use, contexts, or role sets. What they do is communicate with each other in ways that implicate both knowledge and purposeful action, the organizing dimensions and patterning principles of which make up complex systems of interrelationships. This is not the place to attempt the formulation of a comprehensive outline of all the relevant dimensions of such systems; such frameworks are readily accessible elsewhere in the literature (Hymes 1974a; Sherzer and Darnell 1972). I prefer, rather, to indicate the range – though not at all the full extent – of such factors by reference to the concerns dealt with in the chapters to follow. I summarize them here only partially in the order of their presentation in the book, which begins with some of the more constant elements of Quaker communication (Chapters 2 through 4), proceeds roughly chronologically through the shifting fields of action and relationships in which speaking or silence served as significant patterning principles between the first emergence of the Quakers in the early 1650s and the advent of toleration in 1689 (Chapters 5 through 8), and concludes with a processual overview (Chapter 9).

I begin with an elucidation of speaking and silence themselves as cultural symbols, symbolic classifiers of the most fundamental principles of morality and action in Quaker ideology. This, I might observe at the outset, is a dimension thus far missing from the considerations of language-centered social historians; but the Quaker case clearly underscores the great potential importance of grounding an investigation of the social and ideational significance of language in the people's own conceptions of the nature of language and its use. At issue is not simply the expression of symbolic meaning by means of a linguistic code, but the symbolism of the act of speaking – or not speaking – itself: What does it mean to speak or be silent? For the study of the seventeenth-century Quakers, an understanding of the meaning and range of these two key symbols and the tension between them is prerequisite to comprehension of the patterns and functions of Quaker language in all its dimensions of thought or action. Implicated also here is the Quaker notion of how communication works as a process, how it is effected, again crucial to an understanding of how messages were encoded, exchanged, and received. Such conceptions, like all patterns and functions of language, are cross-culturally variable – to be discovered, not simply assumed to be akin to the investigator's own.

I turn next to a consideration of the central speaking role among the early Friends, that of the minister. Not only was the role of the minister the only social role defined by the Quakers themselves in terms of speaking, but non-Quakers too identified the Quaker leaders as "great speakers." Like the symbolism of speaking and silence, the role of the minister provides a thread that runs throughout the entire work. Principles concerning the legitimacy of the ministry constituted a major dimension of contrast and conflict between the Quakers and other contemporary groups, whereas the religious speaking of the ministers represented a link between the spiritual mission of the Quakers out in the world and their own collective worship in the famous Quaker "silent meeting." Moreover, the dynamics of the ministerial role represented perhaps the strongest field in which the tension between speaking and silence was played out, giving powerful experiential substance to this most basic symbolic opposition in Quaker culture. So central was the role of the minister among the early Friends that it ultimately provides the most productive frame of reference for tracing the changes in Quaker speaking during the first four decades of Quakerism, marking the transition from charismatic movement to religious sect in speaking-related terms.

Another major organizing focus of the investigation is the range of specific situational and institutional contexts for speaking in early Quaker life. Basic to my approach in this work is the understanding of speaking as *situated* behavior, situated within and rendered meaningful – both as act and message – with reference to relevant contexts. Such contexts may be identified at a variety of levels, such as setting, for example, the culturally defined places where speaking occurs. Thus, my analysis attends to the significance of a range of settings for Quaker communication: church, street, marketplace, courtroom, meetinghouse. Institutions too may be viewed in terms of the way in which they serve to impart contextual meaning to speaking and condition or determine the entire structure of communication within them. Here, I have emphasized two sets of institutions in particular: the emergent religious institutions of Quakerism and the judicial institutions within which Friends negotiated some of their basic relations with political authority.

Most important as a contextual framework in the ethnography of speaking is the event (or situation or scene) within which speaking occurs. I mean here those culturally defined, bounded segments of the flow of behavior and experience that constitute meaningful contexts for action. Thus I have looked to event as an organizing principle in my analysis of speaking in the public threshing meetings and the meetings for worship, the latter representing the central religious speech events in Quaker culture. I should stress here that the speech event as the unit of analysis is the most comprehensive of all analytical constructs in the ethnography of speaking, for it draws together within one unified and systematically organized frame of reference setting, roles, goals, speech acts and genres, communicative means, principles of interpretation and evaluation, and social interactional ground rules, with all their attendant functions and meanings, in the conduct of speaking. Of course, one or another of these components, or several in combination, may be foregrounded for examination; I have already mentioned setting and role, for example. Thus, the analysis of Quaker trials in Chapter 7 centers around oaths (a genre) and swearing (an act); the investigation of the Quaker plain speech in Chapter 7 is pursued largely in terms of greetings, leave takings, salutations, titles, pronouns (i.e., acts, genres, and other communicative means), and norms of social interaction relating to politeness, deference, and hierarchy. Always, however, the analysis is centered on interrelationships, on speaking as a cultural system or as part of cultural systems defined in other terms, as the unifying nexus of thought and action.

Finally, there is the problem of change. Burke, we recall, in taking up the communication model that informs the ethnography of speaking and other sociolinguistic approaches, makes a point of adding to the basic guiding questions they provide the question of how culturally constituted systems of communication change over time. If we recognize that speaking or any other form of communication may be viewed as a cultural system in its own right or as part of cultural systems defined in other terms, two corresponding dimensions of change open themselves to investigation. I have attempted in this work to attend to both, for in truth they are interrelated.

The seventeenth-century Quakers were but a segment of a complex and heterogeneous larger society, and the formative decades spanned by this study constituted a period of extraordinarily turbulent change. Because speaking was an especially salient link between Friends and society at large as well as among themselves, and because changes within the Quaker social system were inextricably linked to changes in their larger social environment, virtually all the elements, patterns, and functions of speaking treated in this work, as well as their interrelationships, were constantly in flux during the period under review, as relationships between Quaker and non-Quaker, Quaker and Quaker, were rearranged; and so I have treated them.

Nevertheless, the central defining feature of Quaker identity was ultimately their religion; thus, in the larger view I have treated their linguistic ideas and usages as a problem in the historical sociology of religion. Specifically, the period under examination in this study, from the early 1650s to 1689, saw the development of Quakerism from an essentially inchoate charismatic movement to an institutionalized and routinized introversionist sect (Wilson 1970:38–39). Part of my concern, and the focus of my concluding chapter, is to fit Quaker speaking and silence into the scope of this broader problem of historical process. I do so largely in terms of Max Weber's productive concept of the routinization of charisma. But whereas Weber and those who have drawn upon his work have tended overwhelmingly to emphasize the social structural and institutional aspects of this process, my own emphasis, consistent with my primary concern with speaking and silence, is upon the expressive, symbolic *means* of charismatic authority and the routinization of the prophetic ministry. The prophetic ministry is an appropriate subject for such concluding analysis as a structural center of speaking and silence in seventeenth-century Quaker culture and the major thread linking together the work as a whole.

This, then, is the orientation and organization of the work. Undertaken primarily as an exploration in the ethnography of speaking, it has merged along the way with social history and the sociology of religion, winding up, it appears, as an instance of that genre mixing that Clifford Geertz (1980) has identified as part of the contemporary refiguration of social thought. Hence the foregoing lengthy effort at situating it within the scholarly landscape. All framing rhetoric aside, it remains the case, as George Steiner has observed, that "we know next to nothing of the genesis, institutionalization, transformations in the speech-conventions and habits of historical societies" (1978:189).

The immediate need is for detailed, closely focused substantive case studies. The Quaker record allows us to begin to fill in this lacuna in our knowledge for at least one historical case; comparative studies, we may expect, will follow.

One final orientational word. Because this is a book about language as thought about and employed in social life, it has seemed to me more than usually appropriate to quote directly and extensively from my sources. Given the subject matter of the study, the words of the Quakers themselves are not simply sources of information; they constitute relevant data in their own right.[4] The availability of these data, I believe, will enhance the credibility of my own analysis and conclusions. Still more important, I hope that by allowing the seventeenth-century Quakers to speak directly to the reader the immediacy of the work will be enhanced, for the larger issues implicated by Quaker speaking in seventeenth-century England – freedom of conscience, social revolution, the toleration of diversity and dissent – are as timely now as they ever were.

[4] Spelling and punctuation have been modernized in the interest of readability.

2

LET YOUR WORDS BE FEW: SPEAKING AND SILENCE IN QUAKER IDEOLOGY

For the seventeenth-century Quakers, in common with all Christians, the crucifixion was a key symbolic frame of reference, a metaphorical model that organized and served as a standard for both the interpretation of history and the direction of human action. But the crucifixion, as the central symbol of Christianity, has been saturated throughout its history with a multitude of significances, any of which may be selected out and highlighted as semantically and operationally central by a given Christian sect or denomination and used as a base from which to generate further active meanings. Two elements of the crucifixion symbol that served the early Quakers in this way were the doctrine of salvation through suffering – *No Cross, No Crown* as Penn stated it in his famous work (1865) – and the related symbolic opposition between the flesh and the spirit.

As Barbour has pointed out (1964:144), the Quaker contrast between the flesh and the spirit did not carry with it the otherworldly ascetic's extreme renunciation of the former, of man's "natural," earthly existence (cf. Weber 1958:193–194n); nor, as we shall see, did Quaker belief and practice rest on a simple dualistic contrast between the two. It is clear, however, that the early Quakers considered the perfection of the spirit to be the chief end of human existence and the life of the flesh, if not subordinated to this spiritual mission, to be dangerous and corrupting. The proper relation between the two was implicit in the metaphor of crucifixion: As Christ's sacrificial suffering on the cross made possible mankind's spiritual redemption, so the taking up of the cross by every person – the sacrifice of the earthly will – was the means of attaining spiritual salvation for each individual Christian. "If . . . ye quench the spirit, and join to the flesh, and be servants of it," wrote George Fox, "then ye are judged and tormented by the spirit; but if ye join to the spirit and serve God in it, ye have liberty and victory over the flesh and its works. Therefore keep in the daily cross, the power of God, by which ye may witness all that to be crucified which is contrary to the will of God, and which shall not come into his kingdom" (1952:18). The Quakers saw themselves as having been "brought forth in the cross; in a contradiction to the ways, worships, fashions, and customs of this world . . . that so no flesh might glory before God" (Penn [1694]:42).

For the early Quakers, speaking was basically a faculty of the natural man, of the flesh. Fox experienced early in his life the realization that "the people of the world," those who were joined to the flesh and servants of it, "have mouths full of deceit and changeable words" (1952:2).

It is not that languages or speaking were seen as inherently evil. Mankind's earthly existence might be difficult, a time of testing and suffering that must be borne on the way to everlasting salvation, but while on earth one did have to live in society and communicate about earthly matters with others, and "natural" speaking was the legitimate means of doing so: "Natural languages . . . may be serviceable for natural uses, natural transactions in civil affairs betwixt nation and nation, man and man" (Howgill 1676:491). Again, it is not that speaking could not be turned to the service of spiritual salvation, for, as we shall explore at considerable length in the chapters that follow, the early Quakers were known as irrepressible talkers in the service of their religion, and preaching and praying were essential elements of their religious practice. Rather, speaking in the service of the spirit had to derive in a special way from a proper spiritual source, and "carnal talk" (Fox 195:12), talk that did not stem from that spiritual source, was inadequate to comprehend spiritual truth, the service of which was the most important business of man on earth. More than that, carnal talk was dangerous; even as a youth, Fox records, he "was afraid of all carnal talk and talkers, for I could see nothing but corruptions, and the life lay under the burden of corruptions" (1952:12). It is in this context that we must interpret Farnsworth's injunctions that "fleshly speaking is an unprofitable action, and is altogether useless in point of salvation and worship of God" (1663:14), and Howgill's further observation that "although there may be languages, and each have an interpretation and a signification, they are all short to declare the life, the immeasurable being of eternal life" (1676:134). At the foundation of these principles was the powerfully resonant awareness that natural languages came into being at Babel and that only by regaining the "state in which Adam was before he fell" could one comprehend the eternal and "divine Word of wisdom" (Fox 1952:27).

If carnal speaking, as a faculty of the natural man, is inadequate for the attainment of the desired spiritual condition, which are the proper behavioral means by which this condition may be attained? For the Quakers, one of the most fundamental means was *silence*. Silence was very close to the center of seventeenth-century Quaker doctrine and practice, and much of our effort in this work will be devoted to the exploration of its complex range of meanings and implications for action. For now, however, we must begin with the meaning of silence in its most immediate and open sense, as the refraining from outward speaking: "Let all flesh be silent before the Lord, amongst you; cease from a multitude of words . . . cease from those discourses that draw the mind from an inward, deep sense of the invisible, immutable power of the Lord God Almighty" (Marshall 1844:128). The further dimensions of Marshall's injunction will emerge in the course of our further explication of

Quaker belief and practice, but this much at least should be clear: Silence demands a limitation on speaking, though not necessarily a full rejection of it.

But the principle of silence extended far beyond the curtailment of speaking in a literal sense. Outward speaking, as "carnal" activity, became a type case for all fleshly activity, for as some of our earlier quotations from Fox make clear, an excessive reliance on carnal speaking was one of the principal symptoms for the early Quakers of all that was corrupt in the world around them. Accordingly, silence, as the cessation of outward speaking, became a metaphor for the suppression of all joining to the flesh: "Seeing all our joys, pleasures, profits, or other things delightful to the flesh, to be but vanity and vexation, we become silent thereunto, not answering to obey the lusts of the carnal mind" (Britten 1660:6). Insofar as natural, fleshly activity is activity done in one's own will, it is antithetical to the suppression of the earthly self and subjection to God's will that are necessary to the attainment of a proper spiritual state.

Silence, in its broader sense, demands the suppression of self and of self-will. Barclay makes this clear in his *Apology*: "As there can be nothing more opposite to the natural will and wisdom of man than this silent waiting upon God, so neither can it be obtained, nor rightly comprehended by man, but as he layeth down his own wisdom and will, so as to be content to be thoroughly subject to God" (1831, 2:353). Silence as self-sacrifice in a most immediate sense, the sacrifice of self-will through suppression of the earthly self, was one means of reenacting the crucifixion, of "taking up the cross," and thus of attaining the proper state of spiritual grace.

With the salvation of one's soul dependent, at least in part, on silence, and speaking susceptible to fleshly corruption, it is not surprising that the early Quakers, notwithstanding their recognition of the necessity of social speaking during man's sojourn on earth, manifested, like many of their contemporaries (Fraser 1977:31), a pronounced distrust of speaking and a concern to keep it to a minimum. Time and again, throughout the early period of Quakerism, we encounter injunctions such as those of William Dewsbury – "All take heed of many words, at all times let them be few" (1689:175–176) – or Edward Burrough – "It's better to speak little, than to utter multitude of vain words" (1660a:11–12). The implications and consequences of this moral requirement to "let your words be few" (Ecclesiastes 5.2) ramify throughout the communicative system of Quakerism, and its importance as a principle and concern cannot be overstressed.

For one thing, the proliferation of words carried with it the danger of distracting one from the spirit through too great an engagement in worldly affairs. As early as 1652, Farnsworth cautioned that it would "draw your minds out above the cross, to live in words" (in Barclay 1841:355). William Bayly gave fuller voice to the same concern in 1664, adding a caution against the temptations of asserting self-will in speaking by loudness, forwardness, or hastiness of speech, and identifying the devil as the source of all idle words and willful speaking:

> Take heed of discourse among yourselves which are unnecessary; for the enemy hath a secret end to effect among such things, to draw out your minds from the living sense of the precious, tender seed of God in you . . . So my dear friends, be very careful, and let your words be few . . . And take heed of loudness, forwardness, or hastiness of speech in all your discourse about the things of this world. (1830:288)

Warnings such as these were repeated throughout the period (see, e.g., Marshall 1844:57), often grounded in the biblical text from Matthew 12.36: "But I say unto you, that every idle word that men shall speak, they shall give account thereof in the day of judgment." Idle words, to be more specific, are "words out of their service and place, . . . out of the truth," according to Fox (1657:9); "own words," words "not in the life," according to William Smith (1663:15, 18).

Singled out for special condemnation, as we might expect in a radical puritan movement, was talk for its own sake, for the carnal pleasure it afforded. All forms of speech play and verbal art were to be rejected as the idlest of idle and corrupt speaking, all "wicked singing, and idle jesting, and foolish laughter" (Symonds 1656:4), all "foolish jesting, and tales and stories" (Parnel 1675:37; see also Taylor [166]:7). Appropriate, unadorned, minimal speech was called, in the idiom of the period, "plain speech": "Plainness of speech all dwell in . . . and few words" (Camm and Audland 1689:286). The Quaker plain speech was an instance of the tendency on the part of many religious movements to adopt a cultural style "dominated by the cultural idiom of indigence," as Turner has observed (1974:267). "Plain speech" subsequently came to designate primarily those Quaker speech conventions that were most visible and distinctive *vis-à-vis* the speaking of others, such as their pronominal usage and names for the days of the week and the months of the year (see Chapter 4), but the original impulse extended across all Quaker speaking, creating a morally defined speech style for the Friends. This speech style was appropriately accompanied by a characteristic demeanor: "Our words were few and savoury . . . our countenances grave, and deportment weighty" (Marshall 1844:39; cf. Bayly 1830:212; Ellwood 1906:15, 40, 91).

Silence, for the Quakers, was not an end in itself, but a means to the attainment of the defining spiritual experience of early Quakerism, the direct personal experience of the spirit of God within oneself. Birthright membership in the Society of Friends was adopted in 1737, but up to that point membership in the Quaker fellowship had to be achieved, and this could be done only by undergoing a particular kind of religious experience.

The doctrine of the indwelling spirit of God in everyone was distinctive to the Quakers among the religious sects and denominations of the period. The most common metaphor employed by the Quakers for this indwelling spirit of God was – and has remained – the Inward Light.

Writing in 1658, Edward Burrough, one of the most effective of the early Quaker tract writers at systematizing Quaker doctrine for public presentation, outlined the source, nature, and worship of the Inward Light in particularly clear terms in his introductory "Epistle to the Reader" of Fox's *Great Mystery of the Great Whore Unfolded* (Fox 1831, vol. 3). "God," Burrough tells us, "had given to us, every one of us in particular, a light from himself shining in our hearts and consciences; which light, Christ his son, the saviour of the world, had lighted every man withal." The primitive church lived in the knowledge and experience of that Light, but the subsequent history of religion, in the Quaker view, was one of centuries of corruption and decline, in which the Light was obscured by the idolatry, superstition, and formalism of the Catholic church.

In their own day, however, God had brought the Quakers forth "to know and understand, and see perfectly" that his Light was to be found shining within them,

> and by it, in us, we came to know good from evil, right from wrong, and whatsoever is of God, and according to him, from what is of the devil, and what was contrary to God in motion, word, and works. And this light gave us to discern between truth and error, between every false and right way, and it perfectly discovered to us the true state of all things. (Burrough 1658:12)

The Light metaphor, drawing on the light imagery of the New Testament – Christ, the Word, as "the true Light, which lighteth every man that cometh into the world" (John 1.9) – and perhaps colored also by hermetic philosophy, conveys a sense of God's luster and brilliance and of his spirit as a beacon, but it says little of the substance of his message to man or how it is *communicated*. For this, the Quakers resorted to a second metaphor, shifting from the visual to the verbal, the spirit of God within as the *voice* of God, God the *speaker*: "the small still voice, moving in man Godwards" (Marshall 1844:89). Fox frequently referred to God as speaker: "God is become the speaker again, that was the first speaker in Paradise, God hath spoken to us by his Son. Here do people come to hear his voice from Heaven" (see Fox 1972:8–9; Graves 1972:212). Indeed, Barclay, in his *Apology*, the major systematic exposition of Quaker belief and practice during our period, identifies God the speaker as the very object of Quaker faith: "The object of this faith is the promise, word, or testimony of God, speaking in the mind. Hence

it hath been generally affirmed, that the object of faith is . . . God speaking''
(1831, 2:34).

To say that the voice of God within is a ''still'' one is to underscore the
need for man to be in a state of spiritual silence in order to hear it. It is a
voice that ''speaks to our spiritual, and not our bodily ear'' (Barclay 1831,
2:36). Although a direct personal communion with God speaking within was
the core religious experience of early Quakerism, the experience that made
one a Quaker, the religious duties of the early Quakers were far from limited
to a silent waiting upon this small still voice. Again, although outward speaking in one's own will about worldly matters was distrusted at best and dangerous at worst, there remained a central and vital place for properly motivated
religious speaking, both for spiritual edification among Friends and for advancing God's cause in the world. Indeed, as subsequent chapters will show,
the frequently expressed caution to Friends to ''let your words be few'' in
worldly matters did not hold in the same way for religious talk.

Here again, the voice of God the speaker was the measure of appropriateness and power, for God spoke not only *within* the Quakers, but *through*
them. Taking up in their own day an apostolic mission, they accepted Jesus'
charge to his first apostles, including his injunction that ''it is not ye that
speak, but the spirit of your father which speaketh in you'' (Matthew 10.20).

Richard Farnsworth articulated the relationship between the experience of
the voice within and outward speaking in God's service in these terms:

> And as the bodies of men and women subjected unto and guided by
> the spirit of God are the temple of God; therefore the spirit of God
> may speak in and through them; and as the Lord is the teacher of
> his people he may be the speaker in them and through them . . .
> and he may make use of them, and speak in them and through them,
> according to his own good will and pleasure. (1663:15)

This prophetic giving of voice to the Word of God speaking within one,
properly done, was not only legitimate, but necessary (Camm and Audland
1689:293); though outward, it was in polar contrast to ''carnal talk.'' It was,
rather, ''the pure language, which disquiets the birth born of the flesh'' (Fox
1657:7).

The Quaker belief in the voice of God speaking within those who were
attentive to the Inward Light was the basis of a major doctrinal difference
between the Quakers and others of their day, including other Puritan groups
and the Church of England alike. For the latter, the Scriptures were *the* Word
of God, given once and for all – revelation was a closed account. The Quakers,
however, hearing the voice of God speaking in them and through them, knew
the account was far from closed. God's ''immediate speaking never ceased
in any age'' (Barclay 1831, 2:32). For them, the Scriptures were rather the
tangible reports of the Word of God that was in those who spoke and recorded

them (Fox 1831, 3:611), an important record of God's earlier messages to men, and thus serviceable as a guide and a standard, but no more intrinsically valid than the Word of God within themselves, continuously revealed (Bayly 1830:180–181; Farnsworth 1656:3–4). The physical written record that was the Bible could not in itself be *the* Word of God, for ''the Word of God is like unto himself, spiritual . . . and therefore cannot be heard or read with the natural external senses, as the Scriptures can'' (Barclay 1831, 1:155; Fox 1831, 3:611).

One additional term that was part of the Quaker paradigm of the Inward Light, the Voice of God, and the Word, was the *Truth*. In many contexts the terms were synonymous and interchangeable: A Quaker minister might just as well exhort his or her hearers to ''dwell in the Light'' or ''live in the Truth,'' or a tract writer define one in terms of the other (e.g., Penington 1863:501). And certainly, as the speakers of the pure language (Zephaniah, 3.9), the Quakers were bound to *truthfulness*: ''The remnant of Israel shall not . . . speak lies; neither shall a deceitful tongue be found in their mouth'' (Zephaniah 3.13). ''Truth,'' however, tended to be the term of choice in referring to the true, valid (Quaker) religious *way* in its outward, communicable aspect, as in Fox's exhortation to ''live in the life of truth, and let the truth speak in all things'' (1831, 7:192).

Fox's words are also suggestive in another respect. By saying ''let the truth speak in all things,'' Fox makes speaking the primary channel by which Truth is to be communicated. But how does Truth speak in all things? And what is the relationship between living in the life of Truth and letting Truth speak in all things? Fox's words are really the expression of a broader Quaker folk theory of symbolic action in which speaking as a means of communication is metaphorically extended to communication by other forms of behavior and action. Both the primacy of speaking and its metaphorical extension are captured with vigor and economy in Fox's famous exhortation from Pardshaw Crag in 1652: ''Let your lives speak.'' Moreover, communication of (religious) Truth is perhaps the primary function of human social life; on another occasion, Fox urged the Quakers to live in such a way ''that . . . your conversations, lives, practices, and tongues may preach to all people, and answer the good, just, and righteous principle of God in them all'' (1831, 7:191).

There are really two dimensions of the communicative process discussed here: the ''preaching'' of the Truth by word and deed, and the means by which that preaching is rendered effective. To this point, I have been dealing with early Quaker belief concerning the *production* of speech; Fox's statement takes us over into conceptions of the rhetorical process and the hearer's response. Here again, as might be expected, the Inward Light, the ''religious principle of God in . . . all,'' is the key.

The Quaker doctrine of the Inward Light was universal in its scope; the

Holy Spirit shone in every person – Quaker or non-Quaker, Christian or pagan – lighted by Jesus Christ. Such was the spiritual state of mankind, however, that the Light shone unrecognized and unheeded by most, obscured by the corruption of empty and formal religion and the life of the flesh. Nevertheless, by virtue of the presence of the Light within, every person was potentially responsive to the Truth: "Truth hath an honour in the hearts of people that are not Friends" (Fox 1952:341).

If Friends themselves were attentive to the Light within themselves, and spoke or acted according to its leadings, their behavior would arouse the spirit of God in those who witnessed it, provided they were ready to receive the Truth, because the spirit was everywhere unitary and identical. It was not necessary to belabor, threaten, cajole, or reason people into belief or persuasion, but simply to "bear the testimony of the Lord as we have received it from him," in the confidence that the spirit of Truth within the hearer would respond to it (Furly 1663:i). "Words that come from the life will go to the life," wrote Farnsworth, "and raise up that which is pure in one another" (Barclay 1841:355). God's words did not suffer from the communicative defects of natural language.

Again and again, one finds the early Quakers employing such phrases as "to that in your consciences do I speak, which changeth not" (Anon. 1654:14); "to the Light in all your consciences I speak, which will let you see whose servants you are" (Audland 1655:22); "to that of God in you I speak" (Fox 1831, 7:29); or "let that of God in you answer these things" (Burrough 1658:23). The rhetorical model was clearly recognized and acted upon as a frame of communicative reference. The confidence of the early Friends in the power of the Light as a communicative channel was tellingly expressed in Burrough's challenge to the world to acknowledge the power of the Quaker mission: "And do not they preach in the power of God, and reach to your consciences, when you hear them? And doth not the light in you answer that they speak the truth?" (1658:24).

This same confidence accounts for those instances in which Friends seem to have relied on a capacity for xenoglossia (Samarin 1972:109–115) to communicate the Truth across the barrier of natural languages, as in the case of the two missionaries who were found in Paris in January of 1657, "half-starved with cold and hunger, and said that 'they were ambassadors from the Lord to the Duke of Savoy . . . they despaired not of the gift of tongues, and the Lord had told them they should have success' " (Braithwaite 1955:416). Fox himself recounts in his journal how "there was a young man convinced in Scarborough town whilst I was in prison, the bailiff's son: and he came to dispute and spoke Hebrew to me and I spoke in Welsh to him and bid him fear God, who after became a pretty Friend" (1952:505).

This rhetorical model I have outlined obtained in all Quaker communication, for all purposes, whether explicitly sacred or secular. Here, for example, is Thomas Ellwood's account of his proposal of marriage to his future wife: "I used not many words to her, but I felt a divine power went along with the words, and fixed the matter expressed by them so fast in her breast, that . . . she could not shut it out" (1906:214). Or Charles Marshall's advice to those engaged in trade: "After you have put a price on your commodities, which is equal, as you can sell them, then if the persons you are dealing with multiply words, stand you silent in the fear, dread and awe of God; and this will answer the witness of God in them you are dealing with" (1844:57). Indeed, if your own spiritual power was strong enough, communication could be effected without the overt intention of sending any message at all. Fox recorded in his journal concerning his passage in 1654 from Swarthmoor to Lancaster: "And so through many towns, and felt I answered the witness of God in all people, though I spoke not a word" (1952:177).

The rhetorical stakes were highest, of course, in the effort to bring people into the Quaker fold, to "convince" them of the Truth by turning them inward to the Light. Convincement was the culmination of the rhetorical process in religious discourse with non-Friends. Most commonly, the term "convincement" was employed for the full conversion experience, but some Friends drew a distinction between convincement and conversion, as in Dewsbury's critical observation: "Many [are] convinced that are not converted" (1689:319). This suggests the possibility that some could feel the Light within themselves respond to the Truth, but resist or refuse outright to follow it through to full spiritual submission to its leadings. Others, clearly, required time before they were fully ready to take up the cross, though the process was begun when they felt the first inward response to the Truth (e.g., Ellwood 1906).

Convincement was the most powerful experience of their lives for the early Quakers and figures prominently in the spiritual journals of the period. A typical example is Stephen Crisp, convinced by the young James Parnel in 1655: "When I saw this man, being but a youth, and knew not the power nor spirit that was in him, I thought to withstand him . . . but I quickly came to feel the spirit of sound judgment was in him, and the witness of God arose in me, and testified to his judgment, and signified I must own it" (1822:27).

Some Quaker ministers were noted for their special sensitivity to the spiritual state and responsiveness of others, thus enhancing their rhetorical power still further. But this sensitivity was also seen in terms of the spiritual/rhetorical link between the Light within themselves and the others. To cite just one of many possible examples, it was recorded of Robert Withers, an early Quaker minister in Pardshaw, Cumberland, that "several was convinced by him, for his service was to speak to particular persons, he having the spirit of discerning by which he could read the states and conditions of many" (Penney 1907:36). One often sees in the early Quaker journals the phrase, "he spoke to my condition," to describe the hearer's sense of the striking personal relevance of a Friend's message, seen as a confirmation on both sides of the power of communication in Truth. When spiritual communication was taking place, the channel was felt to be open in both directions, and the speaker could sense the responsiveness of others to his message. George Whitehead records of another Friend, William Barber:

> I first met him . . . at Diss in Norfolk, and declared the Truth to him and some others present . . . William was very tenderly affected, and broken into tears; and his spirit bowed and humbled, though he had been a great man and captain in the army: Truth was near in him, and I felt him hear it; and my heart was open and tender toward him, in the love of Christ. (1832, 1:57)

*   *   *   *

Let me attempt to draw together in synthetic fashion some of the principal elements making up the symbolic complex of speaking and silence in early Quaker ideology. I use ideology here, after Geertz and Burke, to designate a symbol system that is a guide for understanding and behavior (Geertz 1973:218, 220), that names the structures of situations in such a way that the attitude expressed toward them is one of commitment (Geertz 1973:231).

Many historians of modern Christianity have observed that the emergence of Protestantism was accompanied by a progressive interiorization of the word (see, e.g., Ong 1967:262–286), as intermediary symbols, rituals, and functionaries that stood between the individual and the experience of the Word of God were stripped away from religious practice. Mary Douglas sees this in anthropological terms as part of a more general process that marks an alienation from current social values:

> A denunciation not only of irrelevant rituals, but of ritualism as such; exaltation of the inner experience and denigration of its standardized expressions; preference for intuitive and instant forms of knowledge; rejection of mediating institutions, rejection of any tendency to allow habit to provide the basis of a new symbolic system. (1973:40)

Though not written specifically about the early Quakers, Douglas's description could hardly apply more closely to their mission and ideology.

In these terms, Quakerism may be seen as a carrying of the Protestant tendency to its logical extreme. The spirit of Christ, for whom Christian tradition already made available the symbolic identification as the Word of God – the Son as "the primary 'utterance' of the Father" (Ong 1967:185) – was located *within* the individual. God spoke his Word anew within the soul of every person, doing away with virtually all mediating agencies in the ultimate exaltation of inner experience. The experience of God speaking within was the spiritual core of Quakerism.

As this most important act of speaking took place inwardly and was spiritual, it required that one refrain from speaking that was outward and carnal. Hence the motivation toward silence in Quaker ideology, consistent too with the alienation from current social values; as Susan Sontag has observed: "Behind the appeals for silence lies the wish for a perceptual and cultural clean slate" (1969:17). It is important to emphasize, though, that the resultant outward silence did not represent a complete cessation of speaking or its polar opposite. It involved rather a shifting of the locus and character of religious speaking from outward, human speech to the inward spiritual speaking of God.

By making the speaking of God within man the core religious experience of their movement, the Quakers elevated speaking and silence to an especially high degree of symbolic centrality and importance. Victor Turner has suggested that iconoclastic religions, by eliminating iconic symbols, place ever greater stress on the Word (1975:155). Again, the early Quakers carried this tendency close to its extreme among contemporary radical puritan sects by the symbolic weight they attached to speaking and silence.

But speaking is a potentially problematic symbolic resource for religious purposes. When the speaker is God, speaking can represent the vehicle and essence of spiritual Truth. Under the best of conditions, in Quaker belief, that Truth might be communicated – within individuals, and even between them – without outward speaking. However, in a world that was seen to be just emerging from a long period of spiritual degeneration, and in which all people were manifestly *not* attuned to the voice of God within them, outward speaking might be seen as necessary to bear a public witness for God and to help others reach to the Light within them. The problem was that outward speaking was basically a human faculty, susceptible to the impulses of fleshly will and the service of fleshly indulgence. How could this be controlled against?

One means of control was to make outward speech in the service of religion the giving of voice to *God's* Word, speaking *through* man. This will be a major focus of the next several chapters. The notion of silence may continue to apply here by metaphorical extension: When outward speaking represented a giving of voice to God speaking through man, a silence of the flesh and self-will could continue to prevail. For the rest, however, it was best to neutralize the susceptibility of speaking to carnal impulse by minimizing speaking as much as possible: "Let your words be few."

To be sure, speaking was not the only element of the human condition subject to carnal impulse. Indeed, all of life on earth was seen as susceptible to natural indulgence and therefore to be kept under control in the conduct of the godly life. Here is where the key symbols of speaking and silence were drawn upon by the Quakers for metaphorical extension beyond their primary verbal referents. Accordingly, speaking became a metaphor for all human action – "let your lives speak" – which was thereby encompassed by the same moral rules that governed verbal activity, that is, the stripping away of superfluity and carnal indulgence and the maintenance of a "silence" of the flesh in all things.

Notwithstanding the symbolic extension of speaking and silence beyond the verbal, the centrality of these symbols in Quaker ideology made for an especially heightened awareness of verbal activities and forms on the part of the early Friends and the elevation of speaking into a cultural focus. In the chapters that follow I attempt to elucidate the significant aspects of this cultural focus as it found expression in ideas and actions that gave shape to Quakerism during its formative period.

3

THE TRUE MINISTRY OF CHRIST: SPEAKING AND THE LEGITIMACY OF RELIGIOUS AUTHORITY

Some of the best modern research on the history of Quakerism has been devoted to the problem of tracing the relevant lines of influence and interrelationship between the early Quakers and such other radical Protestant groups as the Baptists, Seekers, Familists, Ranters, Behmenists, Diggers, and Levellers (see Barbour 1975). As close as some of these connections have been shown to be, however, it is readily apparent that the energies of the early Quakers – and indeed of many of their descendants since the seventeenth century – were devoted centrally to asserting the *differences* between themselves and all others and to advancing their own distinctive vision of the proper spiritual life. The first Quakers viewed this task as central to their ministry, and at every level – from the definition of the minister's role, to the content of the message, to the targets of the efforts – speaking was a central organizing principle and focus of what they did. Almost from the very beginning, the Quaker ministers had two spheres of operation: out in the world among the unconverted, and within their own fellowship among the "gathered" Quakers. Nevertheless, activity in the former sphere was historically antecedent to a ministry among Friends, so I will deal with it first, reserving discussion of the ministry within the Quaker society for a later chapter.

The Quaker ministry may be said to have begun with George Fox's realization, in 1648, that "the Lord commanded me to go abroad into the world . . . to proclaim the day of the Lord amongst them and to preach repentance to them" (1952:33–34). It was not until his journey to the north of England in 1652, however, that an actual Quaker movement began to coalesce, in the sense of a collectivity with a unified sense of a common mission and common identity. From 1654, when the staunch group of ministers who have come to be called the Valiant Sixty undertook their mission southward, until the end of the decade, the period was one of intense engagement out in the world, in which Friends spread themselves abroad to "be serviceable for the Lord and his truth, and get over the head of the wicked" (Fox 1831, 7:78).

Filled with the revelations of the Light within them, these "first publishers of Truth" eagerly carried God's Word throughout the length and breadth of England and beyond. Thomas Symonds, one of the first Quakers in Norwich, expressed the sense of mission of this first generation of Quaker ministers in terms drawn from Jesus' charge to the apostles (Matthew 10.26–27) that make clear the prophetic nature of their ministry: "The command to me is, what is revealed, to thee in secret, that preach thou on the house tops, and what is made known unto thee in thy closet, that publish abroad and let my secrets to thee be no longer hid" (1656:1). So rapid and dramatic was their early impact, and so energetic their ministry, that one anti-Quaker pamphleteer was moved to complain in 1655 that "they are much like to mushrooms and toad-stools springing up in a night . . . they hate idleness, for they put themselves to work as soon as they are whelped" (Anon. 1655:4).

The fundamental goal, of course, was, in Fox's words, "to turn people to that inward light, spirit, and grace, by which all men might know their salvation, and their way to God" (1952:35). The major obstacle to the advancement of their effort was the hegemony of the "world's religions," bogged down with the accumulated weight of their vain, corrupt, and man-made forms, degenerated from the pure integrity and power of the primitive church of Christ and the saints. These corrupt professions distanced people and kept them off from the Truth within them, so the central instrumental goal of the Quaker ministers was to sweep away the error and corruption they stood for – like Paul and Silas (Acts 17.6) to turn the world upside down, a figure frequently employed by the early Quakers (e.g., Fox 1831, 3:175; Howgill, 1676:223; Nayler 1716:41; Parnel 1675:89). Accordingly, they declared war on "the beast and false prophet which have deceived the nations" (Burrough 1658:14) with the Word of God as their weapon: "And the Lamb's war is begun, who will kill with the sword, and slay with the sword, which is the word of his mouth" (E. M. 1658:12). Thus the first Quakers moved out against the opposing armies, in the person of the priests of the corrupt religions of the world.

Writing in 1658, in one of the first retrospective stocktakings of the first years of the Quaker movement, Edward Burrough described the efforts and priorities of the first publishers of Truth in these terms:

> And first of all, our mouths were opened, and our spirits filled with indignation against the priests and teachers, and with them and against them first we began to war, as being the causers of the people to err . . . and against them we cried aloud . . . And in steeplehouses we visited them often, and in the markets and other places, as the Lord moved and made way for us, showing unto them and all their people, that they were not lawful ministers of Christ, sent of him, but were deceivers and antichrists, and such whom the Lord never sent. And we spared not publicly, and at all seasons, to utter forth the judgments of the Lord against them and their ways, and against their churches, and worships, and practices, as not being of God . . . And this was our first work which we entered upon, to thresh down the deceivers

and lay them open, that all people might see their shame, and come to turn from them, and receive the knowledge of the truth. (1658:17)

One would be hard put to find a clearer instance of the classic confrontation, illuminated by Max Weber (1978:439–467) between the prophet and the priest, the charismatic leader's emphatic rejection of the legitimacy of a priesthood founded on traditional authority. What is of special interest to us, however, from a sociolinguistic point of view, is that – consistent with the Quakers' cultural focus on speaking – their strongest attacks against the "false ministers" of the world's religions were framed precisely in terms of legitimate and illegitimate uses of language and speech.

In his own work and that of subsequent scholars, Weber's typology of legitimate authority– charismatic, traditional, and rational – has been elaborated chiefly in structural and processual terms, emphasizing the political dimension of authority and its legitimation. The principal question has been a structural one: On what basis does a leader claim legitimacy for his leadership?

Though some analysts do occasionally make note of the force of personality that is characteristic of the charismatic leader, the focus of attention remains relentlessly structural, the problem one of role legitimacy and power relations. Missing from such considerations is any attention to the expressive dimension of authority, either in terms of the *means* of exercising claims to legitimacy or employed in the exercise of leadership itself, or in terms of the *substance* of authority in cases where legitimate authority resides in control over expressive resources. In the sphere of political authority, what is at issue is control over the determination and implementation of public goals having to do with such matters as power relations and the authoritative allocation of social resources (Swartz, Turner, and Tuden 1966:7).

At least one recent collection, however, *Political Language and Oratory in Traditional Society*, edited by Maurice Bloch (1975), opens the way toward the focused study of the expressive dimension of political authority. A concern with the *observable* elements of the public exercise of power and control led Bloch and his colleagues to the study of "the observed speech acts of political leaders, [the] speech . . . involved in political action" (1975:4).

The contributors to Bloch's collection have much of interest to say about the role of effective speaking in the political processes of the respective societies they examine. A recurrent point, running like a leitmotif throughout the book, is the relationship between skill as a speaker and the claim to and exercise of authority. For example, Ann Salmond writes of the Maori: "Any man in Maori society with ambition to influence his fellows must master the oratorical forms" (1975:50). Likewise, among the Tshidi of South Africa, according to John Comaroff, "oratorical ability is seen to be both a significant component of political success and the means by which politicians demonstrate their acumen" (1975:143). To cite just one further example, Andrew Strathern notes that among the Melpa speakers of Mount Hagen, New Guinea, "a man . . . cannot effectively influence his fellow-men unless he can use speech persuasively" (1975:187).

This is not to put effective speaking forward as the essence of politics; obviously the role played by expressive skills in political action varies considerably from one type of political structure to another and from one culture to another. Nevertheless, Bloch's collection leaves no doubt that effective speaking demands attention in any consideration of how people actually go about establishing claims of legitimacy and exercising authority in the political sphere and of the cultural means they employ in doing so.

If expressive factors have such clear potential relevance to political authority, what of religious authority? Recalling that for Weber the prototypes of charismatic and traditional leaders were, respectively, the prophet and the priest, we may appropriately ask what role expressive factors play in the claim to and exercise of legitimate religious authority. Indeed, to the extent that Burke is correct in maintaining that whatever the unifying nature of religion may be, it rests upon verbal modes of persuasion, and that "whatever else it may be . . . theology is preeminently *verbal* . . . '*words* about "God" ' " (1961:v–vi), we should *expect* claims to legitimacy of religious leadership to be framed in terms of control of the verbal means of religion and the exercise of religious authority to rest centrally in the effective management of words.

The point at issue between the Quaker ministers and their priestly antagonists was fundamentally one of the legitimacy of religious *speaking* and the source of legitimate religious words. What is the nature of God's Word in the practice of religion? How does one become a legitimate speaker of God's Word? These were the questions that lay at the heart of the conflict.

The model of the true Christian ministry on which the Quakers based their own was that of the primitive Christian church. This was not, as it might seem, an appeal to a traditional authority of their own, but rather a search for the charismatic origins of contemporary institutional roles (see Hill 1973:154). The apostles, in whose image the Quaker ministers conceived themselves, experienced a direct, immediate call to the ministry: "They were called by power from on high, and were made ministers by the gift of the holy spirit received from God, and their ministry was an absolute gift from God . . . and they were anointed of the Father, by his spirit of promise, to preach the gospel" (Burrough 1658:8). They were, moreover, the prototypic "mechanic preachers," lay preachers who lived by the labor of their own hands, receiving no remuneration for their ministry (Weber 1978:440–441); "labouring and mechanic men" (Barclay 1831, 2:316); "unlearned men, fishermen, ploughmen and herdsmen" (Nayler 1716:43); "tradesmen, who are base and contemptible in the eyes of the proud" (Fox 1831, 7:290). True prophets, they neither had nor required special learning or training, preaching rather from the ability God gave them.

One of the most noteworthy implications of the Quaker belief that true ministers were not made by human agency, but were called and served by the ability God gave them, was that women were equally eligible to serve in the ministry. This, of course, was anathema to the priests and professors of the world's religions, who noted with shock that "sometimes girls are vocal in their convents, while leading men are silent" (Higginson 1653:11). Those who were critical of the Quakers justified the exclusion of women from the ministry by appeal to Paul's misogynist dictum: "Let the woman learn in silence, with all subjection. But I suffer not a woman to teach, nor to usurp authority over the man, but to be in silence" (1 Timothy 2.11–12).

The Quakers rejected this argument, insisting, like many other sects of the day, on the spiritual equality of the sexes (Thomas 1958:44). They held that the sexual distinction between male and female was a distinction of the flesh, "the carnal part" (Farnsworth 1655c:3), whereas the source, the fountain-head, of the true ministry was the Spirit of God, and that "power was one in the male and in the female, one spirit, one light, one life, one power, which brings forth the same witness and ministers forth itself, in the male as in the female" (Blackborow 1660:13–14). As Fox warned those who would forbid women to preach: "Christ is one in all, and not divided; and who is it that dare stop Christ's mouth?" (1831, 4:109).

Though the unity of Christ in male or female was the Quakers' principal argument for women in the ministry, they also answered the challenge of Paul with scriptural arguments of their own. For example, they argued that as "man and woman were helps-meet in the image of God . . . before they fell," so were they to be helps-meet "in the restoration by Christ . . . as they were before the fall" (Fox 1831, 8:39). They also cited numerous instances from the Bible in which women did preach and prophesy, Paul notwithstanding. Margaret Fell, in her forceful and important treatise, "Women's Speaking" (1710), challenged the false ministers with using those women's words as they used the rest of the Scriptures, while yet denying contemporary women the right to speak in the service of religion: "You will make a trade of women's words to get money by, and take texts, and preach sermons upon women's words; and still cry out, women must not speak, women must be silent" (1710:349; see also Speizman and Kronick 1975).

Finally, the Quakers pointed to the obvious efficacy of women's ministry as proof of its validity. "It hath been observed," suggested Barclay, "that God hath effectually in this day converted many souls by the ministry of women; and by them also frequently comforted the souls of his children; which manifest experience puts the thing beyond all controversy" (1831, 2:328).

Lest one gain the impression that women were wholly equal to men in the ministry, however, evidence to the contrary should be cited. Ann Camm, one of the mainstays of the early Quaker movement, was remembered with approval for deferring to men in the service of the ministry:

> She had the wisdom to know the time and season of her service, in which she was a good example to her sex; for without extraordinary impulse and concern it was rare for her to preach in large meetings, where she knew there were brethren qualified for the service of such meetings; and she was grieved when any, especially of her sex, should be too hasty, forward, or unseasonable in their appearing in such meetings. (Braithwaite 1961:286)

Ultimately, although deep-rooted patterns of sexual subordination could not be overturned completely, it is still fair to say that among all the seventeenth-century sects in which women played a disproportionately large role, "it was . . . among the Quakers that the spiritual rights of women attained their apogee" (Thomas 1958:47).

In the Quaker view of the spiritual history of the world, the purity of the primitive church was trodden under in the period of apostasy that followed, a period of darkness, idolatry, and corruption "that hath reigned through all this time of apostasy, which hath been since the days of the apostles" (Burrough 1658:8). The decline of Christianity was nowhere more strongly marked for the Quakers than in the ministry. When the gift of preaching by the Holy Spirit was lost, ministers came to be made by men, "by natural learning, and arts, and languages, and human policy" (Burrough 1657:12) – traditional authority, in Weber's terms – the life and the power went out of the ministry, and only the form and the shadow of a false ministry were left: "The public ministry as now it stands generally, is wholly degenerated from what the true ministry of Christ once was" (Burrough 1658:15). In mid-seventeenth-century England, the universities of Oxford and Cambridge were the established centers where ministers were made, and the early Quakers, like other religious reformers of the day (Graves 1969:125–136), made the institution of a university qualification a major battleground in the Lamb's War.

What did the process of a university training for the ministry consist in? The Quakers saw it, not unrealistically and not surprisingly, in terms of speaking and languages, and challenged its validity on those grounds. They saw the scholars of Oxford and Cambridge devoting themselves preeminently to the study of languages – Latin, Greek, Hebrew – as a means of mastering the Scriptures and commentaries in the original and establishing thereby the doctrinal and substantive basis of their ministry and their preaching. In terms of the prophetic Quaker vision, this was the height – or perhaps the depth – of spiritual emptiness.

For the Quakers, the Scriptures were simply the reported record of the saints' and apostles' words, genuinely given to them by God, but insufficient as a means to true spiritual enlightenment for others, which could only come through a direct personal experience of the Word of God speaking within oneself. The Quakers were intensely devoted to the Bible, not as a source of traditional authority, but as historical validation of the patterns and dynamics of their own charismatic prophetic mission.

In terms of their vision, the work of the scholars was fundamentally misconceived. Greek, Hebrew, Latin were but natural languages, and, as Fox insisted, "none are made ministers of Christ by arts, nor by languages, let them get all the languages upon the earth, they are still but naturalists, and men learning other men's natural language" (1831, 3:203). University study could not be a means to spiritual understanding or priestly legitimacy in Quaker terms. Indeed, if the mastery of languages was an essential qualification for the ministry, as the priests and professors maintained, "so the devil may be as good and able a minister as the best of them; for he has better skill in languages, and more logic, philosophy, and school-divinity than any of them . . . and can talk more eloquently than all those preachers" (Barclay 1831, 2:316). So much for the spiritual validity of university education! Natural learning and natural languages were accessible to the corrupt as well as to the saintly and could not, therefore, be essential to the true ministry. The point was that the world's languages came into being at Babel, and God's Word, the expression of his spirit, was independent of and prior to its linguistic manifestation in any natural language (Fox 1831, 7:290). Learning old languages to read other men's words in old books in order to understand God's Word in the original was the extreme of folly, for "tongues are not the original"; "the word which was in the beginning before Babel was" was the original (Fox 1831, 7:290), and that Adamic language, in which "all things had their names given them according to their nature and virtue" (Fox 1952:27), was accessible only by attending to the Light within.

There was a special irony in the labors of the false ministers of Oxford and Cambridge to understand the Scriptures. "But what rule walk you by," Nayler taunted them,

> who must have them to such a pitch of learning, and so many years at Oxford or Cambridge, and there study so long in books and old authors? And all this to know, what unlearned men, fishermen, ploughmen and herdsmen, did mean, when they spoke forth the scriptures, who were counted fools and madmen by the learned generation when they spake them forth. (1716:43)

The apostles needed no natural learning to proclaim the Word of God speaking within them, nor did the mechanic preachers of Quakerism.

The scholars' time would have been far better spent attending to the Light within themselves, for this was the authentic source of a true prophetic religious ministry. "If any man speak, let him speak as the oracles of God; if any man minister, let him do it as of the ability which God giveth" (Farnsworth

1663:9). Instead, by relying on old books and old authorities for the stuff of their religion and their preaching, perhaps fleshing them out with their own studied imaginings, the world's ministers were in effect dealing in stolen goods, and so the Quakers accused them (Adamson 1656:4–5). This was doubly damnable. Stealing other men's words in the name of religion was spiritual crime enough, but to sell those stolen goods for money by demanding to be paid for this false ministry, including extorting tithes from the people in addition to a ministerial wage, was wholly contrary to the way of the apostles and Christ's true ministers (Burrough 1658:9). The false ministers had no legitimate right to preach the words of others for their own gain. God's Word was not to be sold, but freely received and freely given.

The Quakers could be bitter and mocking in their condemnation of the made ministers, not only accusing them of being thieves, but comparing them to entertainers and shopkeepers, as in this cutting diatribe by Furly:

> They put you to the university to learn the art of speaking-by-rote, and trading in words; and when any of you hath been a competent time there, and is grown pretty cunning at cutting out of discourses, wresting plain words, and handling your tongue deceitfully, then you are fitted for the work of your ministry; and the next thing is but to seek out for a stage to shew your art to the people, first in one place and then in another, as mountebanks, till you can meet with some so silly as to bargain with you for your ware by the year, and allow you a shop to sell it in, and this is your call to the ministry; for till some or other will thus buy your merchandise, you have no call: but let the Scriptures with which you trade, bear witness whether this was ever the call to the Ministry of Christ. (1663:57–58)

The falseness of the made ministry of the world's ministers did not rest solely in the illegitimacy of their calling and the barrenness of their stolen message. Part of the Quakers' understanding of the efficacy of the spiritual ministry rested on their theory of communication and rhetorical power. They believed that the spiritual truth of a religious message stemmed from its source, God speaking within. Because the Inward Light was everywhere unitary and identical, true communication and persuasion were effected by the reaching of the Light in another person. Truth was felt in the resonant chord struck within one's conscience by another's message. Accordingly, "the true ministers need no human authority, to authorize their ministry; for they have a witness in every man's conscience" (Aynsloe 1672:6). The power of the true minister resides in his "being able to speak, from a living experience, of what he himself is a witness; and therefore knowing the terror of the Lord, he is fit to persuade men . . . and his words and ministry, proceeding from the inward power and virtue, reach to the heart of his hearers, and make them approve of him, and be subject unto him" (Barclay 1831, 2:280).

But the false ministers did not "speak as the oracles of God" (Farnsworth 1663:9), but in their "own will" or "as they are ordered by men" (Aynsloe 1672:7), preaching on subjects of their own choosing, without concern "whether it be fit or seasonable for the people's condition or not" (Barclay 1831, 2:349). Further indication of their will worship was their preaching at appointed times and places (Aynsloe 1672:7); the false minister preaches and prays "by the hour-glass, and tells the people when the glass is run, the time is spent" (E. M. 1658:2). Thus corrupt, the false ministers were in fact *incapable* of speaking the Truth. Ann Audland, when asked on one occasion in 1655 what was untrue in the preaching of the Banbury vicar, replied that when men were out of the doctrine of Christ everything they spoke was untruth, and though they should say "the Lord liveth," they would speak falsely (Braithwaite 1955:199).

Sinful and corrupt in the pulpit, the false ministers were equally corrupt outside it. The true minister preached by conduct as well as by conversation (Fox 1831, 7:167; Whitehead 1832, 1:46); what, then, did the conduct and conversation of the false ministers communicate? Here again, it was their speech behavior that witnessed their degeneracy, their indulgence in the fleshly pleasures of frivolous, vain, idle talk. "Do not your teachers join with the world," charged Payne, "in feastings, in idle speeches, and in foolish jestings that do administer no grace to the hearers, telling tales and stories which are pleasing to the flesh?" (1655:28).

What is worse, the false ministers indulged in and valued those vain and degenerate politeness forms that fed the carnal pride of the natural man (this will be discussed in detail in Chapter 4), like the scribes and the Pharisees (Matthew 23.12) who, loving "salutations in the market places" and "being called of men Master" (Aysnloe 1672:7), were condemned by Christ. The true ministers of God were servants, and "that is one clear mark by which they be known from those hypocrites, dogs, and hirelings that have greetings in the markets, and are called of men Master" (Adamson 1656:19). As the servant of God, a minister should be an example of humility, suppressing all earthly pride; yet "if a poor labouring man come before one that you call a minister," Parnel charged, "though he be one of his hearers, and one who helps to maintain him [by tithes and other contributions], yet he must *You* the priest, and the priest Thou him: And here the heathen lord over one another by their corrupt wills" (1675:94). Francis Howgill's scornful account of a group of the world's ministers engaged in a politeness display is especially devastating:

> It so came to pass that I was amongst a company of these that would be called ministers of the Gospel, in number no less than ten, and in the room I was when they all came in, and they courted, and bowed, and scraped with their feet, with their hats to the ground

many of them one to another, and reeling up and down the house in this manner, and one striving to outstrip another in compliments; and though they all had intentions to sit down, yet they strave among themselves who should be last, and in this posture they continued half an hour altogether, at the which I admired, and indeed was ashamed, that men who professed godliness should be found in such transgression. (1676:353)

Clearly, at issue in those battles of the Lamb's War fought on the grounds of the true and false ministry was the matter of role legitimacy: Who were the legitimate spokesmen of God? As we have noted, the conflict was framed in terms of the classic tension, illuminated by Weber, "between the prophets and the representatives of the priestly tradition" (1978:457). The early Quaker ministers were a type case of the prophetic leader in Weber's terms; indeed, Weber himself identified Goerge Fox as "a prophet type" (1978:446).

Not just Fox, however, but all Quaker ministers exercised a prophetic ministry. In true prophetic fashion, their authority rested on charisma, their powers being of divine origin and not conveyed by any human agency. Called to the ministry directly by the Holy Spirit, they relied for their preaching only on direct personal revelation. Moreover, they served freely and without remuneration, as true mechanic preachers. In terms of Weber's typological distinction between ethical and exemplary prophets, the Quaker ministers represented a merger of the two. In their vital, emotional preaching, they demanded obedience to divine commandment as an ethical duty, but they also felt called upon to demonstrate to others by personal example the way to religious salvation. One of Weber's principal concerns in developing the concept of charismatic authority was the interesting structural and processual problem of the routinization of charisma, and we will need to deal with that issue in tracing the course of Quakerism subsequent to the period of its first emergence as a charismatic movement. During the 1650s, though, it is clear that the first generation of Quaker ministers took the field as essentially unfettered bearers of a prophetic ministry.

In polar contrast to the Quaker ministers, the false ministers against whom they did battle were bearers of a priestly tradition, claiming authority by virtue of their service in that sacred tradition. Made ministers, trained for the priesthood at Oxford or Cambridge, they interpreted for pay the closed canons of their scriptural tradition. The Lamb's War, then, was in one major outward sense a struggle between the charismatic prophets of Quakerism and the upholders of the priestly tradition of established religion, as rival claimants to exclusive religious legitimacy as spokesmen of the divine Word.

In religion, authority has to do with the control of the symbols that give access to spiritual power, and the exercise of authority involves the management and manipulation of those symbols. In the actions of the Quaker ministers, a central sacred symbol and its outward manifestations as ministerial means were merged into a unitary whole. The sacred symbol was God's living Word, and the essential duty of the ministers was to speak it abroad, serving as the oracles of God. Their mission was to give voice to the Word of God speaking directly in them and through them, unmediated by human agency. For them, this was the only legitimate religious speaking and the essence of legitimate religious authority.

Their position, as we have seen in detail, put them directly into conflict with the traditional authority of the "false ministers." For the latter, the issue was no less one of legitimate control over God's Word in the world, but that Word was embodied in the Scriptures, a closed account. What made one a legitimate spokesman of the Word was mastery of the sacred canon, which qualified one to be brought into the sacred tradition. Proper religious speaking demanded a body of acquired knowledge, including linguistic knowledge, and the human ability to interpret the Scriptures for the uninitiated. Of course, for the priests of the established religions authority also rested in control over the management of a range of essential rituals, not necessarily wholly verbal, although all with a verbal component. What is noteworthy is that from the Quaker perspective, which is our primary concern, these other ritual trappings were determinedly stripped away. Religious practice was systematically reduced to the Word, and the sole function of the religious specialist was to open that Word to the world. Thus, legitimate speaking was not only important to Quaker ministerial practice, for the Quaker ministers it was their sole *raison d'être* and the only basis and means of their authority.

I am not, of course, suggesting that the Quaker case is in any way typical of the nature of legitimate religious authority. Rather, in their exclusive concentration on the speaking of God's Word as the essence of religious experience, they represent a rather extreme case. Examination of this case, however, highlights the place of speaking in the claim to and exercise of religious authority, a dimension of even more importance perhaps in religion than in politics. Authority is more than simply a matter of structures and role relations. Whether in politics or religion, a full understanding of the means and perhaps often the substance of legitimate authority must be founded also on the social control of communication.

4

CHRIST RESPECTS NO MAN'S PERSON: THE PLAIN LANGUAGE AND THE RHETORIC OF IMPOLITENESS

The early Quakers, like all the radical sects of their day, defined themselves in opposition to established institutional religion. Inasmuch as the dominant political issues of the day centered around religion, to be in opposition to prevailing religious practice was also to challenge dominant political and legal structures. Because speaking was a major symbolic focus of early Quakerism, and distinctive ways of speaking represented the principal visible means by which the Quakers differentiated themselves from others, much of the religious and political conflict surrounding Quakerism implicated speaking in some way. For example, Quakers were beaten for speaking out against the legitimacy of parish priests in their own churches (see Chapter 5) or jailed for refusing to swear legal oaths or oaths of allegiance (see Chapter 7), all actions motivated by religious convictions concerning the place of speaking in the godly life.

Of those Quaker speech usages that elicited hostile and violent reactions, however, there was one class, no less religiously motivated, that challenged not so much religious or political institutions as the very fabric of social relations and social interaction. The forms in question were those that sociolinguists have come to call politeness phenomena: greetings and salutations, titles and honorific pronouns. At issue was the Quakers' refusal to use them.

Doctrinal discussions, religious challenges and debates, legal proceedings, and the like were intense, public events, framed as confrontations on religious grounds. They were dramatic, heightened, invested with importance, but not part of the routine of daily life, even during the most intense periods of Quaker proselytizing, as in London in 1654 or Bristol in 1655. Moreover, central participation in such events was limited to a relatively small group of people, those moved to undertake the propagation and defense of Quakerism out in the world. The distinctive Quaker usages in regard to politeness phenomena, however, were part and parcel of the conduct of everyday life, figuring even in secular interactions, and they implicated all Quakers without exception. By constantly violating norms of deference and politeness especially in regard to greetings and leave takings, titles, and pronouns, Quakers aroused hostilities stronger than any of the other radical puritan groups of the period. This chapter is an examination of the nature of the Quaker "plain speech," its ideological underpinnings, and the consequences of its practice.

Before proceeding to those aspects of the plain speech that represented politeness phenomena, however, it should be noted that the Quaker plain style included other distinctive usages as well, most notably special terms for the days of the week and months of the year. The days were labeled "first day" through "seventh day" in place of Sunday through Saturday, and the months, in similar fashion, were designated "first month" through "twelfth month."[1] This usage, held to also by the early Baptists, had a dual charter, both biblical and moral. To number the days was to designate them "as they were given forth and called by God in the beginning" (Fox 1831, 7:63), in Genesis. The moral issue, implicating both days and months, was that their common labels were derived from the names of pagan gods and were thus idolatrous: "And by all these idolatrous names is our English people calling the days and the months, notwithstanding they make a profession of God and Christ, and have the Scriptures, which they say is their rule to walk by, which saith, ye shall not do after the matter of the heathen" (Clark 1656:19). But these usages were seen largely as quibbling peculiarities by others; it was the Quaker practice of refusing to employ politeness forms that was of real social importance.

*   *   *   *

One Quaker usage that constituted a particular affront to those with whom they came into contact was their practice with regard to greetings and leave takings, such as "good morning," "good evening," "good day," "good morrow," "God speed you," "farewell." The Quakers' refusal to use these forms was seen, not surprisingly, as marking a serious lack of civil courtesy. An early anti-Quaker commentator remarked that when the Quakers meet someone by the way, "they will go or ride by them as though they were dumb, or as though they were beasts rather than men, not affording a salutation, or resaluting though themselves saluted" (Higginson 1653:28). Again, this time underscoring the Quakers' lack of manners with regard to leave taking, "they use no civil salute, so that their departures and going aside to ease themselves are almost indistinguishable" (Higginson 1653:28). Greetings and salutations are part of the social duty of fully socialized people; to fail to use them is the mark of someone not fully human, either lacking the ability to speak at all or a beast. They are also ceremonial acts (Goffman 1967:54), conventionalized means of communication by which an individual expresses his own character and conveys his appreciation of the other participants in

---

[1]   By the Julian Calendar, employed in England until 1752 when the Gregorian Calendar was adopted, the new year began on March 25. Accordingly, by the seventeenth-century Quaker reckoning, March was First Month, April Second Month, etc.

the situation. To refuse to greet someone, especially someone who has offered a greeting first, is not only to mark oneself as unsocialized, but to signal a lack of social regard for the other person, a serious face-threatening act (Brown and Levinson 1978) in a society and a period in which much emphasis was placed on elaborate etiquette (Wildeblood and Brinson 1965:177). I will develop this theme further as our discussion proceeds. For now, we must ask what were the Quakers' grounds for refusing to perform these fundamental courtesies.

When challenged for their refusal to observe the etiquette of greeting, the Quakers' basic appeal was to the demands of Truth, both in its literal sense and as it designated the proper, godly, spiritual way. To live in the way of Truth was to do the work of God and thus to do good. Not to do so was by definition to be out of the good life, whether by omission – not witnessing the Light of God within – or by commission – "evil workers, cursed speakers, drunkards, and cheaters, cozeners, them that use false weights and deceitful measures in their merchandising in their common occasions and works" (Fox 1657:1).

We have seen that the early Quakers were distrustful of speaking, as a fleshly faculty. One consequence of this distrust was the impulse to limit worldly speaking as far as possible and thereby to reduce one's susceptibility to being corrupted; hence the frequent injunction to "let your words be few." A principal function of greetings, however, is to open access to talk (Goody 1972:40). It follows naturally that if one has no real need to talk to another person, greetings are to that extent rendered unnecessary and become an entrance to the trap of sinful "idle words." As articulated by Caton:

> When [Quakers] have occasion to speak to any man, they speak unto him whether it be on the way, or in the street, or upon the market, or in any other convenient place; but to salute men in a complementary way, by doffing their hats unto them, and bowing before them, and giving them flattering titles . . . that they are not free to do. (1671:27)

Another manifestation of the Quaker demand for truthfulness in all things was a resort to extreme literalness, that is, a refusal to accept any verbal usage, no matter how conventional or no matter how strongly sanctioned by the canons of etiquette, if it violated the standard of Truth at any level. Indeed, as we have seen, the Quakers viewed custom and the use of what they saw as empty ceremonial forms as fundamentally incompatible with spiritual rigor. Thus, if they identified a particular kind of customary behavior as contrary to the Truth, it was to be shunned as a lie. To wish somebody a good day when he was in an evil day, because he was not in the Light, was both to speak a lie and to partake of his evil deeds oneself. To say "God speed" to him was to invoke the blessing of God on his evil; to wish him farewell was to wish his evil well (Fox 1657:1–2; Howgill 1676:228). "Now we which be in the Light," wrote Fox, "and know the day, who witness the Father and the Son, and to such as are here we can say God speed, and not be partakers of their evil deeds . . . but to say the evil day is a good day, is to speak a lie" (1657:1–2).

Students of greeting behavior emphasize its essentially phatic function of establishing interactional contact (Malinowski 1923:313–316), its lack of literal referential meaning (Ferguson 1976:147); but the seventeenth-century Quakers were not willing to make this concession. If the surface-level referential meaning of an expression could be construed as a lie, no element of conventional or functional meaning could render it acceptable. Moreover, mere phatic use of greetings might lead one to use them insincerely or hypocritically, also a lie (Fox 1657:9, 14; Furly 1663:11–12). Customariness was of no consideration, if by observing custom one violated one's duty to God. Nor was the fact that by flying in the face of civil politeness one might offend others: Pleasing men was not what one was here for, but rather, obeying God (Caton 1671:28; Howgill 1676:353).

*   *   *   *

A similar principle was invoked in regard to another set of politeness forms as well: namely, honorific or deferential titles of address such as "your grace," "my lord," "master," "your excellency," or self-referential salutations, such as "your humble servant," "your most obedient servant," and the actions that accompanied them, including bowing and scraping and putting off one's hat by men, and curtsying by women. It is worth repeating that this was a period in which "the rules of etiquette . . . attained a zenith of artificial complexity" (Wildeblood and Brinson 1965:177). For Quakers of the lowest classes, the niceties of such social graces were of somewhat lesser moment, but among the early Friends were people of the yeoman or middle classes (Reay 1980a; Vann 1969) where the cultivation of good manners was expected; others, like Thomas Ellwood or the Peningtons or the Penns, were from the upper classes, in which the arts of good manners were assiduously cultivated, and good performance of the social graces was constantly subject to evaluation. Ellwood, for example, looking back at the period before he became a Quaker (in 1659), says that the giving of gracious titles "was an evil I had been much addicted to, and was accounted a ready artist in" (1906:25).

Quakers, however, were biting in their characterization of such customs, the

> artificial, feigned, and strained art of compliment, consisting in bundles of fopperies, fond ceremonies, foolish windings, turnings, crouchings and cringings with their bodies, uncovering their heads,

using multitudes of frothy, frivolous, light, vain, yea, and most commonly lying words . . . by which all honour, respect, reverence, esteem or love must be measured; being so enamoured upon it, that they deem it their glory and crown, to be exact in it. (Furly 1663:7; cf. Howgill 1676:353)

At one level, the Quakers rejected such forms because, like the customary greetings, they were not literally true, that is, they did not describe the true relationship between the interlocutors. To call someone "your grace," when he was not in a state of grace, or "master," when he was not your master, or to greet someone with "your humble servant, sir," when you were not his servant, was to lie, and this the Quakers would not do (Barclay 1831, 2:519; Ellwood 1906:25). Again, custom and fear of giving offense were of no consequence here. Fox records in his journal a dramatic encounter between himself and a Major Ceely, the keeper of the prison at Launceston Castle when Fox was a prisoner there in 1656. While walking on the castle green, Fox encountered the major, who doffed his hat to him and said, "How do you, Mr. Fox? Your servant, Sir," to which Fox replied, "Major Ceely, take heed of hypocrisy and a rotten heart, for when came I to be thy master and thee my servant? Do servants use to cast their masters into prison?" (1952:250). The truth must be affirmed, even at a risk to one's personal welfare.

Unwillingness to lie, however, was only one reason for rejecting honorific and deferential titles; at least as important was another set of grounds, which struck closer to the essence of the custom itself. Titles, and the accompanying deferential acts of bowing, taking off the hat, or curtsying, represented forms of worldly honor, honor of men's persons and gestures of deference to their fleshly pride. The way to salvation, the Quakers held, was not to glorify the earthly self, but to suppress it that the spirit might prevail: "Christ respects no man's person" (Fox 1831, 7:318–319).

It is not clear what address forms and gestures the Quakers employed to open and close encounters in place of the "fond ceremonies" they rejected. They did use "friend" as a term of address, apparently to non-Quakers as well as among themselves, anticipating the solidary "comrade" of the revolutionary socialists, although "Friends" was current as a label for separatist groups as early as 1646 (Barbour 1964:36). As regards gestural forms in secular interaction, still less information is available. Furly (1663:13) recommends "giving the hand, falling on the neck, embracing, kissing . . . [as] more infallible demonstrations of true honour, than those dirty customs" of bowing, curtsying, and doffing the hat; and the handshake did become the customary gesture of leave taking at the close of a Quaker meeting. It is far from clear, however, how widespread these forms were among Friends, although it seems safe to assume that they were unlikely to be used with non-Quakers.

*   *   *   *

The best known of the Quaker speech testimonies was that which rejected the use of "you" in the second person singular, insisting instead upon "thou" and "thee." The most superficial justification for this usage, though inherently accurate and logical, was that the use of "you" to designate the singular was simply ungrammatical and in this sense not true: "*I* is a particular, *Thee* is a particular, *Thou* is a particular, single, pure proper unto one. *We* is many, *Ye* is many, *They* is many, and *You* more than one" (Farnsworth 1655b:6).

The argument was advanced in a number of tracts, *A Battle-Door for Teachers and Professors to Learn the Singular and Plural, etc.* (Fox, Stubbs, and Furly 1660), in which Fox himself had a hand, chief among them. The burden of the argument in this famous work, as in other tracts that focused on the issue of grammaticality, consisted in the main of evidence from other languages, often quite extensive and involved, to support the contention that the singular and plural forms should be distinguished. It is interesting that the Quakers should have devoted so much energy to the justification of their pronominal usage by appeal to other languages and resorted to that line of reasoning so persistently, because it was not inherently a strong argument. It disregarded completely the formal and honorific use of the second-person-plural form for the singular in the other languages they cited in support of their case, including French, Spanish, and German. Nor did the Quaker polemicists deal with the relativistic counterargument raised by critics of their usage, namely, that

> though all the world, save England should use to say, *thou* to a single person, yet is that no Law to us, nor is our phrase and custom to be judged hereby . . . There is no one nation or language that can claim authority over another and judge them for forms and phrases of speech, much less over all nations and languages. (Cheyney 1676:3)

The force of the Quaker argument on the basis of grammar was undermined even by the Quakers themselves. In his preface to the *Battle-Door*, which was the most extensive and ambitious statement of the grammatical argument by appeal to other languages, Fox himself makes one of his strongest statements concerning the earthly nature of languages and their ultimate irrelevance to the establishment of spiritual truth: "All languages are to me no more than dust, who was before languages were, and am comed before languages were and am redeemed out of languages into the power where men shall agree" (1660:ii). If all earthly languages are no more than dust, one might ask, why argue in linguistic terms?

But the Quakers were interested in more than linguistic purity for its own sake; their arguments in defense of their pronominal usage ran deeper than mere grammar. Certainly a more important factor in their own eyes was the evidence of the Bible. According to their reading of the Scriptures, the equivalents of "thou" and "thee" were employed by Christ and the primitive Christians as well as in parts of the Old Testament (Caton 1671:26; Clark 1656:21–28). In this light the generalization of "you" was a later corruption, attributed to popes and emperors imitating the heathens' homage to their gods (Ellwood 1676:28; Penn 1865:137) and thus to be done away with together with the rest of the empty customs of the world. Once again, it mattered not at all that "you" had become customary as a singular form (as argued, e.g., by Cheyney 1676:2; Fowler 1676:17–18); one's duty was to be faithful to Truth, not to custom (Ellwood 1676:29).

Most important, however, as with titles and hat honor, was that the form employed to designate the second person singular was intimately bound up with questions of social rank and etiquette. The use of "you" to a single individual communicated deference, honor, courtesy; "thou" imparted intimacy or condescension when used to a close equal or subordinate, but contempt when addressed to a more distant equal or a superior – either that or boorishness. According to a contemporary commentator on accepted patterns of usage: "We maintain that 'thou' from superiors to inferiors is proper, as a sign of command; from equals to equals is passable as a note of familiarity; but from inferiors to superiors, if proceeding from ignorance, hath a smack of clownishness; if from affectation, a tone of contempt" (Hill 1975:247; see also Cheyney 1676:5). Thus, by refusing to use "you" to a single individual because it represented a form of worldly honor, and using "thou" instead, the Quakers provoked the hostility of others, who took their behavior as a sign of contempt (see Brown and Gilman 1960:274–276 on the "thou" of contempt). Besides being grammatically untrue, the use of "you" in the singular constituted a form of worldly honor, which was rendered all the more odious by the circumstance that those who insisted on the use of the honorific "you" to themselves addressed God, to whom honor was truly due, as "thou" in their prayers (Farnsworth 1655b:2).

From this vantage point the use of "thou" to a single person became a means of attacking the fleshly pride that demanded honor and deference. "That which cannot bear thee and thou to a single person, what sort soever, is exalted proud flesh, and is accursed with a curse, and cast out from God" (Farnsworth 1655b:6; see also Farnsworth 1653:29). The honorific form was deliberately rejected to exert a humbling effect upon the person addressed, a reminder of the vanity of worldly honor. Fox expressed the principle clearly: "This 'thou' and 'thee' was a fearful cut to proud flesh and self-honour" (1952:416).

*   *   *   *

Taking up the usages that constituted the plain style was not without its difficulties for the first generation of Quakers. It was not simply a matter of subscribing to a principle and then making one's speaking conformable to it, but rather of learning an entirely new set of speech habits that ran counter in many fundamental respects to common and polite usage. This was no easy matter when one considers that the first generation of Quakers were all adults (Howard 1704:24–25). Indeed, John Gratton compared the experience to being a child again: "I was to enter the Kingdom of Heaven as a little child, and was to learn anew to speak and walk" (1720:44). Coming forth in the plain style was especially problematic for the minority of Quakers, such as Thomas Ellwood and William Penn, who came from those levels of society that placed a high value on the cultivation of polished manners and where elaborate politeness was counted a necessary social grace (Ellwood 1906:25–26; Penn 1865:108–109).

The adoption of the Quaker practices with regard to greetings, titles, and pronouns was rendered still more difficult by the strong reactions, ranging from surprise to violent hostility, that the unconventional Quaker usages provoked on the part of others. In the very early years, before Quakerism had spread very far and people had become more familiar with the Quakers' peculiar ways, the reaction of outsiders was often simply surprise. Fox records an instance in 1651 when he stopped at a house on his travels northward and asked the woman of the house for something to eat, employing "thee" and "thou" to her. She was, he notes, "something strange" in her reaction to his speech (1952:77). Some observers, when they first encountered the unconventional Quaker style, found it so strange that they could only conclude that the Quakers were deranged. Of an incident in which he was brought before a justice in 1652 for disturbing a church service, Fox wrote:

> He bad me put off my hat, and I took it off in my hand, and said to him, "Doth this trouble thee?" And I put it on again; and I said "thou" to him, and he asked the man that rid thither before me whether I was not mazed or fond. And he said, no, it was my principle. (1952:92)

These reactions, however, were comparatively mild. From the very beginning, the plain speech of the Quakers provoked angry and violent reactions from those who saw it as rudeness and felt themselves offended by it (Edmondson 1820:50; Fox 1952:406). Some years later, looking back on that early period, Fox recalled that Friends were "in danger many times of our lives, and often beaten, for using those words to some proud men, who would say, 'Thou'st "thou" me, thou ill-bred clown,' as though their breeding lay in saying 'you' to a singular" (1952:416).

Nor was it only the hostility and scorn of strangers that one risked by adopting the plain speech. More painful by far was the alienation from those with whom one had a close relationship, such as parents or employers, that resulted from the use of the offensive familiar pronoun or failure to use the proper honorific form. In Richard Davies's case, for example, his master was not offended by his use of "thee" and "thou,"

> but when I gave it to my mistress, she took a stick and gave me such a blow upon my bare head, that made it swell and sore for a considerable time; she was so disturbed at it, that she swore she would kill me; though she would be hanged for me; the enemy so possessed her, that she was quite out of order; though beforetime she seldom, if ever, gave me an angry word. (1832:29)

Not only did Davies's use of the familiar pronoun provoke his formerly loving mistress to violence, but his unwillingness to use the worldly forms of honor estranged him from his father as well (1832:33).

Perhaps the most dramatic case on record, and the one most often cited, is that of Thomas Ellwood, a member of the gentry, son of a justice, and at one period in his youth amanuensis to John Milton. Ellwood recalls in detail the beatings, tirades, and other punishments he endured at his father's hands for the use of "thou" and "thee" to him and his refusal to remove his hat in his father's presence (1906:27–54).

Although the hostility and violence visited upon them for their use of the plain speech imposed an often severe burden upon the early Quakers, the suffering they experienced thereby also had a strongly reinforcing effect on individual faith and group solidarity. The Christian doctrine of salvation through suffering – no cross, no crown – the suppression of the earthly self so that the spirit might prevail, was, as we have established, central to Quaker belief and practice. To be subjected to suffering for one's religious convictions represented a spiritual testing, which, if accepted and endured, helped to validate the spiritual rightness of one's existence. As Penn wrote: "There is a hidden treasure in it [despite the] wonder, scorn, and abuse of the multitude" (1865:108). The early Quakers spoke explicitly of the process of adopting the distinctive and controversial Quaker usages as "taking up the cross" of the plain speech.

For the very earliest Quakers, this process does not seem to have involved a moral struggle. Fox, for example, simply records that when the Lord sent him forth on his religious mission, he forbade him from following the honorific and deferential customs of the world and required him to use the plain style (1952:36). But as others were attracted to Quakerism, and the plain style, like other Quaker practices, became institutionalized, it very soon became a part of the process of convincement to undergo a struggle in taking up the cross of the plain speech, dreading the social consequences, temporizing (Furly 1663:51–52), delaying and postponing the adoption of the proper forms, and feeling intensely guilty about one's failure to do the right thing (Stirredge 1810:60), until the breakthrough was finally achieved. Luke Howard, for example, the first Quaker in Dover, struggled for months over the matter of pronouns, worrying that he would lose his trade, be mocked by drunkards and taunted by fools in the streets, and be unable to remain faithful to the Quaker standard (1704:23–24). John Gratton, convinced in 1671, makes very clear both the difficulty of sacrificing the good regard of others and the spiritual satisfaction of taking up the cross of the plain speech, though he suffered for it:

> This language and conversation was hard to flesh and blood, that would have pleased men, and had their praise which I got when I was young, and it went hard with me to lose it all, which I knew I must, though they took offence at me for my obedience to the Lord, so I gave up in obedience to the will of God, in which I found life and peace to my soul, and great encouragement and joy in the Lord, though this way of speaking and carriage went very hard with me, and was a great cross to my natural part, and helped to lay me very low, and to mortify the old man in me, and made me willing to be a fool in the eyes of the world, and to be despised of men. (1720:44)

Indeed, hesitation and struggle in taking up the cross of plain speech came to be so much the pattern that even non-Quakers saw it as conventionalized for newly convinced Quakers, suggesting, with how much justice it is difficult to assess, that a too hasty adoption of Quaker usage would somehow be suspect. In a set of somewhat mocking and sarcastic "directions how to attain to be a Quaker," an anonymous anti-Quaker pamphleteer wrote in 1669: "Be not too hasty to use thee and thou, as their fashion is, but stay till thou hast gained more acquaintance amongst them, and then thou may'st be the bolder to do it. But after thou has once begun it be sure thou never forget it" (Anon. 1669:8–9).

*   *   *   *

As suggested in the foregoing pages, the Quaker plain style was the focus of considerable public controversy and debate. Numerous pamphlets and tracts were published by critics of Quaker practice in which a range of objections was raised against the plain speech, and by the Quakers themselves, marshaling counterarguments in its defense. Examination of the terms of the debate is instructive for what it reveals about the ways in which the plain style conditioned the Quakers' place in the larger society and in which the Quakers' own belief and practice in regard to speaking were formulated partially in response to the wider social and cultural environment.

The thrust of one group of arguments against the plain style was to attempt to impugn its validity by trivializing it, either by suggesting that the politeness forms were a small matter and that the Quakers were misguided to lay so much store in such trifling issues, or by accusing the Quakers of adopting such deviant usages simply as an identity badge, "in affected singularity as a mark of distinction from their neighbours'' (Fowler 1678:59). The Quaker response to this charge that their principled insistence upon the plain style made a mountain of a molehill turned the argument back on their critics: If the Quaker usage was such a small matter, why did the non-Quakers oppose it so vehemently? Moreover, nothing that was required of men by God was trivial. The case is aptly and concisely stated by William Penn:

> To such as say that we strain at small things . . . I answer with meekness, truth, and sobriety; first, nothing is small, which God makes matter of conscience to do, or leave undone. Next, inconsiderable as they are made by those who object to our practice, they are so greatly set by, that for our not giving them, we are beaten, imprisoned, refused justice, etc., to say nothing of the derision and reproach which have been frequently flung at us on this account. So that if we had wanted a proof of the truth of our inward belief and judgment, the very practice of those who opposed it would have abundantly confirmed us. (1865:107)

Although the suggestion that the plain style was merely "a green ribbon, the badge of the party, to be better known" (Penn 1865:107) was clearly controverted simply by the mass of Quaker expressions of the moral grounds for their practice, whether or not one accepted them as valid, it is certainly true that the plain style served as an identity badge for the Quakers. The use of "thee" and "thou" and the avoidance of conventional greetings and titles, together with the sober Quaker demeanor (Symonds 1656:5), were the most visible signs of Quaker affiliation. Richard Davies's experience was typical: "I was now first called a Quaker," he wrote, "because I said to a single person *Thee* and *Thou*, and kept on my hat" (1832:30). Even further, the adoption of these usages came very early to represent a kind of self-induced rite of passage, marking one's "coming out" as a Quaker.

Once again, Thomas Ellwood's account of his personal experience stands as a dramatic instance of this process, rendered the more so by the fact that as a member of the gentry he had especially cultivated the elaborate displays of politeness that signaled good breeding and manners in mid-seventeenth-century England. Ellwood records vividly the occasion on which, meeting a group of his former acquaintances, he refrained for the first time from participating in their greeting ritual. To their puzzled, "What, Tom! a Quaker!" he answered, "Yes: A Quaker," and was immediately filled with joy "that I had strength and boldness given me to confess my self to be one of that despised people" (1906:32–33).

That the plain style was a rallying symbol for the Quakers is made clear by Penn's exhortation that taking up the cross of the plain style "enlists thee in the company of the blessed, mocked, persecuted Jesus; to fight under his banner, against the world, the flesh and the devil" (1865:109). Thus, though the plain style was not consciously adopted as an identity badge, it certainly came by its radical unconventionality to serve that function in the eyes of Quakers and non-Quakers alike.

The second major group of arguments against the plain style has already been alluded to earlier in the discussion: namely, that the politeness forms rejected by the Quakers were sanctioned by custom. Although custom and convention were seen by various anti-Quaker critics as validating the whole range of politeness forms at issue – "usage gives the stamp to speech, and custom is the only law, to make words, or phrases, proper, or improper" (Fowler 1676:17) – the argument was employed most fully and frequently to counter Quaker appeals to other languages as grounds for maintaining a distinction between second-person-singular and plural pronouns, that is, "thou" versus "you" in the singular. In this vein, one anti-Quaker pamphleteer argued:

> It is convenient and proper for us in England to say, *you*, to a single person . . . because custom hath so fixed it, and custom is the great law in speech . . . And whatsoever is the common use, backed by tradition, and universally taught by parents to their children, masters to their scholars, and is ordinary in common converse, this is the most authentic law in speech. (Cheyney 1676:2; see also Fowler 1676:18)

This argument had a certain rhetorical effectiveness in that it countered the Quaker appeal to the precedent of other languages with an appeal to their own national language, meeting the Quakers to a degree on their own terms.

The Quakers, however, had recourse to a further counterargument that was more fundamental than an appeal to mere linguistic appropriateness, namely, morality. It will be recalled that the Quakers' most basic argument against politeness forms was that such forms fed one's earthly pride and were thus destructive of true spiritual righteousness. The early Quakers viewed the course of world history from the days of the primitive church to their own period as one of degeneration and decline through which the pure teachings of Christ and his disciples were overlaid with corrupt, vain, and worldly practices (Burrough 1658:15–16). Their Quaker faith redeemed them out of the corruption, but the rest of England remained mired in sin. It was only to be expected, in their view, that custom and tradition would uphold degenerate and sinful forms of social interaction. "And doth not then the upholding that custom uphold pride, and the upholding pride cause religion to suffer?" charged Ellwood, in rebuttal of an anti-Quaker tract criticizing the plain style. The author, he went on,

> magnifies custom, and builds all upon it; but I impeach that custom itself, as nourishing and cherishing that in man which is not of the

Heavenly Father's planting, and therefore must be plucked up. Let the ax therefore be laid to the root of this custom, which is, pride, ambition, haughtiness, flattery; and no further controversy will ever sprout from it. (1676:29)

The remedy was clear: Proper godly behavior was an eternal standard to be upheld over custom, which was transitory (Caton 1671:28). However strongly conventional the world's politeness forms might be, they ought to be abandoned by everyone in favor of the spiritually appropriate plain style.

If the use of the plain style had struck only at grammaticality or custom, it might still have remained a matter of controversy, because any religiously motivated deviant behavior was a political issue in mid-seventeenth-century England, but it would probably not have generated so intense and heated a body of controversy as it did. The real issue, recognized by Quakers and non-Quakers alike, was that the plain style challenged the social structure and the structure of social relations in very fundamental ways. It was, at least in its beginnings, a manifestation of radical puritanism at nearly its most radical.

The social interactional impact of the Quakers' refusal to offer greetings or titles, or using "thou" to a person of high status, was to make them appear to be "a rude, unmannerly people, that would not give civil respect or honour to their superiors" (Ellwood 1906:37–38; see also Anon. 1655:14–15). Time and again, one encounters judgments of their behavior couched in such terms as "rude," "unmannerly," "uncivil," "discourteous," "disrespectful," "contemptuous," "arrogant," "disdainful," "churlish," or "clownish," imputing to them either ignorance or the flouting of good manners.

It is instructive that the use of the plain style also drew accusations that the Quakers were supercilious, proud, vainglorious (Anon. 1655:14–15), or self-conceited (Furly 1663:23), because that was certainly a plausible reading of their behavior in terms of the contemporary politeness system; the denial of politeness forms was one clear way of asserting one's superiority to others in social interaction. These charges, of course, validated the Quakers' insistence that it was really worldly pride they were attacking through the use of the plain style, not out of pride on their own part, but out of the religious conviction that all flesh must be brought low so that the spirit might prevail. They were obeying God's command "who forbids us to bow" – literally or figuratively – "to the likeness of anything in heaven, earth, or under the Earth" (Fisher 1660:x). For the Quakers, "the ground of all true nobility, gentility, majesty, honour, breeding, manners, courtesy and civility, no more after the flesh, but after the spirit" (Parnel 1675:92), lay in Truth and love in speaking Truth to one's neighbor, in doing unto others as you would have them do unto you (Fox 1831,4:200; Parnel 1675:91).

To accuse the Quakers of rudeness and lack of manners was to see them as destructive of the proper order of social relations at the level of social interaction. At times, however, the argument was raised to a more general level. By refusing to display the proper respect not only to their peers but to their social superiors, "those that are over us in the flesh" (Barclay 1841:5), including often magistrates, officers, or political officials, they were seen as enemies to the social order and civil authority (Ellwood 1906:37–38). One anti-Quaker critic asserted that the casting off of good manners by the Quakers "doth directly tend to overthrow all government and authority amongst men; for, take away outward honour and respect from superiors, and what government can subsist long amongst men?" (quoted in Bohn 1955:348). In the blunt words of another critic, the Quaker is "a professed enemy to all order" (R. H. 1672a:3).

The charges were often expressed in terms of a leveling impulse (e.g., Fowler and Ford 1656:41), after the Levellers, who called for equality of property and the elimination of social and political distinctions based upon wealth; and indeed there does seem to have been a significant Leveller influence upon numbers of the early Quakers (Hill 1975:125–128).

The positions taken by Quakers in terms of these issues and in response to the criticisms that were directed at them were various, reflecting as much the background or rhetorical purpose of the individual or historical circumstance as Quaker religious doctrine. In general, during the first period of Quakerism, through the 1650s, but especially during the period 1654–1656 when Quakerism was at the height of its missionary zeal, their statements were at their most radical, castigating the prevailing system of social and economic inequality and the politeness system that supported it as founded on earthly lust, pride, and self-will. One of the strongest voices was the young minister and early Quaker martyr, James Parnel:

> And here is the ground of the world's superiority, nobility, gentility, honour, breeding and manners; and here they Lord over one another by their corrupt wills; and here is the ground of all tyranny and oppression, rackings and taxings, and wars, and imprisonments, and envy, and murder, and the persecution of the righteous; all arise from proud Lucifer, the lust in man, who would be honoured; and all this is in the fall, and under the curse. (1675:86)

In true leveling spirit, Parnel wanted to do away with a superiority and nobility of the flesh and substitute a nobility of the spirit, in which honor is due to the true in spirit, whether "magistrate or minister, fisherman or ploughman, herdsman or shepherd, wheresoever it rules without respect of persons" (1675:89–90; see also pp. 94–95 and Fox 1831, 4:198).

By the 1660s one can detect a clear tempering of the Quakers' stance on the social implications of the plain style, as their missionary zeal declined, fiery leaders such as Parnel died in prison, and much of their effort had to be devoted simply to surviving the massive legal repression visited upon them after the Restoration and to showing that they were not enemies to authority (see Chapter 7). The statement of Benjamin Furly, for example, in 1663, has a conciliatory and accommodative tone – part of a pattern we will encounter again in later chapters – that contrasts sharply with Parnel's radicalism:

> We say, though after outward power, authority, rule, government or dominion we seek not, nor do desire it, yet we despise it not, but do own it in its place; and do submit unto it for peace and conscience sake, as Christ who was above all outward rule also did. The like for titles, as being distinctions of several offices, as names are of diverse persons, we both own and use them; yet titles there are flattering and blasphemous, in which the honour of God is attributed to man whose breath is in his nostrils, and these, we freely confess we own not, and do trample upon that deceitful mind from whence they came. (1663:54)

Although the social origins of the early Quakers have been the subject of some debate (Reay 1980a; Vann 1969), it is clear that the movement did attract adherents from the gentry and aristocracy, such people as the Peningtons, Thomas Ellwood, William Penn, and Robert Barclay. Penn and Barclay, the two major Quaker apologists of the seventeenth century, came to Quakerism after the zeal of the first period was largely spent, and their response to the charges of social radicalism leveled against the Quaker plain style reflects both their own social backgrounds and the historical circumstances of the Restoration period. Penn seems at times to reduce the Quaker plain style to formalist terms, seeing the symbolic inversion represented by Quaker usage largely as a means of enhancing the rhetorical power of the general Quaker mission:

> The world is so set upon the ceremonious part and outside of things, that it has pleased the wisdom of God in all ages, to bring forth his dispensations with very different appearances to their settled customs; thereby contradicting human inventions, and proving the integrity of his confessors. Nay, it is a test upon the world: it tries what patience, kindness, sobriety, and moderation they have. (1865:108)

Violating custom in these terms is simply an efficient means of trying and testing the powers that be; underlying principle is not much in evidence here.

Barclay, in his *Apology*, contrasts strongly in tone with Parnel twenty years earlier. In place of Parnel's ringing indictment of fleshly lust, oppression, and privilege, we get a calm acceptance of inequality:

> Let not any judge, that from our opinion in these things, any necessity of levelling will follow, or that all men must have things in common. Our principle leaves every man to enjoy that peaceably, which either

his own industry, or his parents have purchased to him; only he is thereby instructed to use it aright, both for his own good, and that of his brethren; and all to the glory of God . . . we know, that as it hath pleased God to dispense [the creation] diversely, giving to some more, and some less, so they may use it accordingly. The several conditions, under which men are diversely stated, together with their educations answering thereunto, do sufficiently show this. (1831, 2:516)

*   *   *   *

The appropriate use of greetings, titles and other honorifics, or formal pronouns is, as I have emphasized, a way of being polite. The Quakers, of course, refused to use these forms. But systematic violation of politeness conventions is no less important to the study of politeness than their scrupulous observation. Moreover, politeness, or the lack of it, was the principal frame of reference for contemporary discussions of Quaker practice within the context of the broader social environment in which they acted.

The fullest and most analytically suggestive framework for the sociolinguistic study of politeness phenomena is provided by Brown and Levinson in their seminal article, "Universals in Language Usage: Politeness Phenomena" (1978). Building upon the work of Goffman, Brown and Levinson conceive of politeness phenomena as means of acknowledging or upholding another person's face, which they see as consisting of two aspects: *positive face*, "the positive consistent self-image or 'personality' (crucially including the desire that this self-image be appreciated and approved of) claimed by interactants," and *negative face*, "the basic claim to territories, personal preserves, rights to non-distraction – i.e., to freedom of action and freedom from imposition" (1978:66). Failure to employ politeness forms and strategies appropriately makes for what the authors term *face-threatening acts*. In the case of the Quaker plain language, it was positive face that was threatened by the Quakers' deviant usages.

The work of Brown and Levinson on politeness, like that of Goffman, is marked by a certain essentially valid eufunctional thrust. Goffman suggests, for example, that "it seems to be a characteristic obligation of many social relationships that each of the members guarantees to support a given face for the other members in given situations" (1967:42). Brown and Levinson, though they give serious consideration to impoliteness, building much of their analytical framework on the notion of face-threatening acts, emphasize most strongly the means and strategies for mitigation and redress of these acts. "In general," they maintain, "people cooperate (and assume each other's cooperation) in maintaining face in interaction, such cooperation being based on the mutual vulnerability of face" (1978:66). And again: "In the context of the mutual vulnerability of face, any rational agent will seek to avoid . . . face-threatening acts, or will employ certain strategies to minimize the threat'' (1978:73).

Acknowledging the general validity of these observations, what are we to make of the seventeenth-century Quakers, who formulated an interactional system built upon the principled contravention of prevailing standards of politeness? At the very least, the Quaker case should be of more than usual comparative and theoretical interest as a system in which the eufunctional generalizations of Goffman and Brown and Levinson do not hold.

As I have observed earlier in this discussion, seventeenth-century English society was characterized by a high degree of preoccupation with deference and politeness. The factors contributing to this preoccupation are various, ranging from the continuing salience of traditional social structures of stratification and hierarchy, to the burgeoning thrust for respectability on the part of the rising middle class, to the influence of elaborate Continental systems for the display of deference. The scope of this study does not allow an extensive or fine-grained analysis of the dynamics of conventional politeness forms during the period under review, but one can certainly say that failures to greet or to use titles and salutations and formal pronouns were strongly marked in a great many social interactional contexts. They represented face-*threatening* acts, whether or not they were taken as affronts by those who came into contact with Friends.

To be sure, there were always some people during that period of religious ferment who were tolerant of behavior, however deviant, that was based on sincere religious principle. Such people – Richard Davies's master, for example (1832:29) – were not threatened by the Quakers' plain language. Moreover, as Barbour points out, there were certain regional differences with regard to pronominal usage; in those parts of the north and west of England (especially in Yorkshire, Lancashire, Westmoreland, Cumberland, Devon and Somerset) where Quakerism arose and was most strong, ''thee'' forms appear to have been standard among equals and are less likely to have caused affront (1964:164–165). When Quakers spread to the other parts of England, to the south and east, where ''thee'' was an insult except to inferiors, their use of this form would naturally provoke strong feelings of hostility. Time was also a factor in the way the plain language was likely to be perceived by non-Quakers to whom it was addressed. As people in various parts of England became more familiar with Quakers and their behavior, through the 1660s, 1670s, and 1680s, and came to recognize the plain language as conventional, they were increasingly less likely to take the Quakers' apparent rudeness personally and be affronted by it.

In addition to the above factors, although direct evidence is scarce, there are indications that the Quakers did employ certain redressive means to mitigate the face-threatening effect of the plain language. The use of ''Friend'' as a solidary term of address, for example, appears to have been a common redressive strategy; by 1672, the phrase, "plainly I tell thee, Friend," was recognized as a formulaic usage of Quakers in trade (R. H. 1672a:4; cf. Brown and Levinson 1978:112–113). Thomas Ellwood's detailed account of his troubles with his father over his unwillingness to use the customary politeness forms indicates that he was at pains to continue to manifest his respect for his father in other ways, though to little avail (1906:47). Certainly, the Quakers' own direct statements of their intent emphasize that they meant no insult, arrogance, disdain, or contempt in their use of the plain speech, urging their critics to examine the rest of their behavior for confirmation of this (Fisher 1660:x; Furly 1663:23).

Even when all such allowances are made, however, there remained the constant potential that the plain language would give affront to those who were zealous guardians of their social position and self-esteem. This was especially true in regard to pronouns, as the experience of Richard Davies with his mistress, Thomas Ellwood with his father, and countless other Quakers with priests and magistrates plainly demonstrates. Whatever redressive means the Quakers were willing to employ, there was a point beyond which they would not go if it meant compromising the integrity of the principles of Truth on which the plain language was based. These religious imperatives, implicating their very spiritual salvation, were far more important than worldly comfort or the willingness to uphold others' face.

The Quakers' behavior with regard to conventional politeness forms and strategies had both an expressive and a rhetorical dimension. By "expressive" here, I mean the Quakers' understanding of the ways in which what they said affected themselves – what they could and could not say, and why. By "rhetorical" is meant their understanding of the ways in which what they said affected others.

The principal expressive factors I have identified are three in number: the requirement always to tell the truth, the prohibition against idle words, and the injunction against paying honor to men's persons. The requirement always to tell the truth operated most centrally with regard to greetings, titles, and salutations, and more peripherally with regard to pronouns. Rejecting the notion that politeness forms are merely phatic and conventional, not to be measured by the standard of referential accuracy, Friends insisted that to address someone as "master" who was not in fact one's master, or "your grace" when he was not in a state of grace, or to salute him with "your humble servant" when you were not his servant, was contrary to literal truth and therefore a lie. Likewise, to wish someone a good day or farewell when he was, like all non-Quakers, in a state of spiritual evil, was again to lie. Worse yet, it was to participate in his evil oneself. The argument of truth against using "you" in the singular was more legalistic and less often voiced.

A single individual was one, not many; hence, to address him or her in the plural was again to lie.

The biblical injunction against idle words – "But I say unto you, That every idle word that men shall speak, they shall give account of in the day of judgment. For by thy words thou shalt be justified, and by thy words thou shalt be condemned" (Matthew 12.36–37) – was closely observed by the Quakers, upholding, as I have established, their distrust of speaking. With regard to politeness, the form most directly implicated by the need to avoid idle words was greetings, insofar as one of the primary functions of greetings is to open access to talk. If one had nothing to engage another person in talk about, no contact need be established. To employ a greeting for its own sake or for the sake of convention was to engage in idle words at a risk to one's own spiritual welfare.

Finally, insofar as the conventions of politeness were keyed to relative social status – "you" for peers and superiors, "thou" to inferiors, titles and salutations a means of signaling deference – to use them was to honor another's person in direct contravention of the biblical injunction to the contrary: "But if ye have respect to persons, ye commit sin, and are convinced of the law as transgressors" (James 2.9). Indeed, the book of James, chapter 2, goes on to establish the irreducible foundation of the Quakers' principle against moral compromise of any kind: "For whosoever shall keep the whole law, and yet offend in one *point*, he is guilty of all" (James 2.10). If politeness is the tending of another's face, and if that face is grounded in self-esteem based on wordly honor, then to that extent to follow custom is to condemn oneself before God; and this the Quakers would not do.

This much establishes why the seventeenth-century Friends would not follow the conventions of politeness for the sake of their own spiritual welfare. But, as I have suggested, there was also a powerful rhetorical motivation to the use of the plain language. Not to pay honor to men's persons by using the world's politeness forms and strategies was motivated by a concern for others' spiritual welfare as well. A central part of the Quakers' mission in the world was to help to redeem the rest of mankind out of the worldly corruption into which it had fallen since the days of the primitive church. The use of the plain speech was a powerful weapon in the Lamb's War, attacking the very fleshly pride that was otherwise fed and exalted by the politeness forms the Quakers rejected. Indeed, the plain language was at its most effective when people *were* offended by it, for that meant they recognized that their pride was at stake. Under the best of circumstances, this recognition opened the way to a fuller spiritual self-knowledge by which "many came to see where they were" (Fox 1952:36) and were able, by the grace of the Inward Light, to move from a lust for the world's honor to a higher state, by a suppression of the fleshly pride that fed upon conventional politeness.

For the Quakers, to be instrumental thus in the salvation of others was to carry out the mission assigned them by God. But, as we have seen, far from all of those who were affronted by the plain language were moved thereby to spiritual insight; anger, violence, and persecution were frequently the consequences of the Quakers' "rudeness." What is important is that this too had its benefits, because the suffering visited upon Friends because of the plain language reinforced their ethic of suffering as a means to spiritual salvation. Bearing the cross of the plain language in a hostile world was a means for the early Quakers to enact and display their faith, shared by the entire Quaker fellowship. Thus, the rhetoric of the plain language served basic Quaker ends both when it succeeded and when it failed. As a people who saw their mission in a corrupt world as one of doing away with the exaltation of the flesh so that the spirit of God might prevail, the early Quakers could scarcely have chosen a more effective means than politeness phenomena as a focus for their religious challenge.

5

SOME PLOUGH, SOME WEED OUT, AND SOME SOW: PREACHING AND PASSAGE IN THE PROCESS OF CONVERSION

When George Fox described the various aspects of the Quaker ministry, even as he embarked on the journey to the north that was to lead to the first real coalescence of the Quaker movement, he did so in terms of the agrarian and pastoral imagery of the Bible. The principal task was to gather people – the seed, the faithful believers (Graves 1972:218–224) – away from the falseness of the world's religions; but this task called forth a variety of efforts, depending upon their prior spiritual condition. Fox outlined the division of ministerial labor thus: "Some speak to the conscience; some plough and break the clods; some weed out, and some sow; some wait, that fowls devour not the seed. But wait all for the gathering of the simple-hearted ones" (1831, 7:18). Elsewhere, he identified the tasks in similar metaphorical terms, as "some threshing, and some ploughing, and some to keep the sheep" (1831, 7:25).

In the early years of the Quaker movement, more or less up to the time of the Restoration in 1660, a relatively large proportion of the ministerial effort was devoted to the mission out in the world – gathering, as opposed to keeping, the sheep. In terms of Fox's agrarian imagery, the convincement and conversion of others to Quakerism required preparing the ground, planting the seed of faith, protecting the growth (by cutting out the weeds and seeing that birds did not devour the seed), and ultimately threshing out the new seed. The Quaker ministers carried out their work in a range of settings roughly functionally correlated with these ministerial tasks; that is, some had more to do with preparing the ground and planting the seed, others with nurturing those in whom the growth had already begun.

The plowing and sowing metaphors identified the tasks of opening people up to the Truth and making them aware how to be responsive to it when they heard it from others and found it within themselves. Because "Truth hath an honour in the hearts of people that are not Friends" (Fox 1952:341), what was needed was to get out among those people and proclaim it. One of the best ways to do this with maximal effect was to locate the places "where people were together" (Penney 1907:296) and work the crowds. Thus, the early Quaker ministers concentrated much of their effort on those settings that provided a ready-made audience for their preaching, especially churches, markets, fairs, and the public streets of cities and towns (Fox 1831, 7:348).

Churches stood out as a special setting for the Quaker ministers because they represented a battleground on which the Lamb's War could be waged in the most direct terms, where people were gathered in observances of the world's religions, led by the false ministers of those corrupted faiths. For the Quakers, the very word "church" was contrary to the Truth in reference to the world's religions, and like the Anabaptists they refused to apply it to the houses of worship maintained by the priests and professors of those religious groups, calling them instead "steeplehouses." The true church consisted in "the people whom God has purchased with his blood, and not the house" (Fox 1952:94). God dwelt not in the outward house, but in the hearts of the true believers (Fox 1952:85). Thus, the Quaker ministers went to speak in the churches "to cry against them, and to exhort people to turn from them" (Briggs 1685:4; see also Fox 1952:50, 85).

Their messages, accordingly, were challenges and attacks against the legitimacy of the priests and their religious practices. John Banks reports a typical instance from his own ministry, in which he challenged his priestly adversary in these direct terms: "If thou be a minister of Christ, stand to prove thy practice; and if it be the same the apostles and ministers of Christ was, and is, in doctrine and practice, I will own thee; but if not, I am sent of God this day, to testify against thee" (1798:48–49). One of the formative influences in Thomas Ellwood's development of sympathy for Quakerism was the visit of a young man to a church service he was attending, who answered the priest's sermon with "the prayer of the wicked is abomination to the Lord" and "God heareth not sinners" (1906:15).

At times, when given the opportunity, the Quaker ministers attempted to controvert the priests' own doctrines. George Whitehead, who appears to have been especially effective at this, recounts an experience in which "in the time the priest was preaching, I took down some of his doctrine; after he had done his preaching, I laid open some of it before his hearers, who were most of them quiet and willing to hear, except two or three professors, and the priest's wife" (Barclay 1841:230–231).

The tone of the Quakers' attacks on the priests in their churches varied considerably from minister to minister and instance to instance. Some, like the young man who challenged the priest of Thomas Ellwood's congregation, were temperate in their manner, "without passion or ill language" (Ellwood 1906:16). Nevertheless, it remains the case that the Quaker opposition to the false priests was strongly motivated and very intense, as discussed in an earlier chapter. Furthermore, the Bible (e.g., Titus 1.13, 2.15) gave them a precedent for rebuking the false priests in their own churches: "And whereas we are accused for going into steeple-houses, it was the practice of the apostles to go into the synagogues, reasoning and disputing about the scriptures, shewing them the substance" (Fox 1831, 4:43). Even more, it gave them a strong vocabulary for the purpose. Among the forms of biblical invective hurled by the Quakers at their priestly adversaries were such phrases as "greedy dumb dogs" (Isaiah 56.10–11), "blind guides," "whited sepulchres" (Matthew 23.16, 27), "sorcerers," "idolators," and "liars" (Revelation 21.8, 22.15). Indeed, one critic was moved to say that the Quaker "reads the Bible only to furnish himself with Scripture-names to call those he intends to quarrel with, 'Reprobate Children of Perdition,' 'Son of Belial,' etc." (R. H. 1672b:37). The accusation leveled most frequently at these vehement early ministers was that of railing: "They are also as horrible railers as ever any age brought forth, a generation whose mouths are full of bitterness" (Higginson 1653:21; see also R. H. 1672b:5). Even allowing for the anti-Quaker bias of such critics, it is clear that the Quakers' language was deeply shocking to the majority of their contemporaries, accustomed to addressing members of the clergy with deference and respect. What others saw as railing on the part of the Quakers reinforced the public image of the Quakers as a rude, unmannerly people, deriving from their refusal to use conventional politeness forms in everyday social intercourse.

Although the priests and professors were the most common targets of Quaker verbal aggression, both oral and in print, Quaker spokesmen also attacked others in similar terms, including people who came to bait or debate them at their own meetings, legal authorities who persecuted them, and people who questioned them in other public places (e.g., Fox 1952:119; Penney 1907:69).

In response to their critics, the Quakers defended their strong language on three principal grounds: truth, biblical precedent, and divine inspiration. Burrough, for example, appealed to all three standards. "And what if the ministers of England be called hirelings and false prophets, and greedy dumb dogs," he wrote, "the practice of some of them doth prove it that they are so; these things you must bear, as coming deservedly, and not unjustly upon you." Moreover, he continued, "the servants of the Lord in all ages ever cried against deceivers, and false prophets, and called them deceivers, and greedy dumb dogs, and serpents, and vipers, and evil beasts, and slow bellies." Christ, the Apostles, and the Prophets were called upon to use such terms against the false ministers in their own time, just as the Quakers were, but "not with revilings and reproachings, but with the spirit of authority from God," the source of all proper religious speaking (1660b:13; see also Howgill 1676:223). Even the normally gentle and mystical Isaac Penington came to the defense of the Quakers' strong language. As "for railing speeches," he wrote: "The false prophets can speak smooth words; speaking in the fleshly wisdom, they can please the fleshly part in their very reproofs; but he that speaks from God, must speak his words, how harsh soever they seem to the fleshly part" (1863, 1:405).

Here is the characteristic Quaker distrust of pleasing language, smooth language, especially as cultivated by the false ministers, and the corresponding sense of the rightness of any speaking that attacked "the fleshly part." If biblical invective discomfited the corrupt, it was all the more appropriate. Coming from God speaking through his ministers, it was beyond criticism:

> And so for the false prophets and teachers: if the spirit of the Lord (in the meanest of his servants) call them idle shepherds, hirelings, thieves, robbers, dogs, dumb dogs, greedy dumb dogs, that cannot bark (though they can speak smooth pleasing words enough to fleshly Israel, and the earthly great ones), generation of vipers, hypocrites, whited sepulchres, graves that appear not, etc., who may reprove him for it, or find fault with the instrument he chooses? Now man judging by the fleshly wisdom, may venture to call this railing . . . but the Lord, being angry with the transgressor, may send a rough rebuke to him, by what measure he pleaseth; and what is the poor creature that he should gainsay his Maker, and desire the message might be smoother? (Penington 1863, 1:405)

Whether temperate or vehement, the Quakers' disruption of church services was seldom met with equanimity by the priests and their congregations. Occasionally, a minister might report that a congregation was "loving" and responsive or that only a few members were strongly opposed to Quaker intrusion (e.g., Barclay 1841:230–231; Fox 1952:74, 76). More often than not, however, the Quakers encountered marked hostility in the churches, frequently in the form of physical violence. Such violence might come at the hand of an angry individual, as in the case of Samuel Briggs, reported by his daughter. At one steeplehouse he visited, Briggs was attacked by a man who took hold of him by the hair and struck his head against a stone until the hair was pulled out, "which my father bore patiently." When his attacker threw the handful of hair to the ground, Briggs "took it up in his hand: and mildly said, 'One hair of my head shall not fall without my Father's providence' " (Briggs 1685:16).

At other times, the Quakers suffered violence at the hands of mobs. A typical example, of the many to be found in the journals of early Friends, concerns Robert Withers in Pardshaw, Cumberland. In 1653,

> the said R. W. was moved to go to Coldbeck steeple house, where he spoke to priest Hutton, when he was in his high place, and the rude people, the priest's hearers, threw Robert down among the seats, and dragged him forth into the yard, and threw him down upon the ground, and punched and beat him until the blood gushed out at his mouth. And he lay for dead some time, but a woman took pity of him, and held up his head till his breath came to him again (as some said who stood by). And on the same day in ye afternoon he went 7 miles to Aikton steeple house, where he spoke to Priest Nichols,

of Aikton, in his high place, and said, "Come down, thou deceiver, thou enemy of Christ, the hand of the Lord is against thee." (Penney 1907:35)

Not all the violence visited upon the Quaker ministers was outside the law, however. From 1656 onward, there were legal constraints against disrupting organized church services. Accordingly, those Quakers who spoke in churches were liable to arrest and were often harshly treated by hostile authorities (see, e.g., Penney 1907:83).

It is worth remarking that women ministers were not exempt from such violence. On one occasion in Starford, for example, when a woman minister appeared in the church to declare against the priest, "she was haled out by these professors, which were then officers, and was led by them to the cage, and there she did sit seven hours, where she was pissed on, and spit on by those brutes of Starford." After being released,

> she came a second time to their meeting where she was haled out like a dog, and the officers did turn her out of the grave-yard, to the mercies of the heathen, who rent her, and did tear her, pulling her head tire off, pulling her by the hair of the head, and throwing her down in the street as she passed along to come to a friend's house, which is nigh half the quarter of a mile from the steeple house, howling and shouting at their fellow creature. (Payne 1655:29–30)

What is especially noteworthy about these accounts, besides the cruelty of attacks visited upon the Friends, is the indomitable spirit of the Quakers in the face of the persecution they endured. Sustained by their conviction that they were sent by God to speak his Word, they refused to be deterred from their purpose as long as they had strength to continue, until they had "cleared [themselves] by speaking to the people" (Penney 1907:72). If they were thrown into jail, they spoke to the other prisoners, or "declared Truth out at the prison windows" (Penney 1907:83). John Banks's determination is typical. After being thrown out of a church on one occasion, he came back in, waited for the priest to finish, and testified against him again, causing a great uproar in the congregation. But, says Banks, "having obeyed the requirings of the Lord, I came away in sweet peace, and spiritual comfort in my heart and soul" (1798:48–49). One must not be deterred by fleshly suffering from speaking out the word of God. Indeed, as we have noted often before, suffering in the service of the Holy Spirit was indispensable for one's own salvation.

Church services were the focus of special concern on the part of the early Quaker ministers attempting to convince others of the Truth because they represented the most tangible embodiment of the religious error against which the Quakers contended. People were gathered in the churches for a religious purpose, engaged in religious practice, and directed by officially constituted religious authorities. In this context the confrontation between Quakerism and established religion was raised to its most direct and dramatic. Other public places – markets, fairs, and town streets – were more diffuse, their social dynamics far more unfocused. Nevertheless, the Quaker ministers were drawn to these secular settings both because they were where the crowds were and, at least in the case of markets and fairs, because much of what the Quakers considered sinful – festivity, sport, popular entertainment, and other worldly and licentious activities – was publicly on display on these occasions. This had still another consequence: In markets and fairs people were especially attuned to novel public performances because the jugglers, actors, rope dancers, and acrobats were drawn to the crowds, just as the Quakers were, and would gather around the Quaker ministers to hear what they had to say (cf. Burke 1978:111–112; Spufford 1974:261).

Of the very large number of early accounts detailing the labors of Quaker ministers in market towns, perhaps none draws together so many elements and conveys a better sense of the dynamic of such occasions than that of William Edmondson, one of the first Quakers in Ireland (1820:71–72). In the course of a ministerial journey in 1657, Edmondson arrived one day at Londonderry. "It was market-day," as it happened, "and there were stage-players and rope-dancers in the market-place, and abundance of people gathered." At this point, Edmondson reports, "the Lord's Spirit filled my heart, his power struck at them, and his word was sharp. So I stood in the market-place, and proclaimed the day of the Lord among them, and warned them all to repent." The effect was powerful: "The dread of the Almighty came over them, and they were as people amazed."

When he had had his say and felt his spirit eased, Edmondson began to walk down the street, drawing the people along with him. This made the stage players "sore vexed that the people left them, and followed me," whereupon they sent to the mayor to have Edmondson arrested and taken to prison, over the objections of his new followers. Edmondson was not to be daunted, however.

> The gaoler put me in a room that had a window facing the market-place, where I had a full sight of the people; and my heart being filled with the word of life and testimony of Jesus, I thrust my arm out at the window and waved it, till some of them espying, came near, and others followed apace; so that presently I had most of the people from the stage-players, which vexed them much. Then they got the mayor to cause the gaoler to keep me close; so he bolted me, and locked my leg to a place where he used to fasten condemned persons. There I sat in much peace of conscience, and sweet union with the Spirit of Truth.

Edmondson's moral victory did not end here, however. He could not resist adding to his account that "as I sat in a heavenly exercise, I heard the people shout and say, the man had broke his back. It was the man dancing on a rope, which broke or gave way, so that he fell on the pavement, and was sorely hurt." So much for the wages of sin. Edmondson closes his account in typical fashion: "Many professors came into prison to see me, and I had much discourse with them, and good service for truth."

Edmondson's account portrays especially clearly the confrontation between the religious faith of the Quakers and the fleshly engagement of "the world's people." His description of his being drawn to speak to the crowd and the gist of his exhortation to the people to repent, for the day of the Lord was at hand, are highly typical of ministerial accounts from this period. Even his arrest and imprisonment are common themes; the element of adversity and suffering enhances the spiritual success of the experience and makes it all the more reportable. The only recurrent theme missing from Edmondson's account is violence. Although the sympathies of the public at large were apparently divided between him and the entertainer, no one attacked him physically, as they did others of his brethren. Again to take just one of many possible examples, we may consider the experience of Ambrose Rigge in Henley-on-Thames, Oxfordshire, in 1658. Preaching from a stool set in the gateway of an inn opposite the corn market with two other Friends, "Ambrose Rigge declared Truth, being many people gathered about them; some were very attentive and sober. And . . . two or three [were] then so reached, that afterward they came to own Truth; yet some were very rude and abusive and throwing things at him, as guts; they got bricks" (Penney 1907:218). As in the churches, the ministers who worked the markets and other public places were susceptible to violence.

The frequency and the regularity of the public markets made them especially well suited to the purposes of the traveling Quaker ministers, who could be sure of finding a large gathering in any vicinity into which they extended their ministerial journeys. But the point was to get the message out to as many people as possible, and other events that drew a crowd were equally serviceable.

One of the great milestone occasions in the early history of the Quaker movement, for example, occurred at a great Whitsun Wednesday fair in Sedburgh, Westmoreland, June 9, 1652. This was an area in the north of England in which Fox found many people receptive to the Truth, including most of those who later constituted the nucleus of the Valiant Sixty, the group that carried Quakerism to the south in 1654. The Sedburgh fair was a fair for the hiring of farm laborers and domestic servants and attracted a great many young people. Fox took advantage of the occasion "and declared through the fair the day of the Lord," going afterward to the steeplehouse yard, where "most of the people of the fair came to me, and abundance of priests and professors." Fox preached to the assembled gathering for several hours, "to bring them off the temples made with hands, that they themselves might know they were the temples of God" (Fox 1952:107). Many people received his testimony on this occasion "and were convinced and turned to the way of Truth" (Penney 1907:243).

Of course, the Quaker ministers did not confine their public efforts to the special occasions of markets and fairs. Between such mass gatherings, people could still be reached, though in less concentrated numbers, on the public thoroughfares of cities and towns. Here, there was less opportunity for lengthy and sustained preaching; instead, the ministers tended to proclaim short, apocalyptic messages as they walked the streets, most commonly exhortations to the people to repent, which came soon to be known as their characteristic cry (Davies 1832:33–34). Though brief, these exhortations were not necessarily lacking in vehemence; preaching through the streets of Selby, Yorkshire, in 1652, Elizabeth Tomlinson was "carried . . . almost off her feet" crying " 'Repent! Repent' for the day of the Lord is at hand; Woe to the Drunkards of Ephraim," which "struck a great astonishment in the people" (Penney 1907:290).

One Friend who tended to specialize in speaking through cities and towns during the mid-1650s was Thomas Briggs (1685:7). Recalling his labors during "Oliver's days," as Friends called the time of Cromwell, Briggs reported that he often went through four or five towns in a single day "to warn people to repent and turn to the Lord, that the Lord might be clear, and I might be clear of the blood of all men" (1685:7). Briggs's account of a visit to Manchester gives us an indication of the message he carried "through many towns, and cities, in England": "Repent, repent, for the mighty day of the Lord God of power is appearing, wherein no worker of iniquity shall stand before him, who is of a purer eye than to behold iniquity; for he wills not the death of a sinner, and if ye repent and turn to him, he will abundantly pardon" (1685:4).

In the streets, as elsewhere, the Quaker ministers were sometimes met with violence. Riding out of Repham, in 1654, George Whitehead was moved to warn the people in the street to repentance, to which they responded by stoning him "in a furious manner." Like his brethren in the churches and markets though, Whitehead stood his ground, so that "I cleared my conscience to the people" (1832, 1:65–66).

The early Quaker ministers worked the public places – the churches, markets, fairs, streets – in order to bring the Truth before those who had not yet received it, to plow the ground and plant the seed of their new faith. For those in whom the process of convincement was already under way, who were already responsive to the Truth, other kinds of contexts were better suited to the task of nurturing the growth and ultimately to carrying through the process of separating them from the world's religions and, to switch to the pastoral metaphor, gathering them into the fold. These other ministerial contexts involved a larger element of voluntarism insofar as they were tailored to the needs of people in whom the seed had already been planted by the Quakers, or those who were already searching for an alternative religious way that suited their spiritual needs, or those already in sects, like the Seekers, with beliefs and practices similar to the Quakers' own. These people often sought out the Quaker ministers voluntarily for further spiritual assistance.

Accordingly, the meetings for cultivation and harvest often grew out of invitations extended to Quakers by already receptive individuals or groups; at other times, Friends themselves appointed meetings in areas where they knew people to be sympathetic, perhaps as a result of earlier work by their own compatriots (for an unsympathetic but reasonably accurate account of the early Quakers' *modus operandi*, see Higginson 1653:14–15).

The gatherings themselves varied considerably in scale and setting, from small and private to large and public. At one end of the spectrum were meetings in people's homes. A nicely typical instance is reported by Richard Farnsworth of his work in Wakefield in 1653. The host was one Doctor Hodgson, whom Farnsworth describes as "shaken a little, and . . . very loving to us," indicating that he was one of those in whom the spiritual ground was broken and the seed of Quakerism planted. Many people crowded into the house, "as many as could thrust," and Farnsworth "was drawn forth much to speak to them," standing upon a table because of the press of people around him. "They were all silent," he reports with evident satisfaction, "and were very attentive to hear me a long time" (Barclay 1841:217).

Separatist congregations also represented a fertile field for the propagation of the Quaker message. At times, then, Quaker ministers found themselves preaching in churches, not to challenge the priests and professors, but at the invitation of the people who "were desirous and in expectation to hear Truth declared" (Penney 1907:124). Indeed, some of these groups, like the Seekers, for example, were already close to the Quakers in belief and practice, conducting silent meetings and relying upon a prophetic lay ministry, "so that the Lord's power was mightily at work in their hearts and great openings there was amongst [them]" (Penney 1907:124).

The largest and most dramatic of the meetings for cultivation and harvest were great public gatherings with participants numbering into the thousands. More than a thousand people were reported to have attended the famous meeting on Firbank Fell, Westmoreland, in 1652 (Fox 1952:108), which is sometimes taken as marking the beginning of the public emergence of Quakerism as a large-scale movement. Howgill and Burrough report a meeting of around two thousand people at the height of Quaker enthusiasm in Bristol in 1654 (Barclay 1841:219), and Fox records in his journal a gathering of between two and three thousand people in Wiltshire in 1656 (1952:272). Even allowing for a considerable degree of exaggeration, these were very large gatherings by contemporary standards.

Gatherings of this magnitude were far too large for any public buildings available for the purpose and were held outdoors. In London, however, Friends' efforts were sustained and successful enough to warrant the taking of a great meeting hall in 1655, called the Bull and Mouth after an adjacent tavern. The hall could accommodate up to a thousand people, and was often filled with a tumultuous crowd drawn by the Quakers (Braithwaite 1955:182).

Of course, not everyone who attended the Quakers' public meetings was a sympathetic participant; the Quakers drew a full share of curiosity seekers and disputants as well. This was a time of great religious ferment, novelty, and conflict, a period in which religion and politics were merged, so that public religious gatherings had an aura of excitement and spectacle about them, much like the mass political gatherings of the 1960s. Moreover, the major Quaker figures such as Fox and Nayler had a certain celebrity that attracted people to the places where they appeared. A significant number of participants were drawn to the public gatherings of the Quakers for their entertainment value, as a form of recreation. Fox certainly recognized this phenomenon; he notes of one meeting in 1653 that "people having notice of it, and not having seen me before, all the country people came in like as to a horse fair, and there came above a thousand people there" (1952:151; see also pp. 154, 242). Women ministers, too, were a novelty, and the appearance of a female Quaker preacher in the neighborhood often sufficed to draw the curious (Hayes 1723:18–19).

Although some came out of curiosity, others came to oppose Friends or "in expectation to hear a dispute" (Penney 1907:124) between Friends and their antagonists. Quakers had a reputation for being a contentious people; one anti-Quaker pamphlet opens with the assertion that "a Quaker is an *everlasting argument*" (R. H. 1672b:1, italics in the original). Religious disputations had a high degree of entertainment value, especially when the confrontation involved one of the major Quaker spokesmen – Fox or Nayler or Burrough – and a local figure noted for his learning or his skill in debate. Fox, for example, records an occasion in 1655 in which Nayler was in a disputation with seven or eight priests, and "all the people saw the priests were nothing and foiled, and cried, 'A Nayler, a Nayler, hath confuted them all' " (1952:223).

There is not sufficient detail in the records to reveal much about the structure of these disputations. Because many of those who came to oppose Friends in public were clergymen and other religious leaders, in some ways the confrontations were like those that took place in the churches, only this time on the Quakers' ground.

Friends measured success in these encounters by two standards: convincement among those who were present and silencing their antagonists, "stopping the mouths of gain-sayers to Truth's honour" (Camm and Audland 1689:n.p.). Here is Fox's summary of a successful encounter: "And a multitude of people was gathered about him, and a priest who was as dark could be began to babble, but his mouth was soon stopped. And I declared the word of life amongst them and turned them to the light of Christ in their hearts'' (1952:304). It was a special triumph, of course, if the opponents themselves, as religious leaders, were convinced; if the illegitimate speakers of the world's religions were brought to physical and spiritual silence. George Whitehead, for example, had a disputation with a Baptist preacher in 1655. ''In a little time,'' he reports, the preacher ''was silent, and seemed somewhat satisfied, and after further serious consideration, came to receive the Truth in an inward sight and sense of the power thereof.'' Ultimately, ''he laid down his former preaching and profession, and became willing to wait upon the Lord among Friends in silence'' (1832, 1:77–78).

In the foregoing pages, I have sketched out the range of principal scenes in which the Quaker ministers operated out in the world in the early years of Quakerism. Their task was to open people to Quakerism, start them on the path to convincement by turning them to the Truth, and nurture them until they were fully convinced and ready to join with Friends. In terms of the imagery employed for this process by the Quakers themselves, the ministers were to plow the spiritual ground, sow the seed of Truth, weed the field, cultivate the tender plants, and bring in the new harvest of souls.

The process was distributed across a range of scenes. The unscheduled confrontations in the steeplehouses and the preaching in public places, such as markets and streets, served predominantly to break the ground and plant the seed. The special meetings for cultivation and harvest – scheduled in advance, more sustained, with a self-selected audience, and more fully under Quaker control – served to complete the process. These are general tendencies, though. If allowed to preach without interruption or violence, an effective minister might convince a receptive hearer in first exposure in a marketplace or at a fair. At this point we may ask ourselves what were the implications for speaking – the principal concern of this study – of this distribution of scenes and functions.

Because of the Quaker belief in a prophetic ministry admitting of no written sermons, whether prepared in advance or recorded in delivery, information concerning the preaching style of early Quaker ministers is extremely scarce. From the viewpoint of the Quakers themselves, the delivery of authentic religious speech was not under human control, could not be learned, and was not to be imitated or planned in advance: It simply happened, through the agency of the spirit within. Accordingly, it was not a matter deemed worthy of or appropriate for close description. Because all religious speaking was spontaneous, we have no prepared texts of Quaker preaching or praying. Nor did the Quakers encourage the recording of religious speech as uttered because it might seem to give undue weight to a single instance of God's communication, through a single human speaker, whereas it was God's agency in the continuing process of revelation that was important to them. There are only ten extant Quaker sermons recorded before 1687, all taken down in some form of shorthand by non-Quakers, all by George Fox (Graves 1972) and thus not fully to be relied upon for conclusive evidence in regard to style, though a few of the early texts contain suggestive traces that seem to be consistent with other evidence that is available to us concerning Quaker preaching.

Ironically, but not altogether surprisingly, one of the very best summary descriptions we have of Quaker preaching is that of a vigorous anti-Quaker critic, the Puritan minister Francis Higginson. As an outsider and ardent heresiologist, Higginson reports features of the Friends' activities that may have been too familiar or self-evident or unreflected upon to find a place in the writings of Friends. Higginson's words are worth presenting in full:

> The matter of the most serious and ablest of their speakers, is *quicquid in buccam venerit*, and for the most part of this nature. They exhort people to mind the light within, to hearken to the voice and follow the guide within them, to dwell within, and not to look forth; for that which looketh forth tendeth to darkness. They tell them that the Lord is now coming to teach his people himself alone, that they have an unction, and need not that any man should teach them; that all their teachers without, the priests of the world do deceive them, away with them; that they speak the divination of their own brain, and every one seeks for gain from his quarter, that they take tithes which are odious in the sight of the Lord.
>
> That they teach for lucre and for the fleece, and live in pride, covetousness, envy, and in great houses, that they sit in the seat of the Scribes and Pharisees, go in long robes, are called of men, Masters; that they scatter people, and delude them with notions of fleshly wisdom, and ways of worship according to their own wills, and not according to the mind of the Lord. They call them out of all false ways, and worships, and forms, and false ordinances (so they call all the ordinances of God used in our public assemblies.) Such stuff as this all their speakings are for the most part stuffed with. Something also they speak of repentance, of living under the Cross; against pride in apparel, and covetousness. But the main subject and design of their speakings, is to inveigh against ministers, and ordinances, to bring ignorant country people to hate or forsake them, to mind only their light within for teaching, which they tell them is sufficient to salvation. (1653:12–13)

One factor suggested by Higginson's description and confirmed by the writings of Friends and others, is the limited range of standard themes the Quaker ministers tended to address. Higginson cites three, all essentially hortatory: apocalyptic exhortations, attacks upon worldliness and the world's religions, and proclamations of Quaker doctrine.

As noted earlier, the early Quaker ministers were much given to apocalyptic exhortations, such as "Repent, Repent, woe, woe, the Judge of the world is come." This was especially true, as Higginson observes, in the streets and marketplaces. Such warnings, coupled with attacks on worldliness and religious corruption, were directed at breaking people loose from their former ways, whether "pride in apparel, and covetousness" or allegiance to "the priests of the world" and their "false ways, and worships, and forms, and false ordinances." The familiar arguments are here: The false ministers are attacked as being made by human agency; speaking their own words in their own wills, preaching for money; being weighted down with pride, covetousness, and envy; and so forth. Finally, the way of Truth is proclaimed, the need to attend for their salvation to the Inward Light of Christ within, to hearken to the Voice speaking directly within themselves, to take up the cross, and so on.

Contemporary anti-Quaker critics considered the Quakers to be confused, undisciplined speakers by comparison with the carefully crafted and polished sermon style of the trained clergy (Anon. 1655:5). Thus Higginson belittles their unplanned speech as *"quicquid in buccam venerit"* ("whatever comes into the mouth"). The Quakers themselves make clear that despite the lack of prior preparation they did not encounter difficulty in preaching out in the world. Speaking of his public mission, William Caton recalled: "And though when I went to such places as aforesaid, I seldom knew what I should say, till I came there, yet behold when I was to speak, I never wanted words nor utterance, for to declare that which the Lord gave me to publish, but often times on the contrary I had fulness to my great admiration" (1689:10). Indeed, references to speaking for an hour are common, and George Whitehead reports an occasion in 1655 on which he preached for nearly five hours (1832, 1:77). More than that, Fox felt it necessary on several occasions to caution his fellow ministers against too much speaking, as in 1658: "Once ye have spoken the Truth to the people and they are come into the thing you speak of, many declarations out of the life may beget them into a form" (1952:341; see also Fox 1831, 7:128). The ministers, of course, credited the Lord with providing them with the fullness of their message, but we may identify other more mundane factors that may have contributed to the fluency of their preaching.

One reason Higginson's account rings true, its anti-Quaker bias notwithstanding, is that it echoes strongly the concerns and the very phraseology of the Quaker documents of the period. He does not place quotation marks around the key phrases he cites, but anyone familiar with the Quaker record will recognize them: "repent, repent," "the Judge of the World is come," "mind the light within," "hearken to the voice and follow the guide within you," "dwell within and look not forth, for that which looketh forth tendeth to darkness,'' and so on throughout the passage. These phrases, rooted in the biblical style of seventeenth-century religious rhetoric, constituted part of a restricted and formulaic register utilized by the Quaker ministers in their labors out in the world, what Jackson Cope has called the ''incantory'' style, characterized by ''an incredible repetition, a combining and recombining of a cluster of words and phrases drawn from Scripture'' (1956:733).

Though Cope identified the incantory style in the written productions of early Friends, the descriptive accounts of Quaker preaching do seem to indicate that it too was characterized by this style. Unfortunately, the earliest Quaker sermons of which we have transcripts of any kind stem from a period after the decline of the early enthusiasm with which the incantory style was most consistent.[1] Nevertheless, there are elements of this style in a few of the recorded sermons we do have; the best example, according to Michael Graves, may be found in a sermon preached by George Fox in 1674, of which the following is an excerpt (Graves 1972:242). In this instance, I have retained the original spelling and punctuation to show how at least this one oral sermon was rendered as a written text:

> So now ffriends, all that are in ye Power, & ye Life Come to be heires of Life, & of a world & kingdim, that hath noe end, so that you may all keep ye Gospell order, for here comes up his Government, in ye Heavenly Seed: that bruises ye head of ye serpent, that bruises ye head of all evill Government; so Now here is ye Government of ye blessed Righteous Seed, which is a mistery,: This is known as every one hath Received Christ Jesus, so walk in him, there is ye Gospell order, that is ye Power of God, which was before ye Devill was, which brings Life, & imortality to Light, ye Power of God, ye Gospell: brings into Life, now in this Power, in this Gospell; is ye order, ye everlasting order, of ye Gospell, which is a mistery. (Fox 1674a:253)

Although we have no way of knowing how faithful a transcript this is of Fox's words, it does show clearly the heavily repetitive quality Cope has identified, and even as transcribed above it has a strongly rhythmical cast that contributes to its incantory quality. If we set the passage out into lines suggested by likely syntactic and prosodic break points (cf. Hymes 1977; Rosenberg 1970; Tedlock 1972), this quality is brought even more sharply into relief. This exercise, though speculative, gains plausibility from the fact that it reveals regularities of form and pattern. We discover two equal sections of ten lines each, both of which begin with a brief introductory phrase and end

---

[1] Michael Graves (1972:239–251) has shown that Quaker preaching in the late seventeenth century was characterized by what he calls a ''catechical'' style, built upon rhetorical questions. See Chapter 9 for further discussion.

with the identical line, "which is a mystery." This rendering of the passage also reveals more clearly Fox's extensive resort to parallelistic constructions and to repetitions and recombinations of key words and phrases (power, life, gospel, order, seed, government), all devices that enhance fluency in spontaneous oral composition, as demonstrated in research on the formal devices that make possible the improvisational composition of oral poetry in the act of performance, by contrast with the performance of ready-made (written or memorized) oral forms (cf. Gray 1971; Lord 1960; Rosenberg 1970). Here I have omitted all punctuation except final periods at the ends of the sections in order to avoid introducing artificial markers of pause.

> So now friends
> · all that are in the power and the life
> come to be heirs of life
> and of a world and kingdom that hath no end
> so that you may all keep the gospel order
> for here comes up his government
> in the heavenly seed that bruises the head of the serpent
> that bruises the head of all evil government
> so now here is the government of the blessed righteous seed
> which is a mystery.

> This is known
> as everyone hath received Christ Jesus
> so walk in him
> there is the gospel order that is the power of God
> which was before the Devil was
> which brings life and immortality to light
> the power of God the gospel brings into life
> now in this power in this gospel is the order
> the everlasting order of the gospel
> which is a mystery.

Comparison of this passage with one from another sermon by Fox, delivered two days after the one from which the above excerpt is taken, demonstrates, at least with regard to Fox's preaching, the formulaic status of certain phrases he employed and the productive capacity of his incantory repetitions and recombinations of a limited set of key words.

> In this gospel the power of God is the glorious order
> this joyful order keeps all hearts pure to God
> an everlasting order feeleth it.
> So to keep the order of the gospel men come to be heirs of the gospel
> which brings life and immortality to light
> and comes to see over that power of darkness
> by him which was before the power of death was. (1674b:271)

If this incantory style was in fact typical of Quaker preaching in the early years, something we can never know for certain, it may provide some clues to the effects of this preaching on those who heard it. Besides contributing to fluency, the heavily repetitive and rhythmic quality manifested in the above passage is very well suited to eliciting the participative involvement of the auditors through the kind of formal appeal illuminated by Kenneth Burke: "We know that many purely formal patterns can readily awaken an attitude of collaborative expectancy in us . . . Once you grasp the trend of the form, it invites participation" (Burke 1969:58). Indeed, to the extent that the auditor of such preaching could begin to anticipate the repetitive words and cadences of the minister and to be caught up in expressive collaboration with him, there might well arise a sense of immediate co-participation in the utterance that would make the listener feel that the minister's words were echoed within himself. This experience would be powerfully consistent with the Quaker belief in the nature and efficacy of the Inward Voice and the unity of spirit to which it testified. The minister, in these terms, may well be understood to be giving outward voice to that which is spoken by the Inward Voice of the Holy Spirit, which may be heard within us all if only we are in the proper spiritual state to hear it.

Even further, of course, as Burke emphasizes, such formal appeal is a powerful agency of persuasion, or we might say in the Quaker context, of convincement: "A yielding to the form prepares for assent to the matter identified with it. Thus, you are drawn to the form, not in your capacity as a partisan, but because of some 'universal' appeal in it. And this attitude of assent may then be transferred to the matter which happens to be associated with the form" (1969:58).

Higginson's account of the *manner* of Quaker preaching is further consistent with the features we have examined. He describes the speaker,

> his countance severe, his face downward, his eyes fixed mostly towards the earth, his hands and fingers expanded, continually striking gently on his breast; his beginning is without a text, abrupt and sudden to his hearers, his voice for the most part low, his sentences incoherent, hanging together like ropes of sand . . . sometimes full of sudden pauses; his whole speech is a mixed bundle of words and heaps of nonsense, his continuance in speaking is sometimes exceeding short, sometimes very tedious, according to the paucity or plenty of his revelations. His admiring auditors that are of his way, stand the while like men astonished, listening to every word, as though every word was oraculous; and so they believe them to be the very words and dictates of Christ speaking in him. (1653:12)

We cannot tell how widely conventional this delivery style may have been, but the abrupt beginnings, the lack of apparent organization, the frequent pauses, and the great variability in the length of the utterances, together with the incantory style we have already identified, might all be expected as consequences of the requirement of spontaneity and flexibility in preaching. This style is also consistent with Mary Douglas's observation that "the confirmed anti-ritualist mistrusts external expression . . . Spontaneous speech that flows straight from the heart, unpremeditated, irregular in form, even somewhat incoherent, is good because it bears witness to the speaker's real intentions . . . incoherence is taken for a sign of authenticity." (1973:74).

The early Quaker ministers seem to have employed an expressive system that was both flexible and functional. It was well adapted to the limited range of rhetorical functions for which it was used: to plow, sow, cultivate, and harvest. It was adaptable to the brevity of crying "repent, repent" through the streets or the hours-long preaching of a public meeting if circumstances allowed and demanded. And, drawing on the capacity of the incantory style, it lent itself equally to fluency, spontaneity, and formal appeal demanded by a prophetic ministry.

As I have noted repeatedly in the foregoing discussion, the culmination of the ministers' efforts out in the world, summarized metaphorically by the agrarian cycle of plowing, sowing, cultivation, and harvest, was usually conceived of as the harvest itself, gathering in the new converts to Quakerism. This tended to occur in most concentrated form in meetings appointed by the Quaker ministers and attended by those who had already arrived at a state of interest in and susceptibility to the Quaker message. However, at the height of the early Quaker enthusiasm, especially in London and Bristol between 1654 and 1656, a series of large public meetings was held for the explicit purpose of capitalizing on this enthusiasm by bringing in new converts in maximum numbers.

It is evident from Quaker accounts of these meetings that they were conceived of strongly in terms of a process of real and symbolic separation – the separation of non-Quakers from their prior religious affiliations and from the fleshly preoccupations of the world, the separation of the truly religious in the assemblage from the sinful and the uncommitted, and the liberation of the individual spirit from the control of the flesh in those undergoing the conversion experience. The Quaker term for these occasions, drawing once again on the imagery of the agrarian cycle, was "threshing meetings," which captured quite effectively the range of separation processes summarized above.

There were, of course, other ways of undergoing the process of conversion. Some were personal, private, and gradual; but for those who made the religious change in the threshing meetings, the experience constituted a clear rite of passage in the classical sense identified by van Gennep: One entered such a meeting as a non-Quaker and emerged a Quaker. Indeed, van Gennep himself discusses the passage from one religion to another among the types of rites of passage (1960:96).

It was in the threshing meetings, as part of the conversion process, that the extreme forms of the quaking behaviors from which the Quakers gained their name played their most clear-cut role, as marking the stage of transition or marginality between separation and reintegration that constitutes the structure of the rite of passage. Again, the fullest and most graphic descriptions of this phenomenon came from the anti-Quaker literature. Allowing, as before, for the obvious negative bias and exaggeration of these accounts, they ring true because the behaviors they describe are so consistent with descriptions of similar altered states of consciousness to be found elsewhere in the anthropological literature (see Bourgignon 1972). Two accounts especially are worth quoting in full. The first comes from Higginson's early pamphlet, published in 1653:

> Now for their quakings, one of the most immediate notable fruits, and accidents of their speakings, though their speakings be a very chaos of words and errours, yet very often while they are speaking, so strange is the effect of them in their unblest followers, that many of them, sometimes, men, but more frequently women and children fall into quaking fits. The manner of which is this: those in their assemblies that are taken with these fits, fall suddenly down, as it were in a swoon, as though they were surprised with an epilepsy, or apoplexy, and lie groveling on the earth, and struggling as it were for life, and sometimes more quietly as though they were departing; while the agony of the fit is upon them their lips quiver, their flesh and joints tremble, their bellies swell as though blown up with wind, they foam at the mouth, and sometimes purge as if they had taken physic. In this fit they continue sometimes an hour or two, sometimes longer before they come to themselves again, and when it leaves them they roar out horribly with a voice greater than the voice of a man. The noise, those say, that have heard it is a very horrid fearful noise, and greater sometimes than any bull can make.
>
> The speaker, when any of them falls in this fit, will say to the rest: (that are sometimes astonished at this sight, especially if they be incipients) let them alone, trouble them not, the spirit is now struggling with flesh, if the spirit overcome they will quickly come out of it again, though it be sorrow now it will be joy in the morning, etc. And when they have said a few words to this effect, they go on with their speaking. (1653:15)

Higginsons's description is suggestive in a number of ways, including the attribution of the quaking trance more to women and children than to men and the detailed description of the behaviors associated with the trance state, all of which have been observed in various combinations in connection with trance states elsewhere, whether or not they were characteristic of the early Quakers (one suspects a degree of sensationalist exaggeration here). For our purposes, rooted in a concern with speaking among the early Quakers, what is especially noteworthy is the fact that the trance state was induced in significant part by the *speaking* of the ministers. That is, the minister's speaking moved the non-Quaker ("unblessed") subject into this penultimate "threshing" stage of the conversion process.

This, of course, was really the culmination of the ministerial effort, which we have traced through the succession of scenes, stages, and functions summarized by the metaphors of plowing, sowing, cultivation, and harvest. The point I would underscore is that it was, in fact, *speaking* by which each stage in the process was effected. A few representative quotations will bring this point into clearer focus.

Thomas Briggs, in summarizing the effects of his ministerial efforts in "Oliver's days," in which, it will be recalled, he made a specialty of crying repentance through the streets of towns, notes that, "several who have heard my voice, who have not seen my face, have confessed since that a power did reach them, and they were convinced by the power, and brought into the Truth, by which I know my labour in the Lord hath not been in vain" (1685:7). Briggs's statement makes especially clear the central role of his speaking in the process of bringing people into the Quaker fold.

An experience of Thomas Ellwood, recorded in his journal, provides an instance of the effect of ministerial speaking upon his own spiritual development toward Quakerism within the context of a meeting for cultivation in the home of Isaac Penington. Recalling his encounter there with the influential Quaker minister, Edward Burrough, Ellwood writes: "I drank in his words with desire: for they not only answered my understanding, but warmed my heart with a certain heat, which I had not till then felt from the ministry of any man" (1906:18). Once again, it was the minister's speaking that brought about the powerful spiritual effect that moved Ellwood along toward his ultimate conversion.

To take one further example from still another of the relevant scenes we have identified, we may consider Charles Marshall's account of one of the great threshing meetings conducted by John Camm and John Audland in Bristol in 1654. Marshall's description provides a Quaker complement to the anti-Quaker observations of Higginson. Speaking of Audland's role in the meeting, Marshall recalls that

> he stood up, full of dread and shining brightness on his countenance, lifted up his voice as a trumpet, and said, I proclaim spiritual war with the inhabitants of the Earth, who are in the fall and separation from God, and prophesy to the four winds of Heaven; and these

words dropped amongst the seed; and so went on in the mighty power of God Almighty, opening the way of life. But, ah! the seizings of souls, and prickings at heart, which attended that season; some fell on the ground, others crying out under the sense of opening their states . . . At this meeting many were effectually convinced, and from darkness to light turned. (Camm and Audland 1689:n.p.)

Here is the process described in terms of the basic metaphor of the seed; Audland's "words dropped amongst the seed" brought about the climactic point of the occasion, inducing people to fall to the ground and cry out in the spiritual struggle that finally carried them from darkness to the Light of God within them.

But having identified the role of speaking as the effective agency that carried people through to the point of conversion, there remains one final step in the process to be traced. For this, we may turn to the second of our two anti-Quaker accounts of the threshing meetings – this one by an anonymous observer of the Quaker efforts in London in 1655. Describing the extreme quaking behaviors witnessed at such occasions, he writes:

> They pretend raptures, ecstasies, swoonings, swellings, groanings tumblings, and prostrations, skreekings, murmurings, trances, sensible feelings, and manifestations of God's Spirit coming into them; and in this politic frenzy, they pretend to have him, he is now within them, and so must speak, and must only be heard, as sent by God to give commands, directions, and advisos to the great ones of the earth. (Anon. 1655:7)

Even discounting the biased caricature of this description, it is perhaps further questionable insofar as it identifies the process as one in which the spirit came *into* the subject, as from without. Although this is a common form of spirit possession and may indeed have been found among other religious enthusiasts of the day, it is not fully consistent with Quaker belief, which held that the Holy Spirit was already present in every person as the Inward Light or Voice of God within. One might also add, with regard to this and other accounts, that the behaviors described do not constitute glossolalia in the narrow sense of linguistically derived "speaking in tongues," though they do represent what Lombard (1910) has termed *phonations frustes* (mumbling, groaning, gurgling, incomprehensible sounds) in his fourfold categorization of glossolalia.[2]

---

[2] The literature on glossolalia is almost as opaque as the phenomena it seeks to describe. Some would extend the term to a wide range of religiously situated aberrant communication, from inarticulate groans to quite comprehensible utterances by spirit mediums to speaking in unknown but real languages (xenoglossia); others would restrict it to linguistically derived but referentially incomprehensible "speaking in tongues," closely dependent on the linguistic competence and

Nevertheless, this anonymous account is significant in documenting a further important function of speaking in the conversion process. What the observer describes is the role of speaking in the ultimate validation of an individual's conversion experience. What better way to demonstrate that one had finally broken through to the essential Quaker experience of the Spirit of God within than by speaking his words, consistent with the Quaker belief in the prophetic nature of all proper religious speech? The experience of quaking was thus an enabling one, bringing the person who underwent it to a state of being able to speak. The Reverend Ralph Josselin, a Puritan clergyman of Essex, understood this and made a point of it in his famous journal, early in 1656, recording the great stir made by the Quakers in those parts: "Divers have fits about us and thereby come to bee able to speake" (Macfarlane 1970:26). In these cases we have the ultimate culmination of the full process toward which the efforts of the Quaker ministers out in the world were directed: by their speaking to bring others through to the point at which they too were able to serve as "the oracles of God."

knowledge of the speaker. My own preference is for the latter, more narrow definition, excluding xenoglossia, in which some Friends apparently did believe (discussed in Chapter 2). Much of the confusion derives from differences of analytical perspective, not to mention religious taste and predisposition; definitional and typological approaches vary, depending upon whether the analyst's concern is with the formal features of the utterance, the psychological states that induce it, the functional load it carries, the comparative range of the attendant phenomena, and a host of other factors. These problems help to account for the apparently conflicting claims in the literature concerning whether or not the seventeenth-century Quakers were glossolalists (cf. Christie-Murray 1978:46, May 1956:75, and Samarin 1972:12–13 with Cutten 1927:68–69). I find no evidence that they were, nor do I find that it illuminates the issues with which I am concerned here to explore these issues with reference to the literature on glossolalia; the notions of altered states of conscience, spirit possession, and trance are more useful. The reader interested in glossolalia should consult Christie-Murray 1978, Goodman 1972, May 1956, Samarin 1972, and Williams 1981, and pursue the references given in those works.

6

GOING NAKED AS A SIGN: THE PROPHETIC MISSION AND THE PERFORMANCE OF METAPHORS

As I have emphasized in earlier chapters, the mid-seventeenth century in England was a turbulent era, a time of revolution and upheaval, which many contemporaries described, in biblical terms, as a world turned upside down. It was also an intensely apocalyptic period, in which many were convinced that a new spiritual day was at hand, presaged by the dissolution of the old order that seemed to be occurring around them. This apocalyptic vision made prophecy, one means of investing the universe with order, a favored mode of religious and social commentary.

This was the milieu out of which Quakerism emerged in the early 1650s, and true to the spirit of this period, the mission of the early Quakers included a strong and steady outpouring of apocalyptic judgments and prophecies. Richard Farnsworth, one of the most vigorous and influential of the early Quakers and also one of the most aggressively apocalyptic, described their mission in 1655 in these terms: "to tell magistrates, priests and people what they are, and reprove them of their transgressions; and for their sins and iniquities, and forewarn them of the judgments to come, except they repent and amend, and turn to the Lord" (1655a:16). *Tell, reprove,* and *forewarn* – these were among the major communicative tasks undertaken by the Quakers out in the world: identification and moral condemnation of the current sinful actions or conditions of others and prophetic warning of the consequences to follow if they did not repent, reform their ways, and come into the Quaker fold.

The means by which this mission was to be carried out were enumerated by George Fox, the dominant Quaker leader of the seventeenth century: "Many ways were these professors warned, by word, by writing, and by signs" (1952:407). The signs to which Fox referred were of several kinds, including natural omens; but there was one class of signs that was produced by the Quakers themselves and that is worthy of special consideration as a prominent feature of Quaker communication in the seventeenth century. Specifically, these signs consisted in the public performance of shocking, dramatic actions, intended to convey, by nonverbal means, an expression of moral reproof and/or prophecy.

The charter for these semiotic enactments was biblical; the Quakers saw themselves in the image of the apostles and prophets of the primitive Christian church and thus found themselves called upon to carry God's message – the Truth – to the world in similar ways. Specifically, the Quakers compared themselves to the prophet Isaiah: "Behold, I and the children whom the Lord hath given me are for signs and wonders in Israel from the Lord of hosts, which dwelleth in mount Zion" (Isaiah 8.18).

In an age saturated with verbal religious discourse, striking nonverbal enactments represented a ready means of attracting attention to the Quaker message, highlighting at the same time the Quaker challenge to conventional communicative norms (cf. Benthall 1975:11). These sign behaviors were especially adapted to the public places – markets, fairs, streets, churches – frequented by Quaker ministers seeking to plant the seed of Truth in others. Then too, the early Quakers' distrust of speaking as susceptible to worldly corruption made them ready to rely on other codes and channels, including physical action, for communicative purposes. Fox, for example, in his remarkable sermon on Pendle Hill in 1652, identified by some as marking the beginning of the Quaker movement as such, exhorted his followers to "let your lives speak." Accordingly, the performance of "signs" was seen by the early Quakers as an appropriate and efficacious means of delivering reproofs and prophecies to the sinful world.

Several types of sign enactments may be distinguished. The simplest type of performance was the direct, nonmetaphorical representation of an action or condition of the viewers by the enactment of an iconic or indexical sign of it. Following Sebeok, I define "icon" as a sign in which there is a topological similarity between a signifier and its denotata (Sebeok 1976:128) and "index" as a sign in which a signifier is contiguous with its signified or is a sample of it (1976:131). For example, not long before the great London fire of 1666,

> a Friend . . . was moved to come out of Huntingdonshire . . . and to scatter his money up and down the streets, and to turn his horse loose in the streets, and to untie his breeches' knees, and let his stockings fall, and to unbutton his doublet, and to tell the people so should they run up and down scattering their money and their goods half undressed like mad people, as he gave them a sign. And so they did when the fire broke out and the city was burning. (Fox 1952:503)

Here, the prophesying Friend, Thomas Ibbott, made of himself an iconic sign by simulating the distracted appearance and behavior that were soon to characterize so many Londoners in the great fire. This sign performance, like some others, was accompanied by a verbal explanation of the sign relation being enacted; I will return to this latter feature below.

A more complex example that was both reproof and prophecy and involved both iconic and indexical signs took place on the eve of the Restoration, in 1660:

> There was . . . [a] Friend, Robert Huntington, who was moved of the Lord to go into Carlisle steeplehouse with a white sheet about him, amongst the great Presbyterians and Independents to show unto them that the surplice was coming up again; and he put a halter upon his neck to show unto them that a halter was coming upon them; which was fulfilled upon some of our persecutors when the King came in. (Fox 1952:408)

The white sheet here was an iconic sign of the surplice, and the surplice, in turn, was an index of Catholic and Episcopal religious practice. Huntington himself stood in iconic relation to his viewers. Huntington's act was thus a reproof to those religious professors who were compromising their religion with corrupt practices that were anathema to the Quakers. The wearing of the halter was an iconic prophecy that if the viewers persisted in their sinful ways, they would face the prospect of hanging. There is an element of ambiguity in Huntington's performance, insofar as it contained no metacommunicative cues to indicate what was reproof for past or present behavior and what was prophecy for the future. That was apparently left to the viewers to figure out. This was characteristic of many of the Quaker sign peformances, and I will come back to it later.

A further degree of ambiguity, however, was inherent in the other types of Quaker sign performance, all of which were metaphorical in nature. That is, they consisted in the physical acting out of originally verbal metaphors pertaining in some significant way to the condition of the viewers. In this, they represented especially striking instances of the Quaker tendency, noted by Cope (1956:726), to "break down the boundary between literalness and metaphor, between conceptions and things." Fernandez's observation that "metaphors are not only rhetorical devices of persuasion; they can also lead to performance" (1974:125) applies very well to these metaphorical sign performances of the Quakers. Indeed, the physical acting out of the metaphors was intended as a means of enhancing their rhetorical power; the intersemiotic translation from the verbal to the physical codes enabled the act of communication to seize the attention of onlookers especially effectively, by making visible the semantic anomaly inherent in the metaphorical juxtaposition of subjects that belonged together "only by a stretch of the imagination" (Fernandez 1974:123). There is a difference, however, between the Quaker sign performances and those of primary interest to Fernandez: He is concerned primarily with the metaphorical basis of ritual action, whereas the Quaker performances were all done in nonritual contexts. As we shall see below, this had important implications for the communicative success – or lack of success – of the Quaker enactments. The ritual frame contextualizes the performance of metaphor and renders it both intelligible and effective; acting out certain metaphors in other settings may make them more strongly noticeable, but relatively less intelligible as metaphors.

One set of Quaker metaphorical performances involved the manipulation of physical objects. In 1659, at a time of developing political pressure against the Quakers, one "Friend was moved to go to the Parliament that was envious against Friends and to take a pitcher in her hand and break it to pieces, and to tell them so should they be broken to pieces, which came to pass presently after" (Fox 1952:355–356), at the time of the Restoration. Here, once again, the prophecy was made explicit by verbal means.

Two years later, one Richard Sale, from near Chester, "was moved to go to the steeplehouse . . . and carry those persecuting priests and Presbyterians a lantern and candle as a sign of their darkness" (Fox 1952:408). This was an expression of judgment: The candle was an index of literal darkness, which stood in turn as a metaphor for spiritual darkness. As the literal darkness required physical illumination, so spiritual darkness demanded spiritual illumination, by the Inward Light.

An especially revealing example is reported by Thomas Aldam, who, on the occasion of an audience with the Protector in 1655 "was moved to take his cap from off his head and to rend it in pieces before Oliver Cromwell" (1690:10), an action all the more highly marked in view of the Quaker testimony against hat honor. We have no record of Cromwell's interpretation of Aldam's performance, but there are at least three records of how contemporary Quakers understood it, including Aldam's own, and they are all different, though they all have in common the interpretation of the tearing of the cap as standing for some kind of dismemberment or detachment. One interpretation, by George Fox, was that the tearing of the cap was a metaphorical prophecy that the kingdom would be torn away from Cromwell (1952:355). Aldam's own interpretation (1690:10) is more complex, consisting of two parts, a reproof and a prophecy, and incorporating three metaphors. The taking off of the hat, leaving the head uncovered, was a metaphorical reproof to Cromwell, as "head" of state (metaphor 1), for not being "covered" (metaphor 2) with the spirit of the Lord; the rending of the cap was intended to signify that because he and his compatriots were thus uncovered, the government would be "rent" (metaphor 3) from them, as the cap was torn apart.

Edward Burrough and Francis Howgill, two influential early Friends, also based their interpretation on the hat as covering, but in this case the covering was not spiritual, but political, taking Cromwell's political powers as his "covering" (Barclay 1841:28). The rending of the hat was thus a metaphorical prophecy of the rending apart of the government.

The hat-as-covering element of two of the foregoing interpretations is structurally similar to the semantic core of the most common – and controversial – of the early Quaker sign performances, called by them "going naked as a sign." This involved appearing in a public place – the streets or market of a town, or a religious gathering – unclothed, though it is not always clear just how unclothed; some were stark naked, some wore modest coverings about their loins, others wore certain essential undergarments or sackcloth; but by the standards of the period all were naked. Going naked as a sign was thus an instance of what Morris (1977:207–212) calls a deliberate overexposed signal, the performance of an intensely private action in public, motivated in this case by the desire to proclaim an ideological message.

Perhaps the best known of the early Quaker practitioners of going naked as a sign was William Simpson. One account of his activity casts it in terms very similar to Burrough and Howgill's and Aldam's interpretations of Aldam's performance with his cap: Simpson, it was reported, "went three years naked in sackcloth, in the days of Oliver and his Parliament as a sign to them, and to the priests shewing how God would strip them of their power, and that they should be as naked as he was, and should be stripped of their benefices" (Carroll 1978:78). Simpson's nakedness, in these terms, is a metaphor of being stripped of one's outward, worldly coverings, just as Aldam's bare head was. This is only one significance of going naked as a sign, however.

The richness of the clothed and naked human body as a symbolic resource meant that the same act, going naked, for the most part in functionally equivalent contexts, namely, public places, could be used in the construction of a range of possible metaphors. To be sure, not all these meanings were intended or equally plausible in every enactment. Where the performer of a particular instance of going naked as a sign recorded his or her intended meaning or meanings, we have a pretty good idea of at least one side of the communicative transaction, although some attributed different meanings to their acts at different times. Nevertheless, it remains the case that the meaning of specific metaphorical sign performances was often far from transparent to the viewers as metaphor. An examination of going naked as a sign in terms of the structure and dynamics of metaphor will help us to see why.

Briefly, a metaphor may be viewed as a statement of identity between a pair of terms that mediates an analogy or semantic correspondence between them (Black 1979:28–31). Following Max Black, we may call one of these terms primary and the other secondary. According to Black, "the metaphorical utterance works by 'projecting upon' the primary subject a set of 'associated implications' . . . that are predicable of the secondary subject," thereby endowing it with a particular set of semantic attributes derived from and shared with the secondary subject. The operation of predication fills in the semantic contours of the primary subject and transforms it from inchoate to choate, in Fernandez's (1974) apt terms. This gives us, then, three basic elements to be attended to in the interpretation of a metaphor: the primary and secondary subjects and the implicative complex of shared features for which we may employ Richards's (1936) widely adopted term "ground" for the sake of convenience.

Let us now set out a small sampling of instances of going naked as a sign, recorded by those who performed them.

a   Explaining his act of going naked at an Independents' church in Hull, June 24, 1673, Daniel Smith wrote: "As my body was naked, so was that congregation naked, not being clothed with the spirit of the Lord" (quoted in Carroll 1978:79).

b   William Simpson, mentioned earlier as something of a specialist at going naked as a sign, accounted for his actions in these terms in a tract published in 1660: "As naked shall you be spiritually, so my body hath been temporally naked in many places in England, as a sign of the nakedness and shame that is coming upon the Church of England" (quoted in Carroll 1978:79).

c   Thomas Briggs records that "in Oliver's days," he "was moved of the Lord to go through Cardiff for a sign," to convey to the people there that "thus must you be stripped of all your profession, that are not found in the life of righteousness" (1685:8).

d   Writing in 1659 of his going naked through "Walton, London, Colchester, Cambridge, and other Towns about," William Simpson explained his own nakedness as "a figure of all your nakedness, though I am clothed on with immortality" (quoted in Carroll 1978:79).

Examining just these four instances, what metaphorical relations do we find expressed? The secondary subject, of course, is held constant throughout: the naked body of the Quaker engaged in the sign performance. As regards the primary terms, we may identify the following:

> The current spiritual condition of a particular congregation of Independents (example a)
> The future spiritual condition of the entire Church of England (example b)
> The future spiritual condition of the people of Cardiff (example c)
> The spiritual condition of the people of England *plus* the spiritual condition of the Quaker himself (example d, a double metaphor)

Fernandez has suggested that "the inchoate pronouns of social life – the 'I,' 'you,' 'he,' 'it' – gain identity by predicating some . . . metaphor upon themselves" (1974:122). If we follow Fernandez's lead, and consider these various primary subjects in pronominal terms, from the point of view of the Quaker carrying out the act of communication, the range of primary subjects of going naked as a sign emerges in clearer terms. Insofar as the unclad Quaker himself or herself might be the primary subject, the pronoun was *I* (first person singular). When, as in Daniel Smith's enactment (example a), the metaphor was to apply to the witnesses of the act, the pronoun was *you* (second person plural). When, in addition to the witnesses, the metaphor was to be extended to others of their kind (e.g., other people of Cardiff, the Church of England, or England itself), the pronouns included both *you* (second person plural) and *they* (third person plural). For the act of going naked as a sign to be communicatively successful, then, would have required a clear indication in the enactment itself which pronoun or pronouns – I, you, they – were intended.

If we look for the shared features that constitute the ground of the metaphors enacted by going naked as a sign, we see that there are two principal ones and that they are diametrically opposed to each other. In examples a, b, and c the semantic feature meant to be projected from the secondary to the primary subject is the quality of being divested of an appropriate covering (e.g., the spirit of the Lord) and thus being exposed in a shameful state. In example d, however, although the people of England are to appear shamefully naked, Simpson himself is also edenically naked, divested of the *inappropriate* covering of corrupt, worldly religion, in the second of the two metaphors, in which he is the primary subject. What is projected from his naked body onto his spiritual condition is not a shameful nakedness but a good one, like that implied in the term "the naked truth," also employed by the Quakers in connection with going naked as a sign (Braithwaite 1955:192n). As MacRae aptly states in his essay, "The Body and Social Metaphor," "we find – as well as the association of the evil and the base with the image of the body – also the image of its splendor: its exposure as Truth – the naked truth, the bare truth, *nuda veritas*, the confronter of veiled calumny and deceit" (1977:69). Simpson's explication of his going naked as a sign exploits both meanings at once, but his action serves as the secondary subject of two metaphors, each with a different primary subject.

This brief examination of the metaphorical meanings of a limited number of instances of going naked as a sign suggests one dimension of the problem: the potential difficulty of identifying the primary subject and ground of the metaphorical act. Was a given instance of going naked a metaphor for non-Quakers' spiritual condition, the naked Quaker's own spiritual condition, or both? Was it meant to implicate good or evil or both? Did it apply to the present, as judgment, or to the future, as prophecy? Was it intended to relate only to the condition of those who witnessed the act, or was it to be generalized beyond them? If the latter, then to whom? All others of their city? Their religious profession? All non-Quakers? With this range of potential primary terms and grounds – and there were still others – it was not always clear from the act alone which were intended.

Now one of the principal ways in which the primary subject of a metaphor may be identified is through its relation to the surrounding discourse. As Sapir observes, "one of the terms [of the metaphor] will be commensurate or continuous with the topic of discourse'' (1977:7); it is for this reason that he suggests the designation "continuous term" for what Black calls the primary subject. As Black himself observes: "A successful metaphor is *realized* in discourse, is embodied in a given 'text,' and need not be treated as a riddle" (1979:23). Can we look to the context of the various acts of going naked as a sign for a clear indication of what primary subjects were intended?

In certain cases, the answer is yes. In the instance cited above as example c, Thomas Briggs explicated his own metaphor verbally in the course of enacting it: "And this was the message that the Lord put into my mouth, to declare unto them, which was a town of great profession; thus must you be stripped of all your profession, that are not found in the life of righteousness" (1685:8). But although the act of going naked, like other sign performances, was occasionally thus accompanied by words, the verbal messages were not always about the nakedness itself. William Simpson, for example, sometimes blackened his face while going naked and said to the onlookers, "so would the Lord God smut and besmear all their religion, as he was besmeared" (Fox 1952:407), thus explicating this second metaphorical act without reference to the first. Nor does this second metaphor provide sufficient contextual information to clarify the primary subject of the nakedness (cf. the performance of Richard Sale described in Nuttall 1952:15–16). If anything, it may have rendered the nakedness more ambiguous.

What of situational context, then? If the additional components of the Quakers' performances were insufficient to clarify the primary subject, perhaps the situations in which they occurred provided the answer. On examination, however, it is clear that they did not. Going naked as a sign was done in public places; on the streets, in markets, during church services, and so on. Whereas an initiation rite in a tribal society, for example, might contextualize a metaphorical act of going naked as a divestiture of the initiates' social attributes, none of the above contexts could indicate whether the Quaker's act was judgment or prophecy, whether it applied to the Quaker's or the onlookers' condition, or to whom, if anyone, it was to be extended beyond the immediate witnesses. Moreover, it must be remembered that from the point of view of most witnesses, the unclad Quaker simply passed before them in a public place quite unexpectedly. Though appearing thus "out of context," of course, had a contextual meaning of its own, it was not sufficient to make clear the *metaphorical* meaning that was intended.

To summarize the argument thus far, then, I am suggesting that part of the reason the metaphorical act of going naked as a sign was unsuccessful was that it often failed to make clear the primary subject or the ground of the metaphor. This was only part of the problem, though, and perhaps not the most important one.

One of the fundamental requirements of a successful metaphor is that it should be recognizable as one; the juxtaposition of items must be seen to call for a figurative interpretation. This suggests another relevant dimension for our analysis of going naked as a sign. Although students of metaphor have persistently found it difficult to formulate the essence of this feature with precision, few are able to disregard completely the factor that metaphor, like other forms of figurative language, embodies a degree of semantic anomaly. That is, it seems to state an equivalence between terms that is at odds with literal truth values within the meaning system of the given culture. Indeed, it is this lack of surface-level truth value, either in the form of a statement that appears semantically anomalous in its own terms or in relation to the surrounding discourse (Fraser 1979:178–179), that often serves as the principal signal, or key, that the statement should be interpreted figuratively.

With reference to going naked as a sign, although going naked in public may appear to be an anomalous act from the standpoint of morally acceptable behavior, it was nevertheless far from semantically anomalous; if anything, it was oversaturated with literal truth value. The act of displaying one's naked body in public, in mid-seventeenth-century England, was so striking and shocking in its own right that it tended to engage the onlookers' attention so wholly at that level that they were prevented from looking beyond the arresting literal fact for a metaphorical meaning. In other words, the significance of the naked body was so blatant that the attention of the witnesses became fixed on it and seldom moved to the predication of some of its semantic features onto some other primary term to complete the metaphor. Rather than being read figuratively, the Quakers' nakedness was taken literally and widely condemned by anti-Quakers as "immodest," "impudently bold," "obscene," "uncivilized," "heathenish," "brutish," "shameless," and "unseemly" (Anon. 1655:7, 16, 19–20; Ellwood 1906:38; Higginson 1653:29–30; Nuttall 1952:15–16; Penney 1907:213–214). To be sure, the image of the Word made flesh was intensely meaningful to the people of seventeenth-century England (see Broadbent 1977:307), but for most of them its essential meaning depended upon its having happened only once (see John 1.14); they were not prepared to grant special power to going naked as a means of expressing verbal metaphor.

The question arises, How could the Quakers have assumed that their sign performances would be understood at all? The answer, once again, lies in the system of seventeenth-century Quaker belief concerning the nature of the communicative process: namely, that the Inward Light was the source of all spiritually informed communication, that in this sense, God himself was the *sender* of all the Quakers' religious communication, and the Quakers were merely his communicative means and instruments. Moreover, by virtue of the presence of the Light within, every person, Friend or not, was potentially responsive to the Quakers' religious message, the Truth. If Quakers were attentive to the Inward Light and spoke or acted as it moved them, it followed that their message would reach to the Light in those to whom it was directed if the receivers would open themselves to it. In a sense, then, every act of religious communication from the Quaker point of view was an instance of God communicating with himself, but inspiring both human sender and receiver in the process. That of God in me speaks to and is understood by that of God in you.

This is why the Quakers who engaged in the various sign performances we have been discussing could assume that their performances, no matter how ambiguous, would be understood by those ready to receive God's message. In practical terms, however, the sign performances turned out to be notably unsuccessful – even counterproductive – as a means of religious communication. Although some people who witnessed these performances apparently did get the message, it is clear that going naked as a sign shocked and alienated most others and prompted accusations of shamelessness and immorality against the Quaker movement. At the very least, the susceptibility of going naked in public to imputations of immorality was a major factor in its eventual decline and disappearance from the Quakers' communicative repertoire. The violence often visited on the naked Friends, as on the other Quaker ministers, could be borne in the service of Truth, and the riddlelike opaqueness of the sign performances could do little harm in its own right (though it could also do little good), but when the reputation of Truth was compromised, the balance shifted against the behavior in question, and it could not be sustained.

Also contributing to the ultimate failure and decline of the early Quakers' sign enactments in general was the unfortunate episode of James Nayler's entry into Bristol in October 1656, the most extravagant and controversial sign performance of them all. Nayler rode into the city with his followers spreading garments before him and singing "Holy, holy, holy," in a reenactment of Jesus' entry into Jerusalem, "as a sign of the coming of the righteous One" (Braithwaite 1955:251–256).

Participants in the enactment apparently had differing ideas of what they were about. At his subsequent examination before a committee of Parliament, Nayler maintained that his enactment was intended as a prophetic *sign* of the second coming of Christ, but evidence indicates that some of his followers viewed Nayler himself as Christ come again, not merely as a sign. The outcome of Nayler's trial for blasphemy was founded on the judgment that he had in fact put himself forward as the Messiah, and he was convicted and brutally punished for his alleged crime. Nayler's case became a *cause célèbre*, and the entire episode reflected badly on the Quakers in the public eye, helping to discredit sign enactments still further.

Finally, there were other factors as well, on a broader societal and cultural level, that militated against the efficacy of prophetic communication, even as conditions of social crisis called it forth. The second half of the seventeenth century was a watershed era in English intellectual history, the turning point between the dominion of a supernaturalist world view and the emergence of scientific rationalism. Keith Thomas has documented at length these larger developments and their influence on the decline of prophecy in his important work, *Religion and the Decline of Magic* (1971).

In any event, going naked as a sign and other sign performances I have discussed flourished intermittently among the Quakers only during the brief period of the 1650s and early 1660s, declining sharply thereafter, and all but disappearing by the mid-1670s. In 1672, the London Yearly Meeting of Friends issued the following advice to the ministry, advice we will have occasion to consider further in its broader implications for change: ''And avoid all imagined, unseasonable and untimely prophesyings; which tend not only to stir up persecution, but also to the begetting airy and uncertain expectations, and to the amusing and affrighting simple people from receiving the Truth: for this practice, God's wisdom neither leads to, nor justifies'' (Barclay 1841:332). Thus authoritatively pronounced inconsistent with God's wisdom, the enactment of prophetic signs could have no further place in the ministerial repertoire of Friends.

7

SWEAR NOT AT ALL: OATHS, SOCIAL DRAMA, AND THE CONFLICT OVER POLITICAL AUTHORITY

In earlier chapters, we have considered various speech testimonies by which the seventeenth-century Quakers challenged both the religious and social order of their day. The early Friends denied the legitimacy of the world's "made ministers" and upheld the legitimacy of their own charismatic ministry in terms of speaking; they challenged the pride-serving acknowledgment of social hierarchy by means of the plain language. Insofar as no religious testimony was without political relevance in mid-seventeenth-century England, these speech testimonies also colored the role of Friends in the larger political arena of contending religious factions. There was, however, yet another speech testimony that patterned Quaker relations with political authority in a more immediate and fundamental way: the testimony against the swearing of oaths.

As the Quakers themselves observed, their denial of oaths was "now no new doctrine," including among its precedents the example of the early heretics (Besse 1753, 2:16; see also Fisher 1679:811–813). Christopher Hill points out that all those medieval heretics – Bogomils, Albigensians, Lollards, Taborites – who denied the authority of the state gave symbolic significance to the refusal of oaths (1964:383). Hill, Susan Staves (1979:191–251), and Keith Thomas (1971:67–68) have also shown how the mid-seventeenth century was a period in which oaths were widely called into question on a variety of grounds, including the decline of the supernaturalist world view and the emergence of a rationalist, naturalistic one; the demonstrable unreliability of oaths of allegiance in a time of frequent political overturnings and changes in ideas about authority; and the growing reliance of an emergent capitalist society on the motivation of self-interest: "It paid a man to make his word his bond because of the rise in importance of credit, reputation, respectability" (Hill 1964:418).

Thus, the Quakers were far from alone in this period in challenging oaths. They were, however, more extreme and persistent in their collective opposition than their contemporaries, and their testimony against swearing had far greater consequences for their sect, bringing them into open and public conflict with the state. What is important from our point of view is that this conflict was played out to a significant extent in terms of speaking.

The doctrinal basis of the Quaker testimony concerning oaths was simple

95

and direct, drawn from the Sermon on the Mount and cited or appealed to in virtually every argument made by Friends against swearing:

> But I say unto you, Swear not at all; neither by heaven, for it is God's throne: Nor by the earth; for it is his footstool: neither by Jerusalem; for it is the city of the great King. Neither shalt thou swear by thy head, because thou canst not make one hair white or black. But let your communication be, Yea, yea; Nay, nay: for whatsoever is more than these cometh of evil. (Matthew 5.34–37; see also James 5.12)

This same text also served as a charter for the Quaker speech usage best known to economic historians, namely, the setting of a fixed price and the refusal to bargain in trade, identified since Weber as a key element in the emergence of modern capitalism (1946:312). An early statement by Fox shows clearly how the testimony against bargaining, linked thus to the testimony against swearing, was intimately bound up with other Quaker principles concerning speaking, implicating the distrust of vain words, the use of vain compliments, and the insistence on truth in all things:

> Is it not better and more ease to have done at a word, than to ask double or more? Doth not this bring you into many vain words, and compliments, and talk, that fills the vain mind? This is deceitful before God and man. And is it not more savoury to ask no more than you will have for your commodity, to keep yea and nay in your communication, when you converse in your calling, than to ask more than you will take? And so is not there the many words where is the multiplying of sins? (1831, 4:100)

It is interesting to observe that this Quaker principle concerning fixed and fair prices was eminently successful, bringing Friends considerable economic success, and thus conferring "credit upon the account of Truth" (Rigge 1678:3; see also Barclay 1841:367; Caton 1671:27; Edmondson 1820:50; Fox 1831, 7:301–302). This success in turn helped to vindicate Friends' principles, offsetting to a degree the severe persecution occasioned by the related testimony against oaths.

As with all biblical charters, the Quakers did not feel themselves bound by the biblical injunction against swearing simply because it was recorded in the Scriptures, but rather because they felt its truth confirmed by God's Word within their own hearts. Referring to the weight of his own conscience, John Crook declared: "That which it speaks concerning swearing in my heart, is according to Christ's command, Matthew 5.34, who saith, swear not at all" (Crook 1662:33).

When their opponents cited biblical precedents for swearing from the Old Testament, Friends appealed to the general Puritan understanding of human spiritual history, passing from edenic innocence, where there were no oaths, to the new redemption of their own day, where once again no oaths were necessary. The basic argument was laid out early (see Anon. 1654:12) and appealed to frequently thereafter. As summarized by Penington: "The ground or occasion of an oath is the fall of man from truth, from innocency, from the uprightness which engaged him to truth before his fall. This made the Jews to stand in need of this bond under the law" (1863:150). He continued:

> The use of an oath was not for man in innocency, nor for man under the power and virtue of the redemption by Christ . . . but for fallen man, for man erred from the truth and covenant of God: and it is very manifest to us, that for a disciple of Christ, who hath received the law from his lips against swearing, to be brought back again to swearing . . . is no less than a denial of Christ, who is his life and redeemer out of the fallen state, and who also is the substance, which ends the oaths. (1863:154)

Christ was the fulfillment of God's own oath to man; "Christ performed God's oath, and took away the oath of God amongst men, that they were to swear by the Lord, and set up yea and nay instead of it" (Fox 1831, 5:159).

The strength of the Quaker position on oaths may be accounted for in large part by reference to the centrality of Truth in Quaker doctrine. Ideally, all action, whether spoken or otherwise, was to be an expression of Truth, done in God's way and God's will. The Holy Spirit was to be the author of one's words and the guide to right action, through the grace of the Inward Light. All Friends were immediately responsible to God already in word and action. Thus, they had no need to invoke the conditional curse implied by an oath upon themselves for not telling the truth, having already submitted themselves to God's judgment.

Francis Howgill, who died in prison for refusing to swear, made clear the superfluousness of oaths for the Quakers: "Whosoever comes to witness a restoration again into the same image by Christ . . . as all that are born of God and are true Christians indeed do come to, there will be nothing but *Truth* speaking and ruling in the heart, and in the words: and oaths ends" (n.d.:2).

To these basic doctrinal objections against swearing oaths, the Quakers added another objection to contemporary practice, consistent with their condemnation of religious formalism and ceremony. The act of swearing itself was contrary to Christ's command, but it was rendered still more objectionable by the ceremonial form of sealing an oath by kissing the Bible, which the Quakers saw as an idolatrous display (see Crook 1662:41).

During the mid-seventeenth century, there were two principal varieties of oaths implicated in the Quakers' refusal to swear. The simpler of the two was the judicial oath, required as a warrant to the truthfulness of legal testimony. The refusal to swear in court undoubtedly put Friends at a disadvantage in legal proceedings, especially before magistrates hostile to their sect, and was made the target of explicit provisions in the Quaker Act of 1662 and the Conventicle Act of 1664, to be discussed further below. Their testimony against oaths precluded them from giving evidence in court and thus from prosecuting those who infringed their rights; in chancery cases a person who could not file an answer on oath faced the prospect of financial ruin (Cragg 1957:51). For their part, Friends maintained their willingness to give evidence and suggested (to no avail) the institution of the mechanism put forward by Christ to establish the truth of legal testimony (see Fox 1831, 5:155): "In the mouth of two or three witnesses every word may be established" (Matthew 18.16).

An indication of the extremes to which the victimization of Friends could be carried for their unwillingness to take judicial oaths may be found in the case of Thomas Hymans of Bridgewater, Somersetshire. Hymans was robbed on the highway of more than seventeen pounds, but when he came to give evidence against those who had robbed him, the judge refused to accept his evidence without an oath. Still worse, the judge turned the proceedings against Hymans himself, with the result that he spent about five months in jail and paid a fine of five pounds (Besse 1753, 1:616–618). Such blatant injustice notwithstanding, judicial oaths never represented as important and public an issue as the second class of oaths: political oaths of abjuration and allegiance. These oaths, some of them enacted as anti-Catholic measures in the reigns of Elizabeth and James I, were revived and turned against the Quakers and other separatist groups, first under the Commonwealth and more rigorously and devastatingly after the Restoration.

In April 1655, following a Royalist rising, a proclamation was issued requiring suspected Roman Catholics to take an oath abjuring papal authority and the doctrine of transubstantiation, on pain of imprisonment and forfeiture of estate (Fox 1952:220n; Penney 1907:346). An act of 1656 required a still more detailed oath (Penney 1907:346). These oaths were put to Quakers because of the widespread suspicion that they were Jesuits in disguise and subversive agents of the Royalist cause (Penney 1907:346), though they were always as vocal as any in their opposition to Catholicism.

More important were the Oath of Supremacy (St. 5 Eliz. cap. I), enacted early in the reign of Elizabeth, and the Oath of Allegiance (St. 7 Jac. 1 cap. 6), originally enacted in the aftermath of the Gunpowder Plot. The Oath of Supremacy was worded as follows:

> I, A. B., do utterly testify and declare in my conscience, that the king's highness is the only supreme governor of this realm, and of all other (his) highness' dominions and countries, as well as in all spiritual or ecclesiastical things or causes, as temporal. And that no

foreign prince, prelate, state, or potentate, hath, or ought to have any jurisdiction, power, superiority, pre-eminence, or authority, ecclesiastical or spiritual, within this realm: and therefore I do utterly renounce and forsake all foreign jurisdictions, powers, superiorities, and authorities, and do promise, that from henceforth I shall bear faith, and true allegiance to the king's highness, his heirs and lawful successors; and to my power shall assist and defend all jurisdiction, privileges, pre-eminences, and authorities, granted, or belonging to the king's highness, his heirs and successors, or united and annexed to the imperial crown of his realm. So help me God, and by the contents of this book. (Sewel 1867, 1:333–334)

Refusal of this oath was punishable by *praemunire* for the first refusal and high treason for the second. *Praemunire*, taken from the beginning of the writ, *"praemunire facias* A. B. . . . " ("cause A. B. to be forewarned . . . "), denoted a punishment whereby the convicted defendant was put out of the king's protection, remained a prisoner at the king's pleasure, and forfeited his or her estate to the Crown (Penney 1907:354–355).

The Oath of Allegiance, longer and more complex than the Oath of Supremacy, is also worth quoting in full:

I, A. B., do truly and sincerely acknowledge, profess, testify, and declare in my conscience before God and the world, that our sovereign lord king James, is lawful and rightful king of this realm, and of all other his majesty's dominions and countries; and that the pope, neither of himself, nor by any authority of the church, or see of Rome, or by any other means, with any other, hath any power or authority to depose the king, or to dispose of any of his majesty's kingdoms or dominions, or to authorize any foreign prince to invade, or annoy him, or his countries, or to discharge any of his subjects from their allegiance and obedience to his majesty, or to give license or leave to any of them to bear arms, raise tumults, or to offer any violence or hurt to his majesty's royal person, state, or government, or to any of his majesty's subjects, within his majesty's dominions. Also I do swear from my heart, that notwithstanding any declaration, or sentence of excommunication, or deprivation, made or granted, or to be made or granted, by the pope or his successors, or by any authority derived, or pretended to be derived from him or his see, against the said king, his heirs or successors, or any absolution of the said subjects from their obedience, I will bear faith and true allegiance to his majesty, his heirs and successors, and him and them will defend to the uttermost of my power, against all conspiracies and attempts whatsoever, which shall be made against his or their persons, their crown and dignity, by reason or color of any such

sentence or declaration, or otherwise: and will do my best endeavor
to disclose, and make known unto his majesty, his heirs and successors, all treasons, and traitorous conspiracies, which I shall know
or hear of to be against him, or any of them. And I do further swear,
that I do from my heart abhor, detest, and abjure, as impious and
heretical, this damnable doctrine and position, that princes which be
excommunicated, or deprived by the pope, may be deposed, or
murdered by their subjects, or any other whatsoever. And I do believe, and in my conscience am resolved, that neither the pope, nor
any person whatsoever, hath power to absolve me of this oath, or
any part thereof, which I acknowledge by good and full authority to
be lawfully ministered unto me, and do renounce all pardons and
dispensations to the contrary. And all these things I do plainly and
sincerely acknowledge, and swear according to the express words
by me spoken, and according to the plain and common sense and
understanding of the same words, without any equivocation, or mental evasion, or secret reservation whatsoever. And I do make this
recognition and acknowledgement, heartily, willingly, and truly,
upon the true faith of a Christian. So help me God. (Sewel 1867,
1:333–367)

Refusal of the Oath of Allegiance called for imprisonment of the refuser until
the next assizes or quarter sessions, when the oath was to be tendered again.
A second refusal incurred the penalty of *praemunire* (Penney 1907:354).

The first wave of persecution experienced by Friends for refusal to swear
political oaths occurred in 1655–1656. As mentioned earlier, part of the
government reaction to a minor Royalist insurrection in March 1655 was the
issuance of a proclamation requiring suspected Roman Catholics to swear an
oath abjuring papal authority and the doctrine of transubstantiation. In May,
Thomas Salthouse, preaching in Plymouth with his companion Miles Halhead,
gave offense to a priest by publicly rebuking him for insincerity. The priest,
George Brooks, retaliated by securing a warrant for the Quakers' arrest.
Clearing themselves of the initial charge levied against them of denying the
Trinity, Salthouse and Halhead were then tendered the Oath of Abjuration,
which they duly refused. The Proclamation of 1655, however, gave no authority to imprison refusers, so the two ministers were imprisoned as disturbers
of the peace and indicted at the next sessions, six weeks later, "particularly
for divers disgraceful words and gestures against George Brooks, Clerk"
(Besse 1753, 1:147).

Salthouse and Halhead were penalized in two ways for their adherence to
the Quaker testimony against oaths. First, their request for a trial was denied
because they would not use "the common form of words, *By God and my
Country*" in their plea (Besse 1753, 1:147). Then, the Oath of Abjuration

was tendered to them a second time in court, which they again refused. They were convicted and fined five pounds each for the offense against Brooks and for refusing to be tried; that is, their refusal to swear in their plea for trial was turned against them as a charge of refusing to be tried. A threat by the court to have their estates seized for refusing the Oath of Abjuration was dropped, but they spent nearly seven months in prison pending final settlement of the proceedings against them (Besse 1753, 1:147).

The terms in which Salthouse and Halhead refused the oath in court are worth examination:

> In the presence of the Eternal God, and before all this people, we do deny, with as much detestation as any of you do, the Pope and his supremacy, and the purgatory, and all that is in the form of the oath mentioned, we declare freely against; and we do not deny to swear because of any guilt that is upon us, but in obedience to the command of Christ, who saith, "Swear not at all:" and we will not come under the condemnation of an oath, for the liberty of the outward man. (Sewel 1867, 1:155)

Several points are significant here with regard to the public position of Quakers concerning political oaths. We should note that Salthouse and Halhead were quite ready to subscribe to the substance of the oath in clear and strong terms. Important in terms of speaking is that they manifested their readiness to do so by employing other performative verbs – "deny" and "declare" – which, like "swear," name speech acts in which the saying of the expression amounts to accomplishment of the action. I will develop this issue later at greater length. Finally, they declared their intention to suffer rather than violate their consciences. All these, as we shall see, anticipated the Quaker response to persecution for refusing political oaths in the more intense period of the 1660s.

There were several other noteworthy cases of persecution during 1655–1656, one of which involved George Fox himself (Besse 1753, 1:228; Fox 1952:237–266). Nevertheless, as just suggested, the full weight of official persecution of Quakers for refusing political oaths did not fall upon them until the restoration of Charles II in 1660. Ironically, where the Quakers had suffered under the Commonwealth because they were suspected of Royalist sympathies, they faced even more severe persecution by the newly ascendant Royalist authorities, who accused them of disloyalty to the Crown. The plain fact was that the Quakers' testimony against swearing was a ready handle to be used against them by government authorities of any persuasion who were concerned with the far deeper issue of which judicial oaths and political oaths were merely one manifestation, namely, submission to the authority of the state.

The Royalist preoccupation with disloyalty to the government was not surprising, as they returned to power with the memory of Charles I's execution, the Commonwealth's repudiation of the monarchy, and the Puritans' suppression of the Anglican church still very much in their minds (Cragg 1957). Moreover, the Roundhead veterans of Cromwell's army were still a presence, and the Royalist fear of sedition and rebellion, however exaggerated, was far from unfounded, as Venner's Fifth Monarchy rising in 1661 and the Kaber Rigg, or Northern Plot, of 1663 soon demonstrated. Whether motivated by a desire for revenge, or by fear, or by the political conviction that to allow sectarian cleavage in religion was to encourage weakness in the state, the Royalist authorities, led by the Cavalier Parliament, resorted to the oaths of allegiance and supremacy from the very point of their reaccession to power, often singling out dissenters, like the Quakers, in their zeal to reestablish the dominance of the Anglican church in English religious life.

Richard Davies, for example, a leader among Welsh Quakers, reported in his journal that he "was had before the first justices that were made in these parts by the authority of king Charles the second, in the year 1660," and tendered the oaths of supremacy and allegiance (1832:44). Davies's behavior before the authorities at this early point was still regarded as something of a curiosity. The high sheriff, he reported, "told me I was a strange man and of a strange persuasion, to come with my hat upon my head among them, and would not take the oaths nor give bail" (1832:45). Davies was fortunate in that the authorities before whom he appeared were not hostile to Friends, and he suffered no penalty for refusing the oaths. Others were not so lucky: Thomas Goodaire and Benjamin Staples were sentenced to *praemunire* at the quarter sessions at Oxford in October 1660, though both prisoners were later freed, Staples after thirty-five weeks in prison (Braithwaite 1961:14).

The ill-fated rebellion of the Fifth Monarchy Men, in January 1661, intensified Royalist fears of subversion, and a proclamation followed quickly forbidding meetings of Quakers, Anabaptists, and Fifth Monarchists, and commanding justices to tender the Oath of Allegiance to all who violated the proclamation. Those "esteemed to be the most eminent among the Quakers" (Whitehead 1832, 1:157) tended to be singled out for such treatment, a pattern that was to become clearer over the next several years as the lines of confrontation between government authority and Quaker conscience came more sharply into focus.

A brief easing of the pressures of persecution was signaled by a proclamation of grace issued by King Charles at the time of his coronation (April 23, 1661), although the full release of imprisoned Friends was not accomplished for several weeks. The Cavalier Parliament, less tolerant than the monarch, brought the period of respite to an end, however, with the passage of the Quaker Act in May 1662. This "Act for preventing mischiefs and danger that may arise by certain persons called Quakers and others refusing to take lawful oaths," opened as follows:

> Whereas of late times certain persons under the name of Quakers, and other names of separation, have taken up and maintained sundry

dangerous opinions and tenets, and (amongst others) that the taking of an oath in any case whatsoever, although before a lawful magistrate, is altogether unlawful and contrary to the Word of God; and the said persons do daily refuse to take an oath, though lawfully tendered, whereby it often happens that the truth is wholly suppressed, and the administration of justice much obstructed. (Besse 1753, 1:xi)

Accordingly, the provisions of the act made it illegal to refuse a lawfully administered oath, or even to maintain or persuade others that the taking of an oath was unlawful. The act also prohibited meetings of five or more people "under pretense of joining in a religious worship, not authorized by the laws of this realm," which the preamble cast as "endangering . . . the public peace and safety." The penalties for violation of the act were a fine of not more than five pounds for the first offense, up to ten pounds for the second offense, and abjuration of the realm or transportation for the third.

The Quaker Act represented a piece of formal legislation, aimed directly at the Quakers, for tenets and practices seen to be a danger to government, of which their testimony in regard to a particular speech act, the swearing of an oath, was singled out as so subversive as to require legal penalty. As such, the act amounted to a public drawing of the lines, intensifying the confrontation between the Quakers and government over oaths. At stake in this conflict over the legitimacy and necessity of a speech act was the fundamental political issue of the period: Where did one owe one's first allegiance – to God or to the state?

Hugh D. Duncan has suggested, building on the work of Kenneth Burke, that "a principle of social order must always be personified in some kind of dramatic action if it is to be comprehensible to all classes and conditions of men" (1968:64). Moreover, he suggests it is in these social dramas, in which the competition, rivalry, and conflict inherent in the social order are symbolized and made conscious and visible, that these divisive dimensions of social life are most open to observation.

Victor Turner, who has made especially productive use of the dramatistic perspective for anthropological analysis, has suggested that social dramas achieve their fullest elaboration in the arena of politics (1974:33). "Politics," James E. Combs agrees, "more than any other area of social life, is a dramatic magnification of the human condition. Politics is the most theatrical of social arenas" (1980:16). And if politics is the most theatrical of social arenas, trials may well be the most theatrical of political dramas (Combs 1980:59). Dramatists and political figures alike have recognized and exploited the dramatic potential of trials throughout history, as the subsequent construction of theatrical presentations out of the actual dialogue of House Un-American Activities Committee proceedings or the trial of the Chicago Seven demonstrates (cf. Webber 1968:70–72, 1971:287). We are all too familiar in our own day with the staging of "show trials" carried out not only to determine guilt, but to dramatize it, to establish or reinforce hierarchies, or to accomplish the public degradation of individuals or groups (Combs 1980:37; Duncan 1968:64–65; Garfinkel 1956).

All this suggests that it would be productive to look beyond the legal framework and polemical literature relating to the Quakers' refusal to swear political oaths, to the records of the legal proceedings in which the violators of the laws were tried. If the issues at stake were as significant as I have suggested, we might expect them to have provided an apt focus for political drama; and indeed they did. The oath trials of the 1660s involved major Quaker leaders, attracted widespread public attention, and were recorded in some detail by Friends, down to the actual transcription of the courtroom proceedings (apparently from shorthand). Although we cannot be certain of the accuracy of these accounts, the very effort that went into producing and disseminating them is evidence that the Quakers attached great importance to the trials, and their content makes clear that the trials were indeed social dramas. It is certainly the case, consistent with Turner's observation on the nature of social dramas (1974:33), that the oath trials were characterized by a stress upon loyalty and obligation. Indeed, that was the focal issue: Was one's primary loyalty and obligation owed to the state or to God?

I should make clear that I am not employing the notion of social drama here in some vaguely metaphorical sense resting on a conception of life as theater. Rather, I believe it is apt to consider the trials as dramas on the basis of a set of features that they display in common with theatrical drama. They are:

> *Framed*, in the sense of being clearly marked off in time and space from the surrounding flow of activity and experience
>
> *Public*, both in the sense of being on view, played out before and to an audience, and in the sense of implicating public rather than private issues (Combs 1980:12)
>
> *Formalized*, especially in regard to invocation of positional identities and maintenance of a central situational focus (Irvine 1979b)
>
> *Agonistic*, in the sense of revolving around a conflict or competition (cf. Combs 1980:55)
>
> *Symbolic*, in the sense that the participants (including the audience) see themselves and their actions as implicating and standing for larger issues

If these features justify the label "drama" for the trials, it remains to remind ourselves that they were nevertheless not theatrical dramas, but *social* dramas. The important difference is that a theatrical drama is, in Goffman's apt words, a "mock-up [of] social life," a "fabrication" (1974:136); a trial *is* social life – it is framed as "real." Social dramas are symbolic enactments in which social conflicts are personified, placed on view, and publicly played out, "public episodes of tensional eruption" (Turner 1974:33).

The first trial held under the Quaker Act was that of John Crook, who was tried with Isaac Grey and John Bolton, in London, beginning June 25, 1662. Crook was an important north-country Quaker and a leader of Friends until his death in 1699 (Barbour and Roberts 1973:589; Barclay 1841:29). He represented an especially appropriate target for Royalist persecution, for he had been an active Cromwellian and had purchased a confiscated Royalist estate in Buckinghamshire, which became the center of many of Fox's meetings with Quaker preachers in that region. A former justice, Crook's Quaker activity cost him his judicial post.

Crook was violently arrested at a meeting for worship in mid-May, though he was not brought to trial until about six weeks later. When he appeared in court, however, he was immediately asked when he had taken the Oath of Allegiance. This procedure is worth remarking on, for it became a general pattern in the persecution of Friends in the period that followed. The Quaker Act made it possible to arrest Friends for meeting together in groups of five or more. However, because the act provided for a penalty of only five pounds for the first offense, anti-Quaker authorities resorted to the harsher expedient of tendering the arrested Friends the Oath of Allegiance, refusal of which carried the far more drastic penalty of *praemunire*.

Crook's trial clearly warrants the label of social drama. It was staged in London, before the lord mayor, Chief Justice Forster, and a number of other justices and justices of the peace, with many spectators, both sympathetic and unsympathetic, in attendance. Moreover, as the first trial under the Quaker Act, involving a prominent Quaker leader, it was seen as precedent setting and symbolic. Crook himself observed in the course of the trial that he is "like to be a precedent," asserting at one point that "I dare not betray the honesty of my cause, and the honest oaths of this nation, whose liberty I stand for as well as my own" (1662:11–12).

The issues in terms of which the trial was framed are clearly evident in the opening passage of the transcript:

CHIEF JUDGE: Call John Crook to the bar, which the crier did accordingly, he being among the felons as aforesaid.

John Crook being brought to the bar:

CHIEF JUDGE; When did you take the Oath of Allegiance?

JOHN CROOK: I desire to be heard.

CHIEF JUDGE: Answer to the question and you shall be heard.

JOHN CROOK: I have been about six weeks in prison, and am I now called to accuse myself? For the answering to the question in the negative is to accuse myself, which you ought not to put me upon, for *nemo debet seipsum prodere*. I am an Englishman, and by the law of England I ought not to be taken nor imprisoned, nor desired of my freehold, nor called in question, not put to answer, but according to the law of the land; which I challenge as my birthright, on my own behalf, and all that hear me this day (or words to this purpose) I stand here at this bar as a delinquent, and do desire that my accuser may be brought forth to accuse me for my delinquency, and then I shall answer to my charge (if any I be guilty of).

CHIEF JUDGE: You are here demanded to take the Oath of Allegiance, and when you hve done that, then you shall be heard about the other; for we have power to tender it to any man.

JOHN CROOK: Not to me upon this occasion, in this place; for I am brought hither as an offender already, and not to be made an offender here, or to accuse myself; for I am an Englishman, as I have said to you, and challenge the benefit of the laws of England; for by them, is a better inheritance derived to me as an Englishman, than that which I receive from my parents; for by the former the latter is preserved: and this is the 29th Chapter of Magna Carta, and the Petition of Right, mentioned in the 3rd of Car. I, and in other good laws of England; and therefore – I desire the benefit and observance of them: And you that are Judges upon the Bench ought to be my counsel, and not my accusers, but to inform me of the benefit of those laws; and wherein I am ignorant you ought to inform me, that I may not suffer through my own ignorance of those advantages which the laws of England afford me as an Englishman . . .

CHIEF JUDGE: We sit here to do justice, and are upon our oaths, and we are to tell you what is law, and not you us: Therefore sirrah you are too bold.

JOHN CROOK: Sirrah is not a word becoming a Judge; for I am no felon; neither ought you to menace the prisoner at the bar: for I stand here arraigned for my life and liberty, and the preservation of my wife and children, and outward estate, [they being now at the stake]; Therefore you ought to hear me to the full what I can say in my own defense, according to law, and that in its season, as it is given me to speak: Therefore I hope the court will bear with me, if I am bold to assert my liberty as an Englishman and as a Christian: and if I speak loud, it is my zeal for the Truth, and for the Name of the Lord; and mine innocency makes me bold –

JUDGE: It is an evil zeal, interrupting John Crook.

JOHN CROOK: No, I am bold in the Name of the Lord God Almighty, the everlasting Jehovah, to assert the Truth, and stand as a witness for it: Let my accuser be brought forth, and I am ready to answer any Court of Justice – (Crook 1662:6–7)

Drawing on his own legal knowledge as a former justice, Crook was here demanding due process, on the basis of his rights as an Englishman and a Christian. ''It is justice I stand for,'' he insisted a short while later; ''let me have justice . . . as by law you ought to do'' (1662:9). Specifically, his demand was that he be dealt with in terms of the charge for which he was originally arrested under the Quaker Act, boldly challenging the right of the court to shift the proceedings to the Oath of Allegiance in an obvious attempt to entrap him. The judge, not surprisingly, treated Crook's attempt to teach him the law as a presumptuous affront, addressing Crook with the contemptuous ''Sirrah.'' The judge, for his part, insisted on the court's authority to tender Crook the oath, regardless of the grounds on which he was brought to trial. It is especially noteworthy, in symbolic terms, that the judge appealed for this authority to the fact that he and his colleagues had themselves taken oaths of office. In effect, the authorities held, we have the power in this situation because we have taken our oaths as justices; you have none because you refuse to take an oath. The confrontation was thus joined in terms of justice and due process versus power and authority, and this remained the central issue throughout the trial.

Judging from the report of the transcript, the court was determined to push the trial forward to a conviction, denying the defendants' request for a postponement to prepare their defense, rejecting an objection to the composition of the jury, which included several known anti-Quakers, and refusing even to allow the accused to speak in their own defense, going to the point of having them gagged (Crook 1662:19–20).

The bias of the proceedings reached an extreme when ''some men were sworn to testify that we refused to take the Oath, which we never positively did,'' though ''other officers of the court, whom they would have sworn, refused to swear, though pressed to it by the Chief Justice, they desiring to be excused'' (Crook 1662:19). Crook, by contrast, remained conscientious to the end:

> As to conscience, I have something to say, and that is, it is a tender thing, and we have known what it is to offend it, and therefore we dare not break Christ's commands, who hath said, Swear not at all; and the Apostle James said, Above all things, my brethren, swear not – (interrupted) the Court calling again to the executioner to stop my mouth, which he did accordingly with his dirty cloth as aforesaid, and his gag in his hand. (1662:21)

What emerges from the transcript is a set of symbolic oppositions, contrasting those who would not swear – the Quakers and the honest witnesses – with those who did swear – the judges and the false witnesses. Religion (Truth with a capital *T*) versus worldly power, honor and honesty (truth) versus dishonor and lies are all implicated in the contrasts, as shown in the accompanying figure. The outcome of the trial was that Crook and his codefendants were found ''guilty of refusing to take the Oath of Allegiance'' (Crook 1662:22) and sentenced to *praemunire*.

Nonswearers (good)	**Swearers (bad)**
Quakers	*Judges*
Will not swear because religion (Truth) binds them to truth	Swear in order to obtain worldly power
Will not submit to worldly power, but uphold Truth	Use worldly power against truth and Truth
Honest Witnesses	*False witnesses*
Will not swear because the charge is not truth	Swear to charge that is not truth
Will not submit to worldly power (of judges), but uphold truth	Submit to worldly power (of judges) against truth and Truth

It is noteworthy that although the confrontation between religious conscience and worldly authority was certainly dramatized in Crook's trial, the matter of his allegiance to the crown entered in only once, in passing, emphasizing as elsewhere his demand for due process: "I did not, neither do I deny allegiance, but do desire to know the cause of my so long imprisonment" (1662:9). Isaac Grey, however, also pressing for due process and condemning the injustice of the proceedings, addressed the issue of allegiance in a way that prefigured what was to become a significant strategy of Quaker defendants in subsequent trials. Responding to the judge's accusation that "the law supposeth you to be disaffected to the present government, and therefore the Oath is tendered to you"(Crook 1662:38), Grey asserted, "I understand that the fundamental law of England alloweth no man to be accused or condemned upon supposition: I do further affirm, and that in the Light of God, that I am not an enemy to the King, nor to any man living upon the face of the earth" (Crook 1662:39).

The special significance of Grey's statement lies in the form of his expression of loyalty: "I do *affirm*, and that *in the Light of God*, that I am not an enemy to the king." Examination of the Oath of Allegiance reveals that it employs a number of words – "acknowledge," "profess," "declare," "testify," "swear" – that represent performative speech acts, in the sense of the term employed by J. L. Austin (1962): utterances that describe an action by the speaker in which the saying of the expression amounts to the accomplishment of the action. More specifically, in terms of Austin's typology of performatives, they are *expositives*, which "make plain how our utterances fit into the course of an argument or conversation, how we are using words, or, in general, are expository" (1962:151).

Now, "affirm" is also an expositive, not very different in weight from most of the words from the oath listed above; indeed, without going into a detailed semantic analysis, it is instructive to note that all these verbs are grouped together as synonyms or near-synonyms in Roget's *Thesaurus* (see under Affirmation 535.3–535.4). To be sure, "swear" is distinctive in an important way, insofar as it calls upon God to witness, and in effect to guarantee, the utterance. But in making his affirmation "in the Light of God," Grey did as much himself, though, as we have seen, the Quakers assumed accountability to God for all speech. Grey's statement is thus very nearly equivalent to an oath (cf. *Oxford English Dictionary*, "swear: To make a solemn declaration or statement with an appeal to God or a superhuman being, or to some sacred object, in confirmation of what is said"). In fact, to look ahead, the Affirmation Act of 1696 established that a Quaker's affirmation should bear the legal weight of an oath. Grey's declaration is evidence that the sticking point for the Quakers concerning the Oath of Allegiance might indeed be narrowed to an objection to the single speech act, "swear," not to the affirmative expression of allegiance before God.

Although Crook's words before the court contained no expression of loyalty quite like Grey's, his commentary appended to the published transcript of the trial proceedings confirms the line of analysis suggested by Grey's affirmation. Citing a work of legal scholarship, Crook noted:

> An Oath . . . is an affirmation or denial, by any Christian, of any thing lawful and honest, before one, or more, that have authority to give the same, for advancing of truth and right, calling Almighty God to witness that the testimony is true . . . Note, an Oath is an *affirmation*, or *denial*, which was not denied by us: he doth not say by kissing the Book or any such like ceremony. Note again, the end of taking this oath, it is for advancement of truth and right, which is truly done by affirmation or denial, being solemnly spoken in God's sight and presence; and our denial to take the Oath in that way of imposed formality (yielding all just and due obedience) did no way hinder the advancement either of truth or right, obedience answering the end of the Oath, and not swearing. (1662:41)

Thus, insofar as Crook's reporting of his experience to Friends in his published account of his trial contributed to his co-religionists' understanding of the social drama it represented and helped to shape its meaning as precedent, the above statement provides additional warrant for us to be alert for subsequent development of the position among Friends that alternative performative expressions of loyalty should be accepted as equivalent to and in lieu of oaths. As we shall see, this position did in fact become increasingly prominent as Friends experienced further persecutions for their refusal to swear in the years that followed.

Crook's framing of his trial account includes one further element that requires our attention, presented in the introductory "Epistle to the Reader." Much of the epistle is devoted to a presentation of biblical and historical examples of "witnesses that have stood for God, against the imposers on the conscience" (1662:3), from Daniel to the Marian martyrs. Here again are the "model and metaphor" (Turner 1974:36) that gave pattern to the Quakers' actions and responses under persecution and underlay the role they assumed in the social dramas represented by their trials: "Blessed are they forever who are found faithful unto death, for they shall have the Crown of Life" (Crook 1662:3). Bear a faithful and steadfast witness to God's Truth against all attempts to impose upon your conscience; suffer conscientiously rather than compromise the Truth. Most important, in a conflict between "God's command" and "unrighteous laws," the Truth must be upheld and the latter denied, whatever suffering may result. "We ought to obey God rather than men" (Acts 5.29).

Other trials under the Quaker Act followed those of Crook, Bolton, and Grey in rapid succession, including proceedings against such prominent leaders as George Fox, Edward Bourne, John Audland, and John Wilkinson. In these proceedings, the lines of the basic conflict emerged into still greater clarity within the conduct of the legal dramas themselves: "obedience to the King's laws" and submission to the authority of the government as against obedience to the higher authority of "the doctrine of Christ." What was part of the framing matter of the published account of Crook's trial became part of the dramatic enactment itself. As articulated in the trial of Audland and Wilkinson:

AUDLAND AND WILKINSON: We are Christians, and do account ourselves to abide in Christ's doctrine, who absolutely forbids all swearing . . .

MAGISTRATE: You must obey the King's laws. (Besse 1753, 2:44)

Or still more fully in the trial of Robert Smith:

ROBERT SMITH: Shall the example of Christ determine the controversy between us?

JUDGE: I came not to dispute with you about the doctrine of Christ, but to teach you the doctrine of the law.

SMITH: Must the doctrine of the law make void the doctrine of Christ?

JUDGE: Will you answer speedily, whether you will take the Oath or not?

SMITH: Love obligeth to allegiance more than oaths can do.

JUDGE: Then signify your allegiance by an oath.

SMITH: That which obligeth me not to swear, obligeth me to injure no man.

JUDGE: Take him away.

SMITH: Friends, the things required at our hands [by the authorities], are to deny those things which to us are the Lord's truths. The one is, *not to swear at all*. The other is, *the assembling ourselves together*. Rather than so to do, I am here not only to suffer, but to seal those testimonies with my blood, if thereunto required. (Besse 1753, 2:64)

It is all here: the oath required as a sign of loyalty, the Quaker appeal to the greater power of loyalty founded on Christian love and Truth, the conflict between the king's law and Christ's doctrine, and the Quaker readiness to suffer rather than submit.

As regards the tender of other performatives in lieu of the oath, we may note especially Edward Bourne's offer to the magistrates: "What is Truth in the Oath we can promise, and if we do not swear, it is in obedience to Christ's command" (Besse 1753, 2:66). Examination of the Oath of Allegiance reveals that it operates in two principal performative dimensions, requiring both current endorsement of the sovereign's legitimacy and engagement to continue to bear faithful and true allegiance to the king and his heirs in the future. In terms of Austin's typology of performatives (1962:156), the oath requires – indeed, it incorporates – both *expositives* and *commissives* (the point of the latter being to commit the speaker to a certain course of action). Whereas "swear" serves as both expositive and commissive in the oath, Isaac Grey's "affirm," discussed earlier, is only expositive. Robert Smith's commissive, "promise," fills in the other half of the pair. Indeed, "promise" like "swear," may be both expositive (when used in the sense of "assert confidently") and commissive.

*   *   *   *

At the end of 1662, King Charles, ever more tolerant than the Cavalier Parliament, issued his first Declaration of Indulgence, which resulted in the release of many Friends from prison and an abatement of the pressures of persecution under the Quaker Act. By the following summer, however, rumors and fears of a Puritan plot in the north brought this brief period of relief to an end and ushered in a new wave of persecution, reinforced by the Conventicle Act of 1664. This piece of repressive legislation went into effect on July 1, 1664, and continued in force until March 1669. Observing that the Quakers "obstruct the proceeding of justice by their obstinate refusal to take the Oath lawfully tendered unto them in the ordinary course of law," the act provided, among other things, that a mere refusal of a judicial oath was to be recorded as a conviction, subject to the penalty of transportation (Besse 1753, 1:xi–xx). The act also prohibited "any assembly, conventicle, or meeting, under colour or pretence of any exercise of religion, in other manner than is allowed by the liturgy or practice of the Church of England."

For more than a decade, at this point, Westmoreland had been an important center of Quakerism, and official suspicion of Quaker complicity in seditious plots in that northern region focused strongly on Friends, despite their protestations of innocence. And among Friends, suspicion centered most strongly on "their grand speakers" (Braithwaite 1961:32). It was here that the second wave of show trials focusing on oaths took place, most notably those of Francis Howgill, Margaret Fell, and George Fox.

Howgill, one of the earliest of the Westmoreland separatists who came over to Fox in 1652, and one of the Valiant Sixty who carried Quakerism to the south in 1654, was arrested at the end of July 1663. "Being in the market-place at Kendal about his ordinary business, [he] was summoned by the High-Constable to appear before the Justices, then sitting at a tavern, who tendered him the Oath of Allegiance, and committed him to prison till the Assizes to be held in the next month at Appleby" (Besse 1753, 2:11).

At the August assizes, he was again tendered the oath, and, refusing it once more, was indicted. Exercising his right to postpone his trial, he was freed until the next assizes, at Lent. Before his next appearance in court, the abortive rising in Westmoreland in conjunction with the Northern Plot aggravated tensions still further. By the time of the Lent assizes, then, Howgill's trial assumed the full dimensions of a social drama. The concern of Friends is indicated in part by the full recording of the proceedings at the Lent assizes and at Howgill's final court appearance in August 1664. Additionally, the transcripts take careful note of the responses of the public at the trials.

At the Lent proceedings it was clear that Howgill had been singled out by the authorities because they viewed him as "a dangerous person, a ringleader of the Quakers," and "a great speaker," even while admitting that they had no direct evidence of his involvement in the activities of the plotters (Besse 1753, 2:11). The focus of the drama, from the judge's opening statement, was the Oath of Allegiance: "Seeing you did refuse to take the Oath of Allegiance at the last Assizes, the law doth presume such persons to be enemies to the King, and Government" (Besse 1753, 2:11). Refusing the oath once again at the Lent assizes, Howgill was jailed until the next sitting of the court in August because he would not give bond to guarantee that he would not join in religious meetings with Friends.

In August the focus of the conflict was articulated in its narrowest and sharpest terms, as the Oath of Allegiance was insisted upon by the court as the sole acceptable means of demonstrating loyalty to the government. Because the Quakers' testimony against swearing was clearly known, this amounted to a direct counterposition of the authority of the state against the authority of religion.

Other means of accomplishing the purpose of the Oath were not acceptable. Howgill had already suggested that the Quakers' pacifist testimony against bearing arms stood as a warrant against their engagement in seditious plots: "It has been a doctrine always held by us, and a received principle as anything we believed, that Christ's Kingdom could not be set up with carnal weapons, nor the Gospel propagated by force of arms, nor the Church of God builded with violence" (Besse 1753, 2:12). On this appearance in court, Howgill offered a signed statement answering to the substance of the oath:

Now as to the Oath, the substance therof, with the representation of my case, is already presented to the court, unto which I have set my hand, and shall in those words testify the same in open court, if required; and seeing it is the very substance of what the law doth require, I desire it may be accepted, and that I may be cleared from my imprisonment. (Besse 1753, 2:14)

But the court would not compromise on "the form of words" (Besse 1753, 2:15); only the oath was acceptable. The point was to elicit a public display of submission to authority. To compromise on the officially established means of accomplishing this display would only undercut its potency.

I do not wish to be seen as arguing here that the judicial authorities were being unreasonably intransigent in refusing to accept an alternative to the oath. For all the cynicism and expediency that marked the authorities' uses of the oath against the Quakers, it may reasonably be maintained – as Malinowski has done – that in law "the value of the word, the binding force of a formula, is at the very foundation of order and reliability in human relations" (1965:234). The Quakers certainly believed in "the sacredness of words and their socially [and divinely] sanctioned inviolability" (Malinowski 1965:234), and their antagonists' insistence on the proper "form of words" could be warranted by appeal to the same standard. Indeed, the potential for the tragic dramas played out in the oath trials lay precisely here, in the justification of powerfully opposed actions by appeal to the same fundamental principle.

In any event, the judges' response to Howgill's offer effectively foreclosed the matter:

I am come to execute the law; and the law requires an Oath, and I cannot alter it: Do you think the law must be changed for you, or only for a few? If this be suffered, the administration of justice is hindered; no action can be tried, nor evidence given for the King: *Your principles are altogether inconsistent with the law and government.* (Besse 1753, 2:14, emphasis added)

Faced with this irreconcilable conflict, Howgill responded as we might expect: "Well, if we must suffer, it is for Christ's sake, and for well-doing" (Besse 1753, 2:17). He chose to suffer rather than submit. The drama came to a close as Howgill was sentenced to *praemunire*. He spent the rest of his life in prison, where he died early in 1669, at the age of sixty, "steadfast in the Faith in which I lived, and suffered for" (Besse 1738, 3:365).

Howgill was a prominent figure in Westmoreland, one of the earliest and must influential of the Quaker leaders. As such, he was fittingly cast in the social drama represented by his trials. But if any figures among Friends could overshadow Howgill, they were George Fox and Margaret Fell, who found themselves cast in a legal drama about oaths during the same period as

Howgill himself. Fox, as the founder of Quakerism and its most forceful and influential minister, was known throughout England. His gift for exploiting the theatrical potential of public confrontations has been noted by Barbour; among a people marked by their "readiness for dramatic action" (Barbour 1964:1), Fox's own "genius for self-dramatization" (Barbour 1964:35) was unequaled. Margaret Fell, as the widow of the locally prominent Judge Fell and mistress of Swarthmore Hall, was of a leading family in Westmoreland, to the extent that she elicited deference even from the very judges who condemned her Quaker principles.

Not surprisingly, the authorities were especially interested in proceeding against Fox, as chief among the Quaker "grand speakers," and offered a reward for his capture (Braithwaite 1961:32). Appropriately, he was arrested at Swarthmore Hall, in January 1664. The large gathering of Friends at Swarthmore on the following Sunday, "on purpose, as 'tis generally thought, to affront our authority" (Braithwaite 1961:33), drew down the hostility of the officials on Margaret Fell soon afterward.

But if the authorities were ready to make a public example of Fox and Fell, the two Quaker mainstays were equally ready to make the proceedings into a public drama. Throughout their first trial in March 1664, both played strongly to the public and defied the judges in highlighting the agonistic focus of the confrontation. Fell angered the judge into charging that "she had an everlasting tongue, you draw the whole court after you, and she continued speaking on, and he still crying, will you take the Oath or no?" (Fox 1664:6). Fox, for his part, was even more confrontational, provoking this outburst from the judge: "I will not be afraid of thee, thou speaks so loud thy voice drowns mine and the court's, I must call for three or four cryers to drown thy voice, thou hast good lungs" (Fox 1664:9). We should note here that the judge's use of "thou" was a gesture of contempt; though Fox could not easily condemn the judge's pronominal use, he was not bound to tolerate further insult:

JUDGE: Sirrah will you take the Oath.

FOX: I am none of thy Sirrah, I am no Sirrah, I am a Christian, art thou a Judge and sits there to give names to prisoners, thou ought not to give names to prisoners.

JUDGE: I am a Christian too.

FOX: Then do Christian works.

JUDGE: Sirrah thou thinkest to frighten me with thy words, and looked aside, I am saying so again.

FOX: I speak in love to thee, that doth not become a judge, thou oughtest to instruct a prisoner of the law and Scriptures if he be ignorant and out of the way.

JUDGE: George Fox, I speak in love to thee.

FOX: Love gives no names. (1664:9)

The trial of Fell and Fox brought the fundamental issue of conflict more explicitly into relief than ever before. Fell, after stating that she accepted the substance of the Oath of Allegiance, continued:

> I stand here in obeying Christ's commands, and so keeping my conscience clear, which if I obey this law and King Charles' commands I defile my conscience and transgresseth against Christ Jesus who is the king of my conscience, and the cause and controversy in this matter, that you all are here to judge of this day, is betwixt Christ Jesus and King Charles. (Fox1664:14–15)

More succinctly, in terms well chosen to underscore the opposition: "I own allegiance to the King as he is King of England, but Christ Jesus is King of my conscience" (Fox 1664:7).

Not only was the opposition between King Charles and the King of Kings, as Fell framed it, but, as stated in turn by Fox, between the judge in the court and "Christ . . . the Judge of the world" (1664:8). Going on to drive the point home, Fox admonished the judge: "Thou sayest I must swear, whether must I obey Christ or thee" is the decisive issue. Thus, the conflict was openly articulated, the Quakers steadfastly reaffirming their higher loyalty to Christ over the earthly sovereign and their obedience to Christ's command over the law of government, all symbolized by the refusal to perform the crucial speech act of swearing.

To be sure, Fox did resort to additional arguments in defense of his refusal to swear: that recent history had shown how little political oaths were to be relied on and that he himself was loyal to the king – "If I could swear any oath at all upon any occasion, I should take that [the Oath of Allegiance]" (1664:10). More than that, he insisted that Friends were willing to be as fully accountable for their words as if they had sworn an oath: "If we transgress our yea and nay let us suffer as they do that break an Oath" (1664:23). This, of course, was an even stronger gesture than the offering of an alternative performative before God. Insofar as Friends considered themselves always accountable to God for their words, that remained a constant. Here, Fox offered to be accountable to civil authority as well, subject to prosecution for perjury for the breaking of his word. Such double accountability is the essence of civil oaths and penalties for their violation.

At this point, I suggest, the articulation of the conflict between the Quakers and the government in terms of oaths could go no further. The Quakers were willing to subscribe to everything the political oaths required of them in terms of loyalty to the state and to be accountable for their declaration of loyalty before God and man, refusing only to do so by the act of swearing. The authorities, however, insisted on the oath as the only acceptable "form of words," as provided by law. The impasse thus centered on the form of words, a matter of speaking; but this, of course, was symbolic of the more basic conflict between the power of the state and the conscience of its people.

The conflict was not resolved in the trial of Fell and Fox any more than it had been in the earlier trials. Margaret Fell was sentenced to *praemunire*. Though her property was not confiscated, she remained in prison until the summer of 1668. George Fox was also convicted and endured a period of very harsh imprisonment before being released in September 1668 on grounds of the blatant procedural irregularities in his trial.

After 1664 and the trials of Howgill, Fell, and Fox, the high dramatic potential of oath trials diminished. Though the Quakers continued to endure persecution for their refusal to swear up to 1696 and the passage of the Affirmation Act, the setting and the symbolic focus of the social dramas in which their conflict with civil government was played out shifted away from the courtroom and the oath.

Several reasons may be suggested for the shift away from oaths as the focus of social drama. During the early 1660s, in the period immediately following the Restoration, the Oath of Allegiance was especially well suited to use in social drama because it condensed the issues of political legitimacy, monarchy, religious separatism, and the reestablishment of Royalist ascendency into one symbolic focus and appeared to be a potent weapon against that most intransigent of separatist groups, the Quakers. But the use of the oath as a weapon was predicated upon a strategy of attacking the Quakers through their leaders, their "chief speakers," on the premise that bringing down the leaders in public displays of authority would draw the strength from the entire Quaker movement. However, even as the great dramatic trials of 1664 progressed, the authorities began to realize that the strategy of attempting to eliminate Quakerism by dealing harshly with the leaders would not work, for the leaders remained steadfast against swearing, accepting suffering rather than submitting, and the people continued to practice their religion even with the leaders in jail. Because the oath trials had to focus on single individuals, they did not offer an efficient means of exerting pressure on the mass of adherents to the Quaker faith.

The initiative, however, remained with the authorities. If persecution of the Quaker leaders for refusing to swear did not achieve the desired goal, the laws against religious conventicles afforded them an alternative weapon to bring to bear against the Friends in far larger numbers. Accordingly, as the oath persecutions diminished rapidly as the focus of dramatic energy, the authorities stepped up their campaign to destroy the Quaker meetings for worship by breaking up the meetings in progress, subjecting the Friends to violence, arrest, and imprisonment, and often inflicting damage upon the meetinghouses as well. The staging of the social dramas shifted from the courtroom to the meetinghouse, and the immediate issue from the oath to the meeting for religious worship.

It is important to note, though, that whether the issue was oaths or meetings, the fundamental conflict remained the same: the authority of the government versus the integrity of religious conscience. Moreover, the persecution of the religious meetings was no less dramatic than the oath trials, as the many contemporary and subsequent accounts make clear. If anything, the attacks on the meetings, with their attendant violence and mass arrests, were even more accessible to public view than the trials. But the Quaker rank and file, like the leaders, would not submit, sustained by the strength of their religious commitment and the guiding metaphor of salvation through suffering.

After the decline of the oath trials, the persecution of the Quakers continued with intermittent periods of relief for another quarter of a century, until the advent of toleration in 1689. It was during this long, painful period that the Friends developed a conception of the place of their fellowship in the larger society and its relation to civil authority that continued to influence their actions for more than a century thereafter. The social dramas centering around oaths and meetings for religious worship played no small part in this process, objectifying and symbolizing the demand of the government for submission to the authority of the state and the Quakers' determination to preserve the integrity of their religious testimony. A detailed examination of the complex process by which the conflict was resolved is beyond the scope of this book, in which our central concern is the role of speaking as a cultural symbol. Nevertheless, in order to clarify the consequences of the conflict over oaths, it will be useful to outline some of the principal contours of the process.

I have already noted that the Quakers' peace testimony formed part of their defense of their refusal to swear the Oath of Allegiance. They argued that their religious principles against fighting made it impossible for them to engage in armed rebellion against the government. But this was only a part of a more comprehensive response that was not grounded so directly in Quaker religious doctrine, representing rather an adaptive response to the pressures brought to bear on them by government persecution.

The emergent accommodation was clearly suggested in the early 1660s. At the close of an account written by Edward Burrough in September 1661 concerning the parliamentary activity that resulted in the Quaker Act of 1662, Burrough addressed his brethren in these words:

> Let all Friends walk in meekness and humility, and in faithfulness towards God, and in wisdom and practice and good will towards all men; that so you may all be preserved in a clear conscience, and may deserve a repute for inoffensiveness in all matters among your neighbours; that so no just occasion may be taken against us by our adversaries: but that in their consciences they may be forced to confess to our harmless conversations. And if at any time they will act against us, and cause us to suffer, it may be on their part for the

cause of God only, and for his Truth's sake, and not for evil doing. (Barclay 1841:107)

That is, do not give offense to the authorities whenever it can in good conscience be avoided. In order to protect the religious testimonies that are under attack, do not engage in any activities that may be used against Friends. Endure the suffering that may be visited upon you for the sake of Truth and behave in such a way that your harmlessness argues for the rightness of your cause. What this meant, effectively, was: Stay out of public affairs.

One can observe this strategy becoming institutionalized during the decades that followed. A major milestone in the process was documented in the "Epistle from Friends" of the General Meeting held in London in May 1672:

> And we beseech you for the Truth's sake, with the power of God stop all busy, discontented spirits . . . from reflecting upon and meddling with the powers, or those in outward dominion, – and all fruitless discourses of that tendence and nature; which . . . are to be shunned, rejected and reproved, whenever met withal: that all among us walk innocently and peaceably with a good conscience before all the world; – for that gives true boldness and confidence. (Barclay 1841:334–335)

And in 1689, the year of the Toleration Act, the "Epistle to Friends" from the London Yearly Meeting made clear the official position of the Society of Friends:

> And walk wisely and circumspectly towards all men, in the peaceable Spirit of Christ Jesus; giving no offence nor occasions to those in outward government, nor way to any controversies, heats, or distractions of this world, about the kingdoms thereof . . . That, as the Lord's hidden ones that are always quiet in the land, and as those prudent ones and wise in heart, who know when and where to keep silent, you may approve your hearts to God; keeping out of all airy discourses and words, that may any-ways become snares, or hurtful to truth or Friends; as being sensible that any personal occasion or reproach causes a reflection upon the body. (London Yearly Meeting 1806:36)

It is clear from these passages that the Quakers purchased their religious freedom at the sacrifice of engagement in worldly politics. The vigorous engagement of the early Quaker ministers in the Lamb's War was transformed, over three decades, into a policy of disengagement from the world's affairs; the impulse toward silence grew into a social policy founded on quietism, with effects that continued to be felt at least through the end of the eighteenth century (Bauman 1971).

The importance of these events for the study of speaking as a cultural symbol of the seventeenth-century Quakers is that a religious testimony concerning an aspect of speaking – the prohibition on religious grounds of the speech act of swearing – was a major symbolic focus in the process by which the place of the Quakers in the political community, their relationship to government, was played out. The social dramas represented by the oath trials of the 1660s exerted a formative influence on the process by which the conflict between the Society of Friends and worldly authority moved ultimately to the resolution represented by the Toleration Act of 1689 and the Affirmation Act of 1696.

Max Weber, in observing that every ethical religion must experience tensions with the sphere of political behavior, drew support for the proposition from the history of the Society of Friends (Weber 1978:590, 595). His example, specifically, was the conflict experienced by Pennsylvania Quakers in the eighteenth century as their peace testimony was challenged by the pressures of the French and Indian Wars. The response of the Pennsylvania Quakers, however, drew heavily on the experience of their seventeenth-century forebears. For seventeenth-century Friends, speaking was a key symbol, and it is thus consistent that the conflict between Quakerism and worldly government should have been framed in significant part in terms of a way of speaking. During Howgill's trial in 1664, the judge admonished him concerning his conscientious stand against oaths: "Your principles are altogether inconsistent with the Law and government" (Besse 1753, 2:14). In order to establish and protect their right not to swear in the face of such opposition, the Quakers had ultimately to accede to it in a way, by a policy of quietist disengagement from law and government. Thus was the conflict over this speech testimony ultimately resolved, as part of a larger transition from movement to sect (cf. Weber 1978:1208), to be taken up again in the concluding chapter.

8

COME TOGETHER TO WAIT UPON GOD:
THE MEETING FOR WORSHIP AND THE ROLE
CONFLICT OF THE QUAKER MINISTER

We began our earlier consideration of the Quaker ministry out in the world with Fox's early delineation of the ministerial division of labor: "And therefore all mind your gift, mind your measure; mind your calling and your work. Some speak to the conscience; some plough and break the clods; some weed out, and some sow; some wait, that fowls devour not the seed" (1831, 7:18). One might expect that in 1651, with only a small handful of yokemates with whom to plow and break the clods, Fox would emphasize those activities aimed at bringing people into the Quaker movement. But there was also a concern from the very beginning with providing for the spiritual maintenance of the seed, keeping those who did become Quakers, while the effort continued out in the world to bring the rest of mankind to Truth.

Not everyone was to be engaged in the ministry among the world's people. As early as 1652, Fox counseled his fellow ministers who were going out to carry the message to the "unbroken places" against taking whole meetings of Friends with them "to suffer with and by the world's spirit." Rather, "let Friends keep together, and wait in their own meeting place. So will the life (in the truth) be preserved and grow" (1831, 7:22–23).

These meetings of gathered Friends, or gathered meetings, as they came to be called, were very different from those appointed by Quaker ministers to plow and thresh among the world's people. They represented instead the principal ritual event among Friends and a major symbolic focus of speaking and silence among Quakers.

Though of obvious importance for the spiritual maintenance of Friends during the 1650s, the meetings for worship were secondary to the ministry out in the world as a directed focus of Quaker energy and initiative. The gathered meeting was viewed as a refuge from the world, a spiritual haven, a place to recharge one's spirit in fellowship with other Quakers. By the end of the decade, however, conditions changed; harsh legal repression and the consequent imprisonment or death of many of the most energetic of the early Quaker ministers acted to turn the Quakers inward. The 1660s and 1670s became a period of consolidation and routinization of the Quaker way, including far more attention to the cultivation of the meeting for worship – what it meant and how it functioned.

To approach an understanding of the structure and dynamic of the meeting for worship, we must begin with the fact that for the Quakers God was to be found by looking inward to the Inward Light, in silence of the flesh. This was the irreducible element of individual worship and the basic building block of collective worship as well. Our first major concern, then, is with how a movement was effected from the individual and inward to the collective and outward, and why.

The best early account of the workings of the meeting for worship is to be found in an epistle from Alexander Parker to Friends. Written on the eve of the Restoration, at the beginning of 1660, Parker's letter is an early expression of the impulse that was to shape the following decades of Quaker activity, namely, ''be still and quiet'' (Barclay 1841:368) and cultivate the emergent Society of Friends in the face of the massive pressures imposed on them from without. A major portion of Parker's epistle is devoted to the conduct of the meeting for worship as a means by which Friends, like the early holy men of God, might strengthen and renew one another and build their faith (Barclay 1841:365).

Parker's guidelines for the beginning of the meeting are the fullest we have:

> So Friends, when you come together to wait upon God, come orderly in the fear of God: the first that enters into the place of your meeting, be not careless, nor wander up and down, either in body or mind; but innocently sit down in some place, and turn in thy mind to the light, and wait upon God singly, as if none were present but the Lord; and *here* thou art strong. Then the next that comes in, let them in simplicity of heart, sit down and turn in to the same light, and wait in the Spirit: and so all the rest coming in, in the fear of the Lord, sit down in pure stillness and silence of all flesh, and wait in the light. (Barclay 1841:365; cf. Penington 1863, 4:54–55)

At this point what appears to be taking form is an aggregation of individuals, each turned inward in silent waiting. What is it that warrants their meeting together? For the key to what makes this aggregation of separate individuals into something more, we must recall the importance in Quaker belief of the unity of the Spirit. What the Quakers sought within themselves was that of God in every person. Accordingly, the very process of turning inward to the Light in each others' presence was in fact a powerfully unifying one because all were waiting ''in one spirit'' (Barclay 1831, 2:353). Waiting silently together, the participants in the meeting achieved ''communion,'' the word they themselves employed (Keith 1670:10).

The process could begin with two people, ''gathered unto their own measure of life.'' As Keith describes it: ''The measure of life in the one, doth after a secret and unspeakable manner, reach unto the measure of life in the other, and flow forth into it whereby the one is raised and strengthened and enlarged by the other'' (1670:10). As the number of worshippers increases, ''the life and light of God . . . spring up in them . . . uniting in one even as many small streams become as a large river of life, which in the wholeness of universality of it, hath its course, motion and operation, in and through every member'' (1670:10; see also Barclay 1831, 2:353). Where Keith uses the image of streams flowing together into a river, Penington likens the effect of collective worship to ''a heap of fresh and living coals, warming one another, insomuch as a great strength, freshness, and vigor of life flows into all'' (1863, 4:54–55).

This communion represented perhaps the most powerful rationale for collective worship. Not only was the resultant spiritual whole greater than the sum of its parts, but the collective spiritual force generated by the group facilitated and enhanced the ability of the individual to attain the proper state of worship (Keith 1670:13). Indeed, the power of communion could lay hold of a person who came into the meeting ''unwatchful and wandering in his mind, or suddenly out of the hurry of outward business, and so not inwardly gathered with the rest'' (Barclay 1831, 2:355). As soon as the individual retired inward, the spiritual power raised up in the meeting ''will suddenly lay hold upon his spirit, and wonderfully help to raise up the good in him, and beget him into the sense of the same power'' (Barclay 1831, 2:355–356). In a like manner, the power could communicate itself to a worshipper whose mind was wandering, or whose spirit was hardened or distressed or languishing, without any words being spoken. This was possible because the heightened spiritual awareness of the other worshippers made them exquisitely sensitive to the distressed spiritual state of one who was not caught up in their communion, opening the way for God to answer his travail (Barclay 1831, 2:355–356; Keith 1670:11; Penington 1863, 4:55).

Thus, in ideal terms, a complete and perfect meeting for worship could be held in complete silence, without a word being spoken aloud. God's Word, manifested in the inward experience of his presence and the communion of the congregation was sufficient. ''When the first day of the week came . . . we had a silent meeting,'' wrote Richard Davies in 1657 (1832:35), ''and though it was silent from words, yet the word of the Lord was amongst us, it was a hammer and a fire.'' More than sufficient, in fact, the completely silent meeting was held by some to be superior as a form of worship to the meeting in which outward words were spoken. According to Penington: ''The ministry of the spirit and life is more close and immediate when without words, than when with words, as has been often felt, and is faithfully testified by many witnesses'' (1863, 4:56; see also Barclay 1831, 2:352; Bishop et al. 1656:47; Fox 1831, 7:87).

Such a position, of course, was rooted in and reinforced the Quaker belief of the insufficiency of language and speaking for the attainment of true spiritual experience. Keith made this explicit, in articulating the purpose of the meeting for worship:

> The good that Friends look at, and wait for in meetings, and do receive is far beyond all words whatsoever, even the very words of life . . . and that good is life itself, which was before words and will be when words are not, and in which all words are to cease, but the life endureth for ever, in which Friends have fellowship with God, and with one another. (1670:17)

Though the Quakers were not the first of their time to conduct silent meetings for worship, and their practice appears to have been derived in some measure from prior experience in other sects, such as the Seekers, that did so, it is apparent that Friends carried the silent meeting to a level of completeness and institutionalization that was especially distinctive. Their practice was unquestionably a curiosity and a wonder to their contemporaries, who could not understand a religious service being accomplished in complete silence and were apt to see silence as an indication that nothing at all was going on, and thus as a waste of time (Barclay 1831, 2:352). Judgments of this kind provoked Fox to expressions of withering scorn. "The priests and professors of all sorts," he wrote,

> were much against Friends' silent meetings, and sometimes . . . would come to our meetings; and when they saw a hundred or two hundred people all silent, waiting upon the Lord, they would break out into a wondering and despising, and some of them would say: "Look how these people sit mumming and dumming. What edification is here where there are no words? Come," would they say, "let us be gone, what! should we stay here to see a people sit of this manner?" And they said they never saw the like in their lives. Then it may be some Friends have been moved to speak to them and say, "Didst thou never see the like in thy life? Look in thy own parish and let the priest and thee see there how your people sit mumming and dumming and sleeping under your priests all their life time; who keep people always under their teaching that they may be always paying." (1952:446)

Indeed, as we have already established, it was the fleshly, outward, word domination of the world's forms of worship that represented for the Quakers the basic contrast between their own powerfully silent communion and others'. What more was to be expected from the false priests who made a trade of words and the professors who fed upon them? Such "who fed upon words, and fed one another with words, but trampled upon the life'' (Fox 1952:19) could not know the true life of those who wait upon the Lord in silence.

Keith maintained that the overwhelming word saturation of the world's religions made the silent model of the Quakers all the more powerfully effective to a people surfeited with religious talk. ''The very silence and silent meetings of friends reached unto them so convincingly, and reached them,'' he wrote, so that they ''came to see the proportion of the true Religion'' (1670:16–17).

Although the meeting for worship could be complete ''though not a word was spoken to the outward ear,'' and a silent meeting was, in ideal terms, the most perfect kind of meeting, speaking was certainly not excluded from Quaker worship; it was, in fact, an important feature of the meeting for worship from the earliest days of Quakerism. Because of the Quaker distrust of human speaking and the religious imperative of a silence of the flesh, however, speaking in religious worship was a complex and delicately balanced act for the Quakers. The tension between silence and speaking in worship provided an important dynamic to the meeting for worship, as to so much else in Quaker life.

The key to acceptable speaking in worship lay in the source of the motion to speak and of the words spoken – in both cases, the Spirit of God, speaking within (Aynsloe 1672:13). Worshipping in complete silence or with the aid of the spoken word was not a matter of human decision resting with the individual or prescribed by liturgical convention. The motion to speak or to remain silent was to come solely from God. As articulated clearly and succinctly by Penington, ''for absolutely silent meetings, wherein there is a resolution not to speak, we know not, but wait on the Lord, either to feel him in words, or in silence of the spirit without words, as he pleaseth'' (1863, 4:55).

This should not obscure the fact that silence was at all times both logically and behaviorally prior to speaking in the conduct of worship. Silence, as the turning inward of the mind upon God, was the sine qua non of Quaker worship. Just as their worship did not consist in words as words, it did not consist ''in silence as silence'' (Barclay 1831, 2:360). Rather, it was from the ''holy dependence upon God'' that ''silence necessarily follows in the first place, until words can be brought forth, which are from God's Spirit'' (Barclay 1831, 2:360; see also Adamson 1656:5). Silence was necessary for the worshipper to be open to the Word of God within, to be spiritually prepared to receive it and speak it forth.

Indeed, there are even indications that the early Quakers saw silence as *historically* antecedent to their religious speaking. In his illuminating retrospective summary of the early years of Quakerism, Burrough described the collective spiritual activities of the first Friends in these terms: ''We met together often, to wait upon the Lord in pure silence, both from our own words, and all men's words.'' It was only by hearkening to the purifying voice of the Lord, and feeling his word in their hearts, that "our tongues were loosed, and our mouths opened, and we spake with new tongues, as the Lord gave us utterance, and as his spirit led us" (1658:13). George Whitehead, too, noted of the early years between 1652 and 1654 that "we had but little preaching, our meetings being kept much and often in silence" (1832, 1:41). In a later retrospective stocktaking, Keith attributed the early predominance of silence in the meetings to the circumstance that "there were but few who were then attrained unto that soundness and clearness of condition, in their own particulars, so as thereby to be fitted and qualified in the word, life, power and wisdom of God, to minister to others" (1670:8). By the time of Keith's writing, however, in 1670, "few meetings but have some or other, to whom a ministry in words is given more or less, so that seldom or rarely meetings are under a necessity to be wholly silent" (1670:14; cf. Barclay 1831, 2:360). So unusual had the purely silent meeting become by 1678 that Friends in Bristol, remembering "the benefit of such meetings in the time of our first gathering" (Mortimer 1971:131), actually made a formal proposal to reestablish it on a trial basis for "as many friends as finds freedom" to participate. Nevertheless, despite the historical trend toward more and more speaking in the meetings for worship, all meetings were to begin in a state of spiritual silence. That principle did not change.

Not only was silence the state from which all appropriate speaking was to stem in worship, but it was also the ultimate purpose, the desired outcome, of speaking. "Concerning silent meetings," Fox wrote, "the intent of all speaking is to bring into the life . . . and to possess the same, and to live in and enjoy it, and to feel God's presence, and that is in the silence." Accordingly, "words declared are to bring people to it . . . in which fellowship is attained to in the spirit of God, in the power of God, which is the gospel, in which is the fellowship, when there are no words spoken" (1831, 4:134; see also Fox 1952:341). That is, silence, and especially the silent communion of worshippers, is the most desirable spiritual state for the conduct of collective worship. Any speaking that should take place during worship must emerge from the inward silence of the speaker *and* be directed toward bringing the auditors to silence or enhancing the condition of silence in which they already reside. The relationship between speaking and silence in the preaching of the minister is illustrated in the accompanying chart.

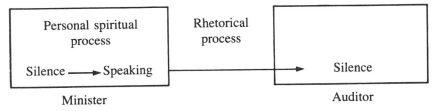

There is something of a paradox in the use of speaking to achieve silence, but the apparent paradox is readily resolvable in the light of Quaker belief concerning man's essential spiritual condition and the dynamics of Quaker worship. Silence is both antecedent to speaking in worship and the end of speaking in worship; silence precedes speaking, is the ground of speaking, and is the consequence of speaking (cf. Sontag 1969:23). Once you have spoken, "retire inward, and sink down into the pure stillness, and keep in the Valley" (Marshall 1677:5).

*   *   *   *

As with so much of Quaker religious practice, speaking in worship was sanctioned in positive terms by appeal to biblical precedent (Farnsworth 1663:11) and by negative contrast by comparison with the practices of the world's religions (Fox 1831, 7:156). The essential point, as we have established, was to proceed solely from the immediate movings of the Holy Spirit within, free of all taint of human will or empty formalism. Accordingly, anything that smacked of human will or customary formalism in worship was to be rigorously excluded. This imperative represented a rather sweeping departure from prevailing religious practice because it precluded any kind of established, formalized liturgy prescribing who should speak, when, and the form of the words spoken (Adamson 1656:6; Barclay 1831, 1:185–186, 213; 2:348–394; Dewsbury 1689: 294; Keith 1687:100). As Barclay insisted, Quakers "cannot . . . prefix set times to pray outwardly, so as to lay a necessity to speak words at such and such times, whether we feel [God's] heavenly influence and assistance or no." Nor were Friends "to rely upon outward performances, or satisfy ourselves as too many do, with the saying of our prayers" (1831, 2:394).

With this insistence on the eschewing of habitual, prearranged, routinized worship, a question might well arise concerning the basis on which the Quakers contrived to come together for collective worship at all. Days and times for meetings for worship were in fact appointed in advance – Sundays (first days) and usually one other – and formally institutionalized as early as 1656, when a meeting of elders in Balby, Yorkshire, issued a minute to the effect "that the particular meetings, by all the children of the light, be duly kept and observed . . . every First-day [Sunday] of the week" (Barclay 1841:277).

The standard Quaker position, when the issue was raised, was that the appointment of a time and place to meet together did not in itself constitute an act of worship, especially insofar as no one was appointed to preach and pray at such set times. The meeting arrangements were, rather, "only an outward conveniency, necessary for our seeing one another, so long as we are clothed with this outward tabernacle" (Barclay 1831, 2:383). Barclay continued: "Our meeting at set times and places is not a part of our worship, but a preparatory accommodation of our outward man, in order to a public visible worship; since we set not about the visible acts of worship when we

meet together, until we be led thereunto by the Spirit of God'' (1831, 2:383).
The regularization of first day as the day for a meeting for worship was usually
rationalized on the grounds that as long as it is necessary to set a time for
meeting, there is no harm in appointing the same day that the apostles and
members of the primitive church used for their meetings, with the understanding that we do not do so because we feel we *must* conform to their
precedent (Barclay 1831, 2:350).

Consistent with their belief in the need to eliminate all self-will in worship,
the Quakers defined the role of the speaker as entirely passive. The speaker
served, in effect, as a conduit or mouthpiece or ''oracle'' for God the speaker
(Farnsworth 1663:9). Not only the impulse to the act of speaking, but the
very words themselves were to be given of God; people were to ''speak as
they are moved by the holy Ghost, and as the spirit gives them utterance''
(Farnsworth 1663:13; cf. Acts 2.4). The terms most commonly used to describe the process were ''motion'' and ''opening'': ''motion'' for the impulse
to the act of speaking and ''opening'' for the clearing of the channel for
God's words to be spoken forth (cf. Ezekiel 3.26, 24.27, 33.22). The passive
role of the speaker and the relationship between motion and opening are nicely
articulated by Charles Marshall: ''When a motion is felt, and openings are
in the heart, and the power of the Lord is prevailing, then sink down in that
in which no vain thought can be hid, and stand single and passive . . . and
then, in the power which warmeth thy heart, and moveth on thy spirit, enter
into thy service'' (1677:5).

At times, as we have discussed, no openings occurred, and the meeting
passed in complete silence. At other times, participants might sit in silence
for as long as two or three hours before someone felt an opening to speak
(Caton 1671:9; Higginson 1653:11).

There were two major genres of verbal expression in the meeting for
worship: *prayer* and *preaching*. The former were addresses of man to God;
the latter, addresses of man to man. Consistent with Quaker belief concerning
inward worship through attendance on the Light within, the prayerful expressions of individual Quakers were inward and silent (Barclay 1831, 1:215).
The exception to this pattern was the prayer of spiritual struggle, in which
the supplicant's travail was manifested in audible sighs and groans (Barclay
1831, 2:359). For example, Luke Howard records of his struggle to take up
the cross of plain speech that it ''made me often cry to the Lord with sighs
and groans (which I could not utter in words) for the help of his Spirit''
(1704:23–24). These sighs and groans counted fully as prayer: ''Nay, though
it be but a groan, or sigh, which cannot be uttered, or expressed; yet that is
prayer, true prayer, which hath an acceptance with the Lord'' (Penington
1863, 2:109).

When an individual felt an opening to utter a prayer aloud, it was not as
one addressing God on his own behalf, but either as a voice for the entire

meeting as a body in spiritual fellowship or on behalf of some other whose spiritual need was opened to the speaker by the Holy Spirit (Shewen 1830:126).

In praying aloud, the speaker knelt and removed his hat (if a man); this signaled to the other members of the meeting to rise or kneel themselves, and the men among them to uncover their own heads, while the women remained covered (hats were kept on while the meeting waited and worshipped in silence) (Blackborow 1660:13; Fox 1831, 7:189; Penington 1863, 4:344). We might recall in this context that the public testimonies of the Quakers included a refusal to uncover the head or bow or kneel to other men as a sign of deference because these were signs of worldly honor and concessions to fleshly pride. Friends believed that such honor was due God alone, and this honor was manifest in the conduct of prayer.

Preaching, as an address to other men, did not require the same deferential forms. Here, the speaker rose, in order to be heard better, while the rest of the meeting remained seated. The speaker (again, if a man) removed his own hat because he was speaking in the Spirit and to the Spirit in others, but the other men kept their heads covered. Preaching was further subdivided into *praise* and *exhortation*: the former an expression of praise for God in his love and power and truth; the latter, exhorting people to proper spiritual behavior.

*   *   *   *

The Quaker doctrine concerning appropriate speaking in worship was straightforward in theory, but, like all oracular prophecy, complex and susceptible to conflict in practice. The first problem confronted by the speaker was to be certain that a motion and opening were genuinely from God and not merely the expression of human will. "All mind to feel the Word of the Lord speaking in you," exhorted Dewsbury, "so you might be fully assured it is not your own work, as man speaking of God, but the Lord alone uttering his own voice in the forcible power of his own Spirit . . . whether it be to pray in sighs or groans, or in words, or to speak in exhortations or praises" (1689:323–324).

Also of concern was the need to be certain that a given message or understanding from the Inward Light was intended for others and not simply for one's own spiritual nurturance: "Some the Enemy hath drawn to speak forth that which they in a retired silence were to feed upon, and grow up in its nature" (Dewsbury 1689:338). To speak aloud what was intended for oneself alone, and thus to violate God's intention and disturb the silence of others, was "judged an unsavory dead thing, unto which God hath no respect" (Whitehead 1852:98).

More subtle, however, was the susceptibility of speaking in religious worship to formalism. Indeed, this problem goes to the very heart of a prophetic ministry. It is the expressive corollary of Weber's trenchant observation that "it is the fate of charisma to recede before the powers of tradition . . . after it has entered the permanent structures of social action'' (Weber 1978:1148). Evidence that this susceptibility was perceived as a threatening factor may be found in the exhortation of the London Yearly Meeting to ministers in 1672 to keep ''out of all mere imitations and formal habits, which are not to edification'' (Barclay 1841:332). Further evidence is abundant; the issue lay at the center of the Perrot schism of the 1660s, which I will deal with at greater length in the final chapter.

A related problem, insofar as it focused on formal elaboration in speaking, was the proscription of verbal artistry in spoken worship, as representing both the indulgence in words for their own sake – idle words, spoken in man's will – and the attempt to titillate the earthly ear and to bend worship to the giving of fleshly pleasure and telling people what they wanted to hear, what the Quakers called (after 2 Timothy 4.3) ministering to the itching ear (Fox 1706:119). The cultivation of verbal artistry was another sin laid at the door of the world's ministers, who ''glory in the expressions, glory in words . . . and delight in words and methods, and curiosity in speech'' (Fox 1831, 4:129). The Quaker, however, ''needs no art nor invention to bring words into metre or rhyme, that they may make a pleasant sound, and a joyful noise; his music doth not stand in outward sounds, made by art and air, but his melody is in the heart, and in the spirit, in the inward man, in the hidden man of the heart'' (Shewen 1830:126). When a Quaker fell into artful language in the meeting, either because of expressive habits rooted in an earlier religious affiliation or ''to seek popularity, applause, or praise of men'' (Barclay 1841:333), it was a clear sign of spiritually invalid speech.

Yet another consideration was the timing of one's utterance in the meeting. It was important not only to be able to recognize a genuine motion to speak, but also ''to know the appointed time and season when the same motion should be brought forth'' (Marshall 1677:2). Finally, there was the related delicate matter of knowing when to stop, of not ''speaking beyond your line or measure'' (Nuttall 1952:90), by adding one's own words to the fullness and sufficiency of God's measure. This was a serious transgression: ''He that utters a word beyond the sense which God begets in his spirit, takes God's name in vain, and provokes him to jealousy against his own soul'' (Penington 1863, 2:111; see also Dewsbury 1689:337).

With speaking thus susceptible to a variety of spiritual pitfalls, how could one avoid falling victim to them? The only guideline for the speaker himself was to wait in pure silence and look to the Light within. But this, of course, was no simple matter, for it could not be accomplished through one's own active efforts. It called for a giving up of self-will, a resignation of all active human effort, and was thus by its very nature not something about which one could feel confident in the sense of having it fully under control. One might have faith in God to do his part, but it was more difficult to be at ease about one's own capacity to give oneself up to his will.

The clearest external standard by which the validity of religious speech might be evaluated was its effect on others. Quaker rhetorical theory, we recall, was founded on the doctrine of the Inward Light and the self-consistency of the Spirit. If one was faithfully attentive to the Light within and spoke only as it allowed, the words would reach to the Spirit of God in those who received them because the Spirit was the same in all people. If the speaker's words produced the necessary resonance in the other spiritually prepared participants, they were genuine; if they aroused no such sympathetic response, they might be judged to have been spoken in the speaker's own will, an intrusion of the fleshly impulse.

The Quaker journals of the period are full of appeals to this standard. To cite only one typical example, we may quote from John Gratton's account of a meeting at which he preached in 1671:

> And the third meeting I was at, the power of the Lord came upon me, and I was pressed in spirit to declare of his goodness . . . so I stood up and spoke to the congregation . . . what was given to me to understand, concerning the creation of man, his dominion, work, state of innocence, fall, and restoration by the promised Seed, Christ Jesus, the Saviour of mankind: All which was to the great joy of Friends, and reaching of the people. (1720:47)

There are also, of course, records of instances in which someone's speaking in the meeting was condemned as invalid; we will return to this later. For now, it is important to realize that this standard of evaluation could only be applied after the fact, that is, after a person had already spoken. The plain fact remained that there was *always* an element of risk in speaking during worship because of the constant human susceptibility to the exercise of self-will. This risk, this tension between the desire to give oneself up to God's will and the susceptibility to self-will that was part of the human condition, lay at the root of the core conflict of Quakerism and profoundly colored Quaker speaking in worship.

Indeed, the very susceptibility to spiritual risk entailed in speaking in worship helped to compound the risk still further, by giving it another dimension. People experienced an understandable reluctance to risk speaking forth an untimely message or one born of their own wills or not intended to be spoken aloud, and so, not surprisingly, there was a tendency to be hesitant to speak at all.

The problem, however, was that to "quench" God's Word was as serious a transgression as being too forward (cf. 1 Thessalonians 5.19). Fox, in fact, considered that many more people were guilty of the latter than of the former (1831, 8:19). Marshall articulated the conflict in dramatic terms:

> And in the day of a beginning of a testimony for the Lord, even in the upright heart, great will be the opposition of the enemy every

way, where he cannot lead out before, for to bring forth an untimely
birth; there he will endeavour to shut up the heart in disobedience,
or rebellion, or raise up so many fears, doubts, and amazements, if
possible to bewilder the soul. (1677:5)

In a more personal vein, John Stubbs, one of the Valiant Sixty and an
effective and influential minister, confessed to Margaret Fell that ''I never
fell into more disobedience than last meeting at thy house, and was warned
of it before, for, when the spring and well was set open, then I did not
speak, but in the dread I spoke, but the life was shut up, and I felt it to
my condemnation'' (Nuttall 1952:184). Not only did Stubbs, one of the
most faithful of the early Quaker ministers, hold back from speaking in
the meeting when he felt an opening, but he compounded his disobedience
by allowing the guilt he felt at his first error to force him to speak after
the opening was closed off.

Not all Quakers, by any means, were equally susceptible to the conflict
potentially attendant upon speaking in the meeting for worship. Although any
member of a meeting, male or female, was eligible to speak in any of the
ways discussed above – prayer, praise, or exhortation – most people spoke
seldom, if at all. No one, obviously, was ever required to speak in meeting.
As Barclay noted, there were good and valued Friends ''who never find
themselves moved to speak a word in public'' (1831, 2:464). Others were
clearly spiritually secure enough to be confident about the validity of their
openings to speak and recorded no doubts or conflicts in this regard. George
Fox, for example, recorded countless instances of his own religious speaking,
with never a suggestion of spiritual misgiving.

For many, however, especially the ministers – the incumbents of the only
role among the Quakers defined in terms of speaking – the conflict engendered
by speaking in worship was a significant enough factor to attain the status of
a conventionalized pattern. The minister was subject to especially great psychological and spiritual pressure in walking the fine line between the normally
contradictory principles of speaking and silence because he or she was moved
to speak in the service of religion more than anyone else. This accounts for
the theme of danger and tension that appears so often in the writings of the
seventeenth-century Quakers on the ministry, emphasizing the risks of the
ministry second only to its positive spiritual aspects. Time and again, one
finds the treatments of the ministry in the seventeenth century framed in terms
of opposing extremes into which the unguarded minister might fall by failing
to keep to the narrow path illuminated by the Light. I am not referring here
to the doctrinal literature on the Quaker ministry, which is more concerned
with differentiating the ministry of Friends from that of other sects and denominations, but to those records that reflect the actual experience and behavior of Quaker ministers, such as personal journals and various kinds of

ministerial guides prepared by leaders of the Society of Friends who were themselves in the ministry. Records of this kind provide insights into the ways in which a minister might fail, as well as the course one needed to pursue in order to succeed in the ministry.

As I have noted, some Quakers never spoke at all in public worship, and others were moved to speak only rarely. The ministers, though, were distinguished by the fact that they felt openings to speak more often than their brethren at large and were effective in articulating the word of Truth and reaching the witness of Truth in others (see, e.g., Bangs 1798:19), though even they might have "but few words, yet [be] very serviceable," as Edmondson remarks of one early minister (1820:52).

In the very earliest years of Quakerism, when the message was being carried solely by Fox and a small handful of others, the ministry involved principally a willingness to preach the Truth of Quakerism to non-Quakers and so bring them into the fold. The first ministers were often spiritually mature and religiously active people, with prior experience in groups not dissimilar to the Quakers: Baptists, Familists, Ranters, Seekers, and so on. But once significant numbers of converts began to be won over to the Truth, the meetings of gathered Quakers began to become the forum in which the minister emerged.

The tensions surrounding the Quaker ministry were present from the very point at which a Friend experienced a concern to come forth in the ministry. This came to be recognized as a stressful and difficult process that had to be accomplished against the current of the general Quaker distrust of speaking in spiritual affairs. One of the earliest accounts of the spiritual trials experienced by one who felt himself called to the ministry may be found in the journal of William Caton. Writing of the period shortly after his convincement in 1652, Caton recounts that

> about that time I begun to know the motion of his power, and the command of his Spirit by which I came to be moved to go to the places of public worship, to declare against the deceit of the priests, and the sins of the people, and to warn all to repent, for I testified to them that the day of the Lord was a coming. But, Oh the weakness, the fear and trembling, that I went in upon this message, who shall declare it? And how did I plead with the Lord concerning this matter? For I looked upon my own weakness and insufficiency, and how unfit I was in my own apprehension, for to encounter with gainsayers, whom I knew would also despise my youth. Howbeit, whatsoever I alleged by way of reasoning against the Lord, concerning this weighty matter, I could not be excused, but I must go, and declare what he should give me to speak, and his promise was, he would be with me.

> Wherefore when I saw it must be so, I put on courage in the name
> of the Lord; and having faith in him which stood in his power, I
> next gave up to his will, and went in obedience to his motion.
> (1689:9)

As Quakerism began to take firmer root, it became the rule that the minister's first call to speak was experienced within the Friends' meeting itself.
John Crook, who emerged in the ministry in 1656, may serve as an example:

> Out of the mouth of [the] seed of eternal life, would words proceed
> within me as I sat in the meetings with God's people, and at other
> times, which I was moved to utter with my tongue often times in
> the cross to my own will, as seeming to my earthly wisdom to be
> void of wisdom, and most contemptible to my natural understanding,
> not knowing the end why I should keep such words: yet I was charged
> with disobedience, and deeply afflicted and troubled in my spirit,
> when I neglected to speak them forth; and sometimes some others
> have spoken the same words, while I was doubting in the reasoning
> about them; and then I was much exercised, that it should be taken
> from me, and given to another that was faithful. (1791:xxiv–xxv)

Crook also feared the prospect that "I should go and appoint meetings, and
gather people together, and should sit as a fool amongst them, having nothing
to say unto them" (1791:xxvi). This pressure to produce was real, for small,
local meetings, which might not even have a member in the ministry, probably
did tend to give place to well-known and widely traveled ministers (Chester
1709:10–11; Higginson 1653:11; Penney 1907:63). But Crook persevered,
and "the Lord made me a minister, and commanded me to publish what I
had seen, felt, and handled (and passed through) of the word and work of
God; the which, I gave up to do, being thereby fired out of all my reasonings
and consultations" (1791:xxvi).

A similar, and equally typical, experience was that of Charles Marshall:

> After many years travail of spirit . . . in the year 1670, and the
> thirty-third year of my age, God Almighty raised me up by his power,
> which had been working in my heart many years, to preach the
> everlasting gospel of life and salvation; and then a fresh exercise
> began: for the enemy tempted me to withstand the Lord, to look to
> my own weakness of body and spirit, and insufficiency for such a
> great work . . . For when the power of God fell upon me, and a few
> words were required of me to speak in the assemblies of the Lord's
> people in Bristol, I reasoned they were a wise people, and how could
> it be I should add to them; also, that I might hurt myself; that
> imagination might be the ground of such requirings, and that many
> wise men therein might look upon me as forward, and so judge me;

and I thus reasoned through some meetings until I was in sore distress. When those meetings were over, wherein I had been disobedient, then great was my burden. Oh, then I was ready to engage and covenant with the Lord, that if I felt the requirings of his power again, I would faithfully give up in obedience unto him. Yet when I was tried again, the same rebellious mind would be stirred by the power of the enemy: then hath the Lord withdrawn the motions and the feeling of his power, and all refreshment with it, and hid his face . . . And when I began [again] to feel the warming power of God stirring in my inward man, I was glad on one hand, but very sorrowful on the other hand, fearing lest I should be rebellious again: and so hard was it for me to open my mouth in those meetings at Bristol, that had not the Lord caused his power so to be manifest in my heart, as new wine in a vessel that wanted vent, I might have perished. (1844:11–12)

Examples might easily be multiplied, each with its own individual nuances, but all basically similar (e.g., Banks 1798:47; Crisp 1822:32–33; Dickinson 1847:96–97; Gratton 1720:47; Richardson 1867:21–22; Story 1829:26–28). In their accounts of their spiritual travails in coming forth in the ministry, the emergent ministers recorded a series of doubts that were typical – ultimately conventional – in the experience of many Quaker ministers. They were beset, first of all, by doubts concerning their physical and spiritual capabilities, and fears of their general insufficiency for the weighty responsibility the ministry entailed. In addition, they were apprehensive that their callings might have stemmed from their own earthly imaginings rather than from true inspiration, that their messages might be judged foolish or worthless by others wiser than themselves, or that their gifts were transitory and that no words would be vouchsafed to them at critical times, to their embarrassment and dismay. The common element that runs through all these accounts is that the troubled ministers were resisting the call to the ministry out of *selfishness*, relying on *reason*, an earthly faculty, to guide their actions. Their trials grew from the fact that they were more concerned about their personal feelings and welfare than about the spiritual mandate to speak they had received. It was only by giving themselves up to God's will and obeying the call to minister to others that they were able to achieve spiritual peace.

In a sense, however, Caton, Crook, Marshall, and the other Quaker ministers who shared this difficult experience, erred on the side of safety; it would have been equally bad to rush forth into the ministry out of the kind of self-will Marshall feared might be operating in his own case, for that would have been injurious not only to himself, but to those who were subjected to his unsound ministry. By going through the painful and chastening battle between self-will and spiritual obedience, the minister was seen to emerge as a better

Quaker as a result of his suffering and eventual submission. Moreover, the struggle might itself then become the subject of his first or later public testimony, when victory, through submission, was finally achieved (Dickinson 1847:97; Story 1829:28).

The trials of the minister did not cease with submission to the motion to speak the Word of God, for there were dangers in the conduct of the ministry of the same kind that beset one in the process of assuming the role and like those encountered by all Friends who were moved to speak in worship. Even further, ministers had the additional problem of adapting to the differences between the two milieus in which they had to operate, at least in the early years: the gathered meetings of Friends and the turbulent world outside. Fox cautioned ministers in 1656: "There is a difference between Friends going into the world, and of coming among them that are come to silent meetings and to feed there; for that which may be seasonable to the world, may not be to them" (1831, 7:128). Repeating his warning in 1658, Fox stressed further the contrast between the "stillness" and "coolness" of the silent meeting and the "dirt" and "heat" of the world outside:

> Friends, be watchful and careful in all meetings ye come into. When a man is come newly out of the world he cometh out of the dirt. Then he must not be rash. For now when he cometh into a silent meeting, that is another state. Then he must come and feel his own spirit how it is, when he cometh to those that sit silent; for he may come in the heat of spirit out of the world. Now the others are still and cool, and he may rather do them hurt if he get them out of the cool state into the heating state. (1952:340)

Ministers were also held to a higher standard of accountability than other speakers. In fact, an overreadiness to judge the ministry of others emerged as a problem fairly early in the development of the Society of Friends. Because the ultimate authority for each individual lay with the Light within himself or herself, words that did not sit well with someone who was spiritually self-assured might easily be judged as being out of the Truth.

Not even the early pillars of the society were immune from criticism. Richard Hubberthorne wrote to Margaret Fell of a meeting in Westmoreland in 1653 at which another man "did judge the words I was moved of the Lord in his power to speak, not to be spoken from the power." Apparently, there were expressions of support for both Hubberthorne and his critic, but Hubberthorne concluded: "I was made to suffer them much, and in the power of the Lord to go on" (Nuttall 1952:94–95).

One finds repeated cautions, throughout the period, against judging others' ministry openly because of the strife and spiritual confusion it engendered and the potential discredit it brought to Friends. Except in cases of those who are "openly profane, rebellious, such as be out of the Truth" (Fox 1952:282),

Friends were cautioned to wait until the meeting was over to speak to the offending party in private and in all meekness and humility (Dewsbury 1689:198; Fox 1831, 7:114–115, 158; 8:13; Marshall 1677:7).

The only solution to such difficulties, as in all things, was a true and faithful attendance upon the Spirit within oneself; ''and all be still, and cool, and quiet, and of a meek spirit, that out of boisterousness and eagerness and feignedness, and self-love you may be preserved in your measures up to God, and if any be moved to speak a few words in your meetings, this we charge you all, that you speak nothing but that which is given in; and in the sense, and in the cross'' (Burrough 1672:74).

The reconciliation of the human necessity of speaking with the spiritual need for silence was a problem every member of the Society of Friends had to contend with throughout his or her life as a Quaker. In one sense, this was the essence of the Quaker religious experience: reconciling one's natural and earthly life with one's eternal and essential spiritual existence. The true Quaker directed his behavior toward making his life maximally expressive of spiritual truth, with the understanding that a silence of the outward person was the best possible way of doing so. Although this was the goal of existence, however, it was also essential that an earthly component be present in one's life in order to maintain an element of spiritual struggle, for the doctrine of salvation through suffering was also central to Quakerism. The tension between the natural and the spiritual faculties – between speaking and silence – was a necessary component of the Quaker experience.

For the Quaker minister, however, the tension took on an added dimension because the role demanded that the minister depart from absolute silence by speaking in the very conduct of a fundamentally religious exercise. This was a mixing of speaking and silence within a single behavioral frame in which both components, otherwise contradictory, were indispensable. The ministerial calling was thus set about with a series of complex pitfalls on either side – for the minister who was too hesitant in using words in the work of salvation on the one hand, and for the one who was too forward in speaking on the other. That most ministers in the early period of Quakerism avoided the pitfalls to the satisfaction and edification of their brethren is amply attested to in the literature. Nevertheless, the conflicts attendant upon the ministry unquestionably had a profound effect upon the evolution of Quakerism during the first few decades of its existence, constituting a major factor in the process of transformation from charismatic movement to religious sect. It is to this development that we will turn in the concluding chapter.

9

WHERE IS THE POWER THAT WAS AT FIRST?
THE PROPHETIC MINISTRY AND THE
ROUTINIZATION OF CHARISMA

Throughout our consideration of the symbolic significance of speaking and silence among the early Quakers, our attention has been drawn again and again to the prophetic minister – in contrast to the false ministry of the priests, as carrier of the Truth to the world's people, as principal speaker in the meeting for worship. In the treatment of the ministry in the foregoing chapters, the analytical emphasis has been on patterns of ideology, meaning, and action, with occasional attention to dimensions of change. In this final chapter, the prophetic ministry will serve once again as a frame of reference in terms of which we may both summarize our analysis and take direct and explicit account of processes of change. The period between the first emergence of Quakerism under the Commonwealth and the advent of toleration in 1689 witnessed some of the most decisive changes in modern English history. The changes undergone by Quakerism were no less decisive.

Historians of Quakerism tend to divide the years between the early 1650s and 1689 into two major periods. The first of these, dominated by the movement to proclaim the Truth abroad to the world and characterized by outwardly directed energy, enthusiasm, and the public waging of the Lamb's War, was brought to a close by the demise of the Commonwealth and the restoration of the monarchy in 1660. The Restoration ushered in an extended period of persecution during which the energies of the Quakers were turned inward, toward forging an ideological and institutional base that would allow their religious survival in a hostile political environment. This adaptive process, in its general, institutional dimensions, has been thoroughly documented by historians (Braithwaite 1961; Lloyd 1950; Vann 1969), tracing the emergence of the system of administrative structures and practices – the men's meetings, women's meetings, Meeting for Sufferings, Yearly Meetings, and so on – that gave form and coherence to Quakerism and enabled it to withstand the massive pressures of the Restoration period.

Within this broader context, however, for which we may rely on the works already cited, the particular focus of this study directs our attention to the implications of this process of change for speaking and silence within the religious fellowship of Friends. As suggested, the prophetic ministry is a productive focus for such an exploration, as a structural nexus of speaking and silence in early Quaker culture. What we will see is the routinization of prophecy, the process whereby a form of speaking by an individual originally responsible only to God is brought under corporate control.

Although I will treat this process of routinization largely in terms of internal adaptations to conflicts attendant upon the prophetic ministry itself in the formative period of Quakerism, I would point out that the developments I will trace were themselves part of a more comprehensive process of routinization and institutionalization of Quaker practice. In broader terms, this was a process of transition from a loosely structured charismatic *movement*, based on common divine leadings to proclaim a particular spiritual vision for the convincement of all mankind, to a classic religious *sect*, a gathered disciplined fellowship, set apart from the wider society by its own special enlightenment.[1] Charisma, as Weber has taught us, "is undiminished, consistent and effective only *in statu nascendi* . . . When the tide that lifted a charismatically led group out of everyday life flows back into the channels of workaday routines, at least the 'pure' form of charismatic domination will wane and turn into an 'institution' " (1978:1121).

This larger process, however, as historians of Quakerism have amply documented, was not impelled solely by the tendency inherent in charisma toward routinization and institutionalization; it was also in substantial part a response to environmental pressures from without. All charismatic movements and sects are situated within complex social milieus, defining themselves in opposition to established religion. Accordingly, all processes of change within them will be related in some measure to environmental factors. From the vantage point of this larger perspective, the changes within Quakerism may be seen to have occurred in response to the need for an organizational structure, an ideology, and a degree of internal cohesion generally that would enable the Quakers to withstand the ruthless pressures of persecution they endured under the Restoration regime. The resultant organization and ideology then came to bear on all aspects of Quaker life, not least the prophetic ministry, whether or not they were linked directly to the larger social environment.

Nevertheless, I have concentrated in this chapter on the internal dimensions of change and on the prophetic ministry for several reasons. First, the effects of the larger social environment on the course of Quakerism during the Restoration period have been treated extensively by others. Second, the prophetic ministry represented a symbolic focus of speaking for the early Quakers, drawing together some of the principal themes of the preceding chapters. Finally, as regards the inward focus, few of the changes undergone by the ministry were in direct and immediate response to environmental factors. How then was the ministry brought under control?

---

[1] I follow the definition of "*sect*" advanced by Wilson (1967:23). My use of the terms "charismatic sect" and "charismatic movement" reverses Yinger's usage (1970:273–274).

Some of the mechanisms of adjustment have already been suggested in earlier chapters: for example, the conventionalization of the struggle undergone by emergent ministers. So numerous are the testimonies to such struggles, marked by a period of self-doubt, resistance, and confusion in both emotion and practice, followed ultimately by a spiritual breakthrough into the ministry, that we may justifiably consider this process a conventionalized adaptive mechanism, a spiritual rite of passage in which the initiate was tested against the structural conflicts inherent in the prophetic ministry, and, if successful, broke through into a state of new spiritual assurance. The process was rendered all the more effective by according so well with the Quaker ideology of salvation through suffering. Spiritual struggle, in these terms, was a means toward a more perfect spiritual state.

The pattern of spiritual struggle in becoming a minister can be traced almost to the very beginnings of Quakerism, as witness, for example, the testimony of Will Caton, quoted in Chapter 8. But conventionalization is only part of the process of routinization. Although conventional patterns give weight to traditional practice, the advent of traditional gerontocratic authority, in Weber's terms, acknowledging the authority of those with acquired experience who were most familiar with the sacred traditions (1978:231), challenges the purely charismatic authority of the unfettered prophet. The entering wedge of such traditional authority for the early Quakers lay in the recognition of the spiritually weighty veterans of the Lamb's War as elders, specially charged as early as the mid-1650s to "feed the flock of God, taking the oversight thereof willingly . . . as examples to the flock of Christ" (Barclay 1841:281).

The influence of these elders over the prophetic ministry is suggested in such testimonies as that of Christopher Story concerning his spiritual travails in breaking through into the public ministry in 1677: "But time after time, though the Lord did appear, I fell short through fear, and quenched the Spirit. And ancient solid Friends perceived it, and spoke to me to give up" (1829:28). That is, the elders were attuned to the struggles of the nascent ministers, alert to the visible signs of such struggles, and ready to intervene in the process to help the young initiates break through. Their guidance came to extend beyond the period of struggle, as they continued to counsel the fledgling ministers through the early stages of their ministry. Benjamin Bangs, for instance, writes of this early stage in his own career as a minister, "there was a tender care in the elders over me, who often would be dropping some seasonable cautions to me, by which I was greatly benefited" (1798:19).

It is important to emphasize that the traditional authority of the elders was in a very basic sense unlike the traditional authority of the made ministers against whom the Quakers campaigned so vigorously. The early elders were themselves prophetic ministers, assisting others who were newly called to the ministry. Still, insofar as acquired experience constituted an essential part of an elder's qualifications, and insofar as one of the elder's functions was the guidance of other ministers, the office of elder represented a step away from the pure prophetic ministry of the earliest period of Quakerism, in which all instruments of God were held equal, and toward a role for traditional authority in the charismatic Quaker ministry. I will have more to say below of the role of the elders in the corporate control of the ministry.

The tendency toward formalization and conventionalization of ministerial *performance* represented a dimension of routinization and traditionality of a different kind. Although the dangers of formalism were present to the Quakers from the very beginning of their movement in the behavior of the made ministers against whom they set themselves, and although the formulaic and conventional elements of ministerial speaking by the Quaker ministers themselves were documented by others as early as 1653 (see Chapter 8), the issue of a *decline* into formalism within their own ranks did not become an open and general concern until the early 1660s, in what has come to be known as the Perrot schism.

John Perrot was a gifted and attractive, if somewhat erratic, Quaker minister who was imprisoned for three years as a lunatic by the Inquisition in Rome. During his harsh imprisonment, Perrot came to be convinced that he had received a commandment from God to "bear a sure testimony against the custom and tradition of taking off the hat by men when they go to pray to God" (Carroll 1971:44). In 1660, shortly before his release from Rome, he sent a letter condemning the practice to Friends in London that stirred a powerful controversy and ultimately triggered a schism that profoundly affected the course of Quakerism during the 1660s and beyond.

Part of the intensity of the conflict engendered by Perrot's position was that his chosen issue of the legitimacy of removing the hat during prayer called up old tensions among Friends. Keeping covered during prayer was a practice of the Ranters, a sect often associated with Friends, but from whom the latter were at pains to disassociate themselves. More important, it was a symbolic gesture employed by James Nayler, who, caught up in the extravagant flush of his own spiritual self-importance before his tragic fall in 1656, refused to remove his hat as George Fox prayed, an offense that Fox only grudgingly forgave and never forgot (Fox 1831, 7:213–215). Indeed, many of Nayler's former supporters were later enlisted in Perrot's cause (Carroll 1971:60). In addition to the issue of the hat, the Perrotonians also challenged other forms of routinization, such as the scheduling of meetings for worship in advance, without waiting for a specific motion to meet together (Carroll 1971:85). They held that unless one were directly moved to uncover or to meet for worship it should not be done (see Carroll 1971:52).

These forms, however, were just the principal symbols of a more fundamental concern on the part of Perrot and his followers. Their basic concern was nothing less than what they perceived as a decline of the spiritual vigor and power that marked the early years of the Quaker movement and a degeneration into formalism and traditional, corporate authority at the expense of individual spiritual guidance (see Davies 1832:79).

In responding to the Perrotonians, the mainstream Quaker leadership was compelled to take a position on formalism in worship. Their response is instructive as an indicator of how far routinization had in fact proceeded among Friends. Indeed, what emerged amounted to nothing less than a rationalization of formalism in Quaker religious practice.

Among the most vigorous opponents of the Perrot faction was the Scottish minister, Patrick Livingstone. Livingstone's tract, *Plain and Downright Dealing with Them That Were with Us, and Are Gone Out from Us*, contains the following revealing passage:

> But the form of Truth we own; that which Truth appears in, that is the form of Truth. Friends do not choose a form for the Truth, but Truth chooseth its own form, and moveth in it at its pleasure. If one speak or pray in the Truth, the words are the form, the form of sound words: but words not coming from the Truth, or actions not proceeding from the Truth in them that speak or act them, these are false forms, though they may be the very same words that Truth hath spoken, or doth speak in his Children; and though they be the same actions that have been, or are acted in and by the Truth in its Children. (1667:12; cf. Fox 1831, 8:16–17)

To be sure, this is not, on the face of it, an endorsement of formalism in worship. For those who had maintained the spiritual ability to judge what was Truth and what was not, it represented no compromise of the original Quaker doctrine that it was the *power* that was important, not the form; what was denied from the beginning was "such as got the form only, and denied the power of godliness" (Fox 1831, 8:17). But for those in whom that critical power had been dulled by drowsiness – sleeping in meetings was a persistent problem (see Barclay 1841:285) – or a cooling of the spirit – which Livingstone himself saw as characteristic of the period of the 1660s in which he wrote (1667:10) – his statement was susceptible to a reading that might suggest an essentially formalistic standard for authentic religious practice. Thus, if "that which Truth appears in . . . is the form of Truth," then it may be inferred that that which has the *form* of Truth must *be* the Truth. Because the words of the Children (Friends) are the Truth, if one employs the forms used by those Friends it follows that what one speaks must be the Truth. Such an understanding could only be reinforced by Livingstone's own subsequent statement: "Now the life of the body leads to unity . . . in outward practices, without imposition; it naturally leads its Children to unity in practises" (1667:11).

Livingstone's emphasis on unity reveals one of the strongest concerns of the more conservative Quakers aroused by the challenge of the Perrot faction. The unity of the spirit was part of the doctrinal bedrock of Quakerism – a corollary of the Inward Light, the basis of silent worship, the foundation of Quaker religious rhetoric. If Friends disagreed irreconcilably about spiritual matters and split into factions, the foundation of the doctrine of spiritual unity was undermined and the credibility of Truth compromised. Fox's strongest epistle against "them that keep on their hats in prayer" (1831, 7:215) high-lights this concern most forcefully: "And ye, with your earthly spirit and earthly form, have given occasion to the world to say, 'that the people of God called Quakers, are divided, some with their hats on, and some with them off, and so they are opposite one to the other.' "

To be sure, the maintenance of public unity was a concern that antedated the Perrot schism and impinged upon the ministry from the earliest years of the Quaker movement. I have noted earlier that in a religious society such as the Quakers, in which virtually every member experiences the Voice of God speaking within, in which any member may feel a motion and an opening to speak God's Word in public, and in which the standard for evaluating the validity of religious speaking rests on the striking of a responsive spiritual chord in others, the exercise of individual judgment concerning the legitimacy of a particular minister or instance of religious speaking may lead to differences of opinion, criticism, and conflict. Records from the early 1650s onward indicate that criticism of the ministry of others was an open and recurrent problem for the early Quakers, socially divisive, publicly compromising of the Quaker doctrine of the unity of the spirit in every person (see Chapter 8), and likely to inhibit still further an untried and struggling minister (Barclay 1841:333). By 1656, a minute of advice from a meeting of elders and brethren "unto the brethren in the north" (Barclay 1841:277–282) – the first surviving document of its kind, representing a corporate statement of Quaker policy – reveals the contours of a mechanism for dealing with the problem:

> And if at such [particular] meetings, any thing at any time be oth-erwise spoken by and out of the light, whereby the seed of God cometh to be burthened; let the person or persons in whom the seed of God is burthened, speak in the light (as of the Lord they are moved), in meekness and godly fear, to him; but let it be done in private, betwixt them two, or before two or three witnesses, and not in the public meetings, except there be a special moving so to do. (Barclay 1841:278)

This policy of deferring criticism until after a meeting and voicing it in private was reaffirmed in subsequent corporate formulations of policy (Barclay 1841:285, 333) as well as by individual Quaker leaders (see Chapter 8). Thus, in order to avoid open disunity and to mitigate potential pressures on inex-perienced ministers, the pure individualism potentiated by the doctrine of the

Inward Light was brought under certain limitations. The regularization, however, was in this instance weighted at least initially in favor of the original speaking minister. When in doubt, let the minister speak anyway and reserve your criticism for later, in private. If your motion is a critical one, a countermessage to the one being voiced, hold it back. Such messages are to be excluded from the meeting for worship and thus from public view. Here, the motivation was at least in part to avoid aggravating still further the already heavy pressure on the neophyte minister, who was, presumably, open to the mature guidance of spiritually experienced Friends. But when the conflict was open, persistent, and public, cleaving the fellowship into factions as in the Perrot schism, the very survival of the movement depended, at least in the eyes of more orthodox Friends, on the strong affirmation of unity and the exercise of traditional authority on a more corporate basis. Under the heavy and protracted pressures imposed upon Friends by the harsh legal persecution of the Restoration period, unity had far more than doctrinal significance. Any internal conflict that fragmented the body of Friends weakened the capacity of the group to withstand such pressures and threatened their very survival as a religious society.

A corporate response of Friends to the Perrot schism came in 1666, in the form of a testimony issued in the name of a specially called meeting of ministers held in London in May of that year. The document was apparently written by Richard Farnsworth, but was signed by eleven of the most weighty Friends of the day who were then at liberty (Fox, Howgill, Dewsbury, and Thomas Taylor were in prison: Braithwaite 1961:248n), including Farnsworth, Alexander Parker, George Whitehead, and Thomas Briggs, all among the original Valiant Sixty who had carried the Truth south in 1654. Braithwaite identifies this epistle as a major milestone marking the narrowing of the Quaker movement into a religious society in which "individual guidance is subordinated to the corporate sense of the Church, which is treated as finding authoritative expression through the elders who are sound in the faith" (1961:248).

For our purposes, the epistle is noteworthy for being in large part a response to the Perrotonians' "slight esteem of [the] declaration or preaching" of "good ancient Friends, who are sound in the faith," of whom the signatories to the document were the principal spokesmen (Barclay 1841:319). Authoritative judgment of the ministry, the testimony declares, belongs to the steadfast body of Friends and the elders:

> We do declare and testify, that the spirit of those . . . who stand not in unity with the ministry and body of Friends, who are steadfast and constant to the Lord and his unchangeable Truth . . . have not any true spiritual right, nor gospel authority to be judges in the church, and of the ministry of the gospel of Christ, so as to condemn

them and their ministry . . . for of right the elders and members of
the church, which keep their habitation in the Truth, ought to judge
matters and things which differ; and their judgment which is given
therein, to stand good and valid amongst Friends, though it be kicked
against, and disapproved by them who have degenerated, as aforesaid. (Barclay 1841:320)

Having asserted this principle of corporate and traditional authority, the
document goes on to make explicit that the ministers, originally answerable
only to the divine guidance of the spirit of God within them, are now accountable for their legitimacy to the church and its elders:

And if any, that have been . . . approved of by the church, do
afterwards degenerate from the Truth . . . then the church hath a
true spiritual right and authority to call them to examination; and if
they find sufficient cause for it by good testimony, they may judge
them unfit for the work of the ministry, whereof they have rendered
themselves unworthy; and so put a stop to their proceedings therein:
and if they submit not to the judgment of the Spirit of Christ in his
people, then ought they publicly to be declared against, and warning
given to the flock of Christ in their several meetings to beware of
them, and to have no fellowship with them, that they may be ashamed;
and the lambs and babes in Christ Jesus preserved. (Barclay 1841:322)

It is difficult to conceive of a more decisive means of bringing a charismatic
ministry under control than the power of disownment. Thus the Perrot schism,
opened in reaction against the power of "men and forms," that is, human
control over the spirit and formalism in religious practice, resulted in a decisive
and authoritative institutionalization of corporate control over the ministry.

Following the testimony of 1666, the next major corporate record documenting the routinization of the ministry was an epistle from a general meeting
of Friends held at the end of May 1672 (Barclay 1841:329–335). This meeting
subsequently became the prototype for the institutionalization of the London
Yearly Meeting, the highest-level agency of Quaker governance (see London
Yearly Meeting 1806:9). The epistle, addressed to the ministers and elders
of the church, articulated and codified standards for the ministry in more
explicit, comprehensive detail than the earlier testimony of 1666.

Some of the principles set out in the epistle were of long-standing familiarity. Ministers were urged to be examples, to let their lives preach as well
as their words. They were to be still and "wait till life arise to bring forth
its own testimony" rather than striving beyond their proper gift by running
on too hastily or quenching the spirit in their spoken ministry. In a related
vein, the epistle cautioned them to avoid all vain repetitions, imitations, and
formed habits, and all impulses to seek worldly popularity, applause, or praise.

Again, the epistle "exhorted" its readers, both ministers and elders, against publicly judging the ministry of others. Elders, for their part, were to stand "as pillars in the house of our God," watchful for "any weakness, want of wisdom, or miscarriage, either in doctrine or practice, by any who came abroad to labour or minister among you" (Barclay 1841:334) and ready to aid in their spiritual preservation and improvement.

As regards these well-established principles, the epistle of 1672 broke no new ground, being of interest chiefly as an official, corporate articulation of guidelines for proper ministerial practice, no small matter, to be sure, in the process of routinizing the ministry. But the epistle did far more than simply codify basic principles. Among the guidelines for the ministers set out in its pages are several that represented a radical departure from the mission of the first publishers of Truth. In giving official voice to these emergent precepts, having to do essentially with the proper stance of the Quaker minister toward those outside the body of Friends, the epistle pointed toward a resolution of an old and basic conflict engendered by the ministers' dual sphere of operation: out in the "heat," "noise," and "dirt" of the world, and among the body of gathered Friends. It did so by placing limits on the range, sphere, and tone of ministerial action.

First, the epistle prescribed a *program* for ministering to those who are not Friends: Proceed "gradually to demonstrate the Truth, to the opening the understandings, and for the conviction of the consciences of the hearers," *before* passing "judgment upon Truth's adversaries or their principles" (Barclay 1841:330). Moreover, do not "cast pearls before swine": Begin with "the first principles of the true light, repentance, and remission of sins through the name and power of our Lord Jesus Christ," only later proceeding to "the highest doctrines, as that of perfection, or height of attainments" that people "may not be stumbled . . . by any hasty or untimely asserting matters beyond their measures or capacities" (Barclay 1841:330–331).

Let us consider the implications of a corporate body formulating a program of this kind. A prophetic minister, bound to speak only as God gives him utterance, cannot adhere to a doctrinal or rhetorical schedule; the first publishers of Truth could not have accepted such restrictions. Again, note that the early ministers out in the world tended, of course, to confront non-Friends in many contexts by passing judgment on them and their principles in churches, markets, streets, and so on. Those were the public battlefronts of the Lamb's War in which they were engaged, and it was only to be expected that such would be the direction of the openings they were given to speak. Moreover, they spoke with vehement intensity, to the extent, as we have seen, that they were frequently accused of "railing." Nor did they deny the vehemence of their attacks, like those of the priests and prophets of the Bible. The Lamb's War was not to be waged with restraint.

Now, however, all was to be moderated. The ministers were cautioned against being "forward or hasty in traversing the ways and principles of professors," but "to take heed of *coming too near* the disobedient, hypo-critical spirit of contentious professors" (Barclay 1841:331). The epistle con-tinues: "Take heed of aggravating reflections and forward clashing at persons or people, with unreasonably and rashly using names of distinctions; which will be resented as reproachful to them, and not only stumble and prepossess their minds with prejudice, but also hinder their convincement" (Barclay 1841:332). This is not war, but diplomacy. One need only try to imagine James Parnel or Richard Farnsworth in the mid-1650s moderating his preach-ing out of a concern for provoking resentment or appearing reproachful to see how enormous a change is represented here. Before long, their adversaries were able to taunt the Quakers with withdrawing from the field:

> That it was the common practice of the Quakers for many years, to pretend they were sent and moved by the Lord, and by the Spirit to come into the parish-assemblies to oppose the ministers, and ac-cordingly did commonly every month, and sometimes oftener, come in and disturb the ministers and congregations, with their messages, visions, and revelations from the Lord, as they said, is so generally known, that I need bring no instances and I think they will not deny it.
>
> But now since His Majesty's happy restoration and government, I do not find but those ORACLES are generally ceased, or at least, for the most part; and now their common practice therein is altered. (Thompson 1675:31–32)

Finally, we may recall that it was this epistle of 1672 that officially dis-couraged the "imagined, unseasonable and untimely prophesyings" (Barclay 1841:333), including going naked as a sign and the related prophetic sign enactments so consistent with the prophetic ministry yet so notably unsuc-cessful in practice.

It is worth observing here that the moderation of tone and action imposed upon the ministry was analogous to the moderated and withdrawn political stance adopted by the Quakers during the same period in the face of legal persecution, as discussed earlier in connection with the oath trials of the 1660s. Both adaptations were strategically motivated by the need to concen-trate their energies and resources within, on the survival of the society and the preservation of essentials, even if this meant curtailing and moderating their activities without. The disengagement from worldly political affairs strengthened the argument that Friends were no threat to the regime and thus need not be compelled to swear oaths of allegiance, while the new moderation in dealing with the professors highlighted the "peaceable" and "inoffensive" (London Yearly Meeting 1806:34) spirit by which the Friends sought to persuade the regime to toleration. Both served to keep Friends from the "noise" and "dirt" of worldly engagement and thus to foster the transition from conversionist movement to introversionist sect (Wilson 1967:27–28; 1970:38–39).

In sum, the epistle of 1672 stands as a documentary testament to the transformation of the prophetic ministry of Friends. Though Quaker doctrine and practice continued to demand prophetic inspiration, the voice of the Holy Spirit speaking through his ministers, the ideal of an unfettered prophetic ministry accountable only to direct divine guidance was routinized and brought under corporate control. Other contemporaneous developments simply serve as confirmation of the transformation.

From the same period, for example, stemmed the practice of requiring certificates from their local monthly meetings for ministers who intended to travel in the ministry beyond their home territory. These certificates, to be presented to each meeting they visited, served as a warrant of their good character and the acceptability of their ministry (Fox 1831, 7:349; Lloyd 1950:125). Again, although a minister's legitimacy still rested ideally on the charismatic base of divine leading, the certificates introduced an element of human corporate legitimacy into the institution of the Quaker ministry. This would have been unthinkable in the first flush of the Quaker movement. Or consider the practice, emerging in the mid to late 1670s, of building within the meetinghouse "a convenient place for Friends to stand on to minister," which developed into the ministers' gallery, a long raised platform facing the assembly at the front of the meeting on which the ministers were seated (Lloyd 1950:129–130). The gallery thus institutionalized the separation of the ministers out of what was formerly an assembly of equals.

This element of incipient hierarchy appears to have been manifested in the form of ministerial preaching as well. In an earlier chapter, I suggested that the incantory style that marked at least some early Quaker preaching and was probably a general feature of much of it was well-suited to eliciting the collaborative co-participation of auditors through the formal appeal of repetition, parallelism, and rhythm, and, further, that such a process was consistent with the Quaker belief in the unified Voice of the Holy Spirit speaking in everyone. Michael Graves's (1972) thorough study of Quaker sermons up to 1700, however, reveals that the incantory style had waned almost to the point of disappearance by the third quarter of the seventeenth century, to be replaced by what he aptly calls the catechetical style, marked by the extensive – at times predominant – use of rhetorical questions as a structural device in the conduct of preaching.

The catechetical style took a number of forms. At times, the ministers furnished answers to their own questions directly after posing them, as in the following excerpt from a sermon preached by John Butcher in 1693:

> For what end hath God concluded all under sin? For what end is it? That we might be destroyed? No, God through Christ . . . hath

extended to you the Day of Visitation, that you might come to the knowledge of life and salvation. But wherein may we come to this knowledge? It is in that way which God hath ordained, even by Christ . . . What is God's end in concluding all under sin? Was it that he might destroy all the children of men? . . . No, but that he might have mercy upon all. (Quoted in Graves 1972:246)

Or, the questions and responses might be rendered as dialogue, in the manner commonly employed by Stephen Crisp:

Go to one place and another place, and ask them what is your way? Our way (say they) is the right way, the most sure and certain way that can be found for people to walk in. But whither will it lead me? It will lead to the Kingdom of God. That is it I would have, but will it lead me to holiness? No, never in this world, you must never come to holiness. Do the best thou canst do here, it is but sin . . . Do you hold out that in your way? Yes. Then I have done with that. (1688, Quoted in Graves 1972:247)

Alternatively, the questions alone were spoken, leaving the answers to be supplied by the auditors, as in this example from George Fox, recorded in 1678, with traces still of the incantory style:

Do you want wisdom? Do you want life? Do you want salvation? From him you must have it. So abide in him by belief in the Eternal Light. (Quoted in Graves 1972:245)

Here, Fox knows that the answers to his questions in his listeners' minds had to be yes, and goes on to tell them how to achieve that wisdom, life, and salvation they seek.

Clearly, like the incantory style, this catechetical style is in its own right a highly effective means of eliciting the expressive collaboration of an audience. The compulsive power of questions has been opened to us by the sociolinguistic explorations of Schegloff and Sacks (1973), Sinclair and Coulthard (1975), Esther Goody (1978), and others. Questions and answers belong to a class of utterance sequences in conversation that Schegloff and Sacks have termed adjacency pairs; these consist of a pair of utterances, spoken by two different participants in the conversation, one elicited by and following directly on the other. The speaking of the first pair part of an adjacency pair exerts a strong compulsive force on the addressee to produce the second pair part; when a question is asked, it is expected that the next thing said will be a relevant answer. As summed up by Goody: "The most general thing we can say about a question is that it compels, requires, may even demand, a response" (1978:23). Rhetorical questions exploit this compulsive power of questions for rhetorical purposes, posing questions that compel known, obvious answers; they give the questioner an especially high degree of control over the dynamic and direction of the interaction. This is true, I submit, even when the questioner supplies the answer, for this answer merely duplicates and reinforces the response that must also be provided – whether spoken aloud or in the mind – by the person to whom the question is addressed.

This collaborative dimension of the catechetical style is very different from that of the incantory style, which elicits collaboration through the appeal of form. In interrogation the collaboration is dialogic, not, as with the incantory style, something verging on simultaneous co-production of the minister's utterance. Moreover, as Samarin (1967:144–145) and Roberts and Forman (1972:184) have suggested, sustained questioning establishes a hierarchy of superordination and subordination in the interaction; the interactional power and initiative lie with the questioner, rooted in the compulsive power of questioning, which is not done to elicit information previously unknown to the questioner, but rather to compel the person(s) being questioned to produce answers that are *already known* by the questioner, who takes on and reinforces through this sustained questioning an ever more authoritative position. I am suggesting, then, that the predominance of the catechetical style in the preaching of Quaker ministers in the last quarter of the seventeenth century is further evidence of the emergence and institutionalization of authoritative hierarchy among Friends, revealing the ministers to be controllers of right doctrine and religious experience vis-à-vis the mass of their co-religionists in the meeting for worship.

By the end of the 1670s the routinization of the prophetic ministry was fully confirmed. The process of emerging into the ministry had become conventionalized; an element of traditional authority had taken hold in the form of accountability to experienced elders; silence and spoken expression had become formalized, with limitations imposed by corporate authority upon the range and tone of the ministerial message; the charismatic legitimacy of the ministers had been tempered by the corporate legitimacy conferred by the issuance of certificates to acceptable ministers; and the separation of the ministers from the body of Friends had been made manifest by the institution of the ministers' gallery.

Weber has suggested that "it is the fate of charisma to recede before the powers of tradition or of rational association after it has entered the permanent structures of social action. This waning of charisma generally indicates the diminishing importance of individual action" (Weber 1978:1148–1149). This was certainly true in the case of the charismatic ministry of the Quakers. As we have seen, there was notably more ministerial speaking going on in the meetings for worship than in the early years: "Few meetings but have some or other, to whom a ministry in words is given more or less, so that seldom or rarely meetings are under a necessity to be wholly silent" (Keith 1670:14).

Nevertheless, by the end of the 1670s, the ministers were speaking in more formalized and constrained ways, in a narrower range of contexts, and with far less independence of action than was open to them in the first vigorous years of the Quaker movement.

Weber's definition of the prophet centers on the quality of charisma: The prophet is "a purely individual bearer of charisma, who by virtue of his mission proclaims a religious doctrine or divine commandment" (1978:439), and again, "the prophet's claim is based on personal revelation and charisma" (1978:440). In turn, however, most of Weber's attention in the development of the concept of charisma is focused on political and structural issues, such as leadership, domination, authority, and the social forms and processes by which they are manifested. Accordingly, his discussion of the routinization of charisma takes up such problems as succession of leadership, the emergence of traditional or rational authority, the development of institutional structures for the continuity of the community, and the like. His treatment of prophetic religion, on the other hand, concentrates essentially on the typological distinction between the prophet and the priest, as bearers, respectively, of charismatic versus traditional authority.

The routinization of prophetic religion is not discussed directly in Weber's theoretical formulations. By implication, it follows the course outlined in his general discussion of charismatic authority, that is, surrendering eventually to traditional or rational authority or a combination of both. Nowhere in Weber's model building – not in the definition of the prophet as a type, not in the suggestion that the prophet's authority must continually be validated by proofs of his power, not in the discussions of the routinization of charisma – does he consider the form or conduct of prophetic practice itself, prophetic communication, presumably the core element of charismatic religion in action. Nor have those many scholars who have built on Weber's foundation filled in the missing element; historical sociologists of religion and anthropological students of religious movements have concentrated almost exclusively on structural, typological, and causal factors, like Weber ignoring the expressive. One might perhaps expect that sociolinguistically oriented studies of language in religious practice would fill the gap, but they do not (though see Samarin 1972:217–218). Although these studies do highlight the importance of the expressive dimensions of religion, such as religious genres, speech acts, and registers, they tend for the most part to deal with social process – where they deal with it at all – in rather limited, ahistorical scope (see Samarin 1976; Zaretsky and Leone 1974:53–219).

I am suggesting that a critical dimension of religious process has apparently evaded attention because of limitations imposed by scholarly tradition and disciplinary orientation; what is missing is the way in which social process – the routinization of charisma – is played out in terms of expressive practice, the conduct of religious communication. I have argued earlier, in Chapter 3, that the conflict between the prophetic ministers of Quakerism and the "priests and professors" of "the world's religions" is best understood as centering around the legitimacy of control over expressive means and the conduct of expressive practice. My argument in this chapter has been an extension of the earlier one: Processes of change in the prophetic Quaker ministry, that is, routinization and the advent of elements of traditional authority, must also take account of prophetic form and practice.

In Quakerism, the prophetic element was not simply a matter of the qualities of a founding leader, although Weber's formulations might lead one to think in those terms (e.g., Weber 1946:295–296) and George Fox has sometimes mistakenly been treated as the prophetic founder of Quakerism. Rather, for the Quakers, *all* religious expression was fundamentally prophetic, an expression of the Voice of God speaking through his chosen instrument, and *every* Friend had the capacity to give prophetic voice to the Word of God by virtue of the Inward Light. The only thing that singled out the ministers from their co-religionists was the circumstance of their being opened more regularly to speak God's Word. These principles were part of the doctrinal bedrock of Quaker faith.

What happened in the course of the process I have traced in this chapter is that the structures and mechanisms of corporate control and the formal and stylistic conventions for ministerial discourse that emerged in the process of routinization came into play to channel, constrain, and guide the originally unfettered *speaking* of the prophetic ministry. The core belief in a prophetic ministry remained, but the legitimacy of ministerial speaking was no longer measured only by reference to the leadings of the Divine Spirit. Authority came to be shared between the ministers and the elders, agents of the corporate authority of the emergent religious society of Friends.

These findings, I submit, demonstrate that the structural dimensions of the process of routinization cannot be separated from the expressive ones. To confine one's attention solely to the former is to ignore the *substance* of routinization, the very sphere of social *action* in which routinization occurred, namely, religious speaking. In larger scope, though, this is only to reaffirm the basic premise of the ethnography of speaking on which this study was undertaken: that speaking is fundamentally *constitutive* of social life, in religion as in all other domains.

*   *   *   *

As the Quakers approached the end of the Restoration period and the advent of toleration, older Friends began to voice their awareness of the changes that had taken place since the early days of the movement. There is a certain poignancy to some of their writing, betraying a realization that Friends might have purchased their survival at the sacrifice of the energy and power of the direct inward spiritual experience that had energized the first publishers of Truth.

Stephen Crisp was distressed as early as 1666, during the time of the Perrot schism, by signs that Friends were relaxing their adherence to ''the single pure language, learned in the light'' and falling into a ''loose and careless kind of speaking'' (1822:101). His *Epistle of Tender Counsel and Advice to All That Have Believed the Truth*, written in 1680, is a clear expression of his concern that Friends had not only relaxed their standards but lost the spiritual essence of the way of Truth, to be left with only the outward form. ''Take heed, my Dear Friends,'' he wrote,

> of holding the Truth in a bare formality, satisfying yourselves that you have for a long time owned the way of Truth, and the assemblies of the Lord's people, and appeared as they have done in all outward things, and have hereby obtained the repute to be one of them; and under these considerations sit down at ease, as to the inward man, unacquainted with the inward travels [travails?], either for thy self or others. (1694:426)

As we would expect, Crisp was troubled by a decline in the intensity of Friends' regard for speaking: ''Too many have let in a false liberty since their first convincement, and have not that respect to their words as they ought to have, to the great dishonour of God, and grief of the righteous, and wounding their own souls'' (1694:432). And later: ''If your faith be such an one as stands in words and terms, though never so true, yet it will fail you . . . and you will not be able to stand'' (1694:436). Crisp was especially strongly concerned as well with the children of Friends, that they ''may take heed that they rest not in a bare educable form of the Truth'' (1694:435).

John Crook, another veteran of the Lamb's War and of legal persecution for refusing to swear, was even more centrally concerned with the new generation in his 1686 *Epistle to Young People Professing the Truth* (Barbour and Roberts 1973:545–549). He too deplored the condition ''that the Quakers nowadays are not like those at the beginning''; as in the ministry, so in the rest of Quaker life, it was ''as if in these latter times the efficacy of Truth was not the same as at the beginning, and as if the cross of Christ, that was so powerful then, was now become of no effect'' (Barbour and Roberts 1973:547).

Crook's postscript to his epistle captures the essence of the contrast between the days of the first Children of the Light and the opening of the new era in which the major problem for the future of Quakerism would turn on how to accommodate to *their* children; fittingly, Crook's concern is couched in terms of language, still felt to represent something essential about Quaker faith and practice. ''Let none despise these lines for their plainness,'' he wrote, for we were a plain people at the beginning. I know some of the younger sort are apt to be taken with fine words and fashionable language, as with other things in fashion, but experience shows that that which tickles the outward ear commonly stops there, very seldom coming so low as to the truth in the inward parts; therefore this epistle is sent abroad in so plain a dress on purpose, answerable to a plain seed in them that are puffed up, but ought rather to have mourned; which seed being reached, and the souls relieved, my end is answered. (Barbour and Roberts 1973:549)

From a plain people at the beginning to a people whose children were showing signs of rejecting that plainness of speech and life, the Quakers had traveled a long and painful course to arrive at this turning. The very principle of plainness in speech by which the early Friends had challenged the fleshliness and vanity of the world had brought them to the economic prosperity that threatened to undermine that principle. The prophetic ministry that had waged the Lamb's War against the priests and professors had been turned inward and brought under corporate control; the plain style of speaking that had warred against fleshly pride had become the mark of an introversionist sect; and the intense engagement in the public sphere of religion and politics had been turned to a sectarian cultivation of a withdrawn, inoffensive posture toward the world. Yet here, on the eve of toleration as at the beginning, we find Crook concerned with the power of plain speech to reach to the spirit of those caught up in the vanity of the world. The great irony is that it was no longer the priests and professors he sought to reach, but a target much nearer at hand: the children of the Quakers themselves.

But the power of special ways of speaking and silence to evoke the essence of Quakerism did not disappear with the coming of toleration. In those later periods when Quaker identity was most problematic or most under stress, as in the moral crisis and revival of the mid-eighteenth century and the separations of the nineteenth, attempts at reaffirming or adjusting the meaning of Quaker faith and practice often returned again to the same communicative symbols and ways of enacting them that have figured centrally in this work: the plain speech, the ministry, the meeting (see, e.g., Bauman 1974a; Jones 1921:171–174, 496). The formative period of Quakerism, from the early 1650s to 1689, in which the key symbols of speaking and silence gave shape to a unified system of belief, action, and meaning, has continued to serve in its own right as a significant symbolic resource ever since.

REFERENCES

Aarsleff, Hans. 1970. Boehme, Jacob. In *Dictionary of Scientific Biography*, vol. 2, pp. 222–224. New York: Scribner.

   1976. Wilkins, John. In *Dictionary of Scientific Biography*, vol. 14, pp. 361–381. New York: Scribner.

Adamson, William. 1656. *An Answer to a Book, Titled, Quakers Principles Quaking*. London.

Aldam, Thomas. 1690. *A Short Testimony Concerning that Faithful Servant of the Lord Thomas Aldam*. London.

Anon. 1654. *The Glorie of the Lord Arising*. London.

   1655. *The Quaking Mountebanck or the Jesuite Turn'd Quaker*. London.

   1669. *The Quakers Court of Justice*. London.

Audland, John. 1655. *The Innocent Delivered Out of the Snare*. London.

Austin, J. L. 1962. *How to Do Things With Words*. New York: Oxford University Press.

Aynsloe, J. 1672. *A Short Description of the True Ministers and the False*. N.p.

Bangs, Benjamin. 1798. *Memoirs of the Life and Convincement of . . . Benjamin Bangs*. London.

Banks, John. 1798. *A Journal of the Life . . . of . . . John Banks*. London.

Barbour, Hugh. 1964. *The Quakers in Puritan England*. New Haven: Yale University Press.

   1975. Ranters, Diggers and Quakers Reborn. *Quaker History* 64(1):60–65.

Barbour, Hugh, and Roberts, Arthur O. 1973. *Early Quaker Writings, 1650–1700*. Grand Rapids, Mich.: Eerdmans.

Barclay, A. R. 1841. *Letters, &c. of Early Friends*. London.

Barclay, Robert. 1831. *Truth Triumphant*. 3 vols. Philadelphia.

Basso, Keith H. 1970. "To Give Up On Words": Silence in Western Apache Culture. *Southwestern Journal of Anthropology* 26:213–230.

Bauman, Richard. 1970. Aspects of Quaker Rhetoric. *Quarterly Journal of Speech* 56:67–74.

   1971. *For the Reputation of Truth: Politics, Religion and Conflict Among the Pennsylvania Quakers, 1750–1800*. Baltimore: Johns Hopkins.

   1972a. An Analysis of Quaker–Seneca Councils, 1798–1800. *Man in the Northeast*, no. 3, pp. 36–48.

   1972b. Quakers, Seventeenth Century. In *Prolegomena to Typologies of Speech Use*. Regna Darnell, ed. Austin: Texas Working Papers in Sociolinguistics, Special Number.

   1974a. Quaker Folk-Linguistics and Folklore. In *Folklore: Performance and Communication*. Dan Ben-Amos and Kenneth S. Goldstein, eds. The Hague: Mouton.

1974b. Speaking in the Light: The Role of the Quaker Minister. In *Explorations in the Ethnography of Speaking*. Richard Bauman and Joel Sherzer, eds. Cambridge: Cambridge University Press.

Bauman, Richard, and Sherzer, Joel, eds. 1974. *Explorations in the Ethnography of Speaking*. Cambridge: Cambridge University Press.

1975. The Ethnography of Speaking. In *Annual Review of Anthropology*, vol. 4. Bernard J. Siegel, ed. Palo Alto, Calif.: Annual Reviews.

Bayly, William. 1830. *A Collection of the Several Writings of . . . William Bayly*. Philadelphia and New York.

Benthall, Jonathan. 1975. A Prospectus as Published in *Studio International*, July 1972. In *The Body as a Medium of Expression*. Jonathan Benthall and Ted Polhemus, eds. New York: Dutton.

Besse, Joseph. 1738. *An Abstract of the Sufferings of the People Called Quakers*. 3 vols. London.

1753. *A Collection of the Sufferings of the People Called Quakers*. 2 vols. London.

Bishop, George, et al. 1656. *The Cry of Blood*. London.

Black, Max. 1979. More About Metaphor. In *Metaphor and Thought*. Andrew Ortony, ed. Cambridge: Cambridge University Press.

Blackborow [Blackbury], Sarah. 1660. *The Just and Equall Ballance Discovered*. London.

Bloch, Maurice. 1975. *Political Language and Oratory in Traditional Society*. New York: Academic Press.

Bohn, Ralph P. 1955. *The Controversy Between Puritans and Quakers to 1660*. Ph.D. diss., Edinburgh University.

Bourguignon, Erika. 1972. Dreams and Altered States of Consciousness in Anthropological Research. In *Psychological Anthropology*. Francis L. K. Hsu, ed. Cambridge, Mass.: Schenkman.

Bouwsma, William J. 1981. Intellectual History in the 1980s. *Journal of Interdisciplinary History* 12:279–291.

Brailsford, H. N. 1961. *The Levellers and the English Revolution*. London: Cresset Press.

Braithwaite, William C. 1955. *The Beginnings of Quakerism*. 2d ed. Cambridge: Cambridge University Press.

1961. *The Second Period of Quakerism*. 2d ed. Cambridge: Cambridge University Press.

Briggs, Thomas. 1685. *An Account of . . . Thomas Briggs*. N.p.

Britten, William. 1660. *Silent Meeting, a Wonder to the World*. London.

Broadbent, John. 1977. The Image of God, or Two Yards of Skin. In *The Body as a Medium of Expression*. Jonathan Benthall and Ted Polhemus, eds. New York: Dutton.

Brown, Penelope, and Levinson, Stephen. 1978. Universals in Language Usage: Politeness Phenomena. In *Questions and Politeness*. Esther N. Goody, ed. Cambridge: Cambridge University Press.

Brown, Roger, and Gilman, Albert. 1960. The Pronouns of Power and Solidarity. In *Style in Language*. Thomas A. Sebeok, ed. Cambridge, Mass.: MIT Press.

Burke, Kenneth. 1961. *The Rhetoric of Religion*. Boston: Beacon Press.

    1969 [1950]. *A Rhetoric of Motives*. Berkeley and Los Angeles: University of California Press.

Burke, Peter. 1978. *Popular Culture in Early Modern Europe*. New York: New York University Press.

    1979. Back to Burkhardt. *New York Review of Books* 26(15):35–37.

    1981. Languages and Anti-Languages in Early Modern Italy. *History Workshop*, no. 11, pp. 24–32.

Burrough, Edward. 1657. *A Measure of the Times*. London.

    1658. Epistle to the Reader. In George Fox. *The Works of George Fox*, vol. 3. Philadelphia, 1831.

    1660a. *A Vindication of the People of God, Called Quakers*. London.

    1660b. *A Returne to the Ministers of London*. London.

    1672. *The Memorable Works of a Son of Thunder and Consolation*. London.

Camm, John, and Audland, John. 1689. *The Memory of the Righteous Revived*. London.

Carroll, Kenneth. 1971. *John Perrot, Early Quaker Schismatic*. London: Friends' Historical Society.

    1978. Early Quakers and "Going Naked as a Sign." *Quaker History* 67:69–87.

Caton, William. 1671. *The Moderate Enquirer Resolved*. N.p.

    1689. *A Journal of the Life of . . . Will Caton*. London.

Chester, Elizabeth. 1709. *A Narrative of the Life and Death of Edward Chester*. London.

Cheyney, John. 1676. *The Shibboleth of Quakerism*. London.

Christie-Murray, David. 1978. *Voices from the Gods: Speaking with Tongues*. London: Routledge & Kegan Paul.

Clark, Henry. 1656. *England's Lessons*. London.

Clark, Michael. 1978. The Word of God and the Language of Man: Puritan Semiotics and the Theological and Scientific "Plain Styles" of the Seventeenth Century. *Semiotic Scene* 2:61–90.

Cohn, Norman. 1957. *The Pursuit of the Millennium*. Fairlawn, N.J.: Essential Books.

Comaroff, John. 1975. Talking Politics: Oratory and Authority in a Tswana Chiefdom. In *Political Language and Oratory in Traditional Society*. Maurice Bloch, ed. New York: Academic Press.

Combs, James E. 1980. *Dimensions of Political Drama*. Santa Monica, Calif.: Goodyear.

Cope, Jackson I. 1956. Seventeenth Century Quaker Style. *PMLA 76:725–754*.

Cragg, Gerald R. 1957. *Puritanism in the Period of the Great Persecution, 1660–1688*. Cambridge: Cambridge University Press.

Creasey, Maurice A. 1962. *"Inward" and "Outward": A Study in Early Quaker Language*. London: Friends' Historical Society.

Crisp, Stephen. 1694. *A Memorable Account of . . . Stephen Crisp*. London.

    1822. *The Christian Experiences . . . and Writings of . . . Stephen Crisp*. Philadelphia.

Crook, John, 1662. *The Cry of the Innocent for Justice*. London.

    1791. *The Design of Christianity*. London.

Cutten, George B. 1927. *Speaking with Tongues*. New Haven: Yale University Press.

Darnell, Regna. 1970. The Second Person Singular Pronoun in English: The Society of Friends. *Western Canadian Journal of Anthropology* 1:1–11.

    1972a. *Prolegomena to Typologies of Speech Use.* Austin: Texas Working Papers in Sociolinguistics, Special Number.

    1972b. Quakers, Modern. In *Prolegomena to Typologies of Speech Use.* Regna Darnell, ed. Austin: Texas Working Papers in Sociolinguistics, Special Number.

Davies, Richard. 1832. *An Account of . . . Richard Davies.* Philadelphia.

Descamps, Marc-Alain. 1972. *Le Nu et le vêtement.* Paris: Editions Universitaires.

Dewsbury, William. 1689. *The Faithful Testimony of . . . William Dewsbury.* London.

Dickinson, James. 1847. *Journals of the Lives, Travels and Gospel Labours of Thomas Wilson, and James Dickinson.* London.

Douglas, Mary. 1973. *Natural Symbols.* New York: Random House (Vintage Books).

Duncan, Hugh D. 1968. *Symbols in Society.* New York: Oxford University Press.

Edmondson, William. 1820. *A Journal of . . . William Edmondson.* Dublin.

Ellwood, Thomas. 1676. *Truth Prevailing and Detecting Error.* N.p.

    1906. *The History of the Life of Thomas Ellwood.* S. Graveson, ed. London: Headley Brothers.

Estrich, Robert M., and Sperber, Hans. 1952. *Three Keys to Language.* New York: Rinehart.

Faldo, John. 1673. *Quakerism No Christianity.* London.

Farnsworth, Richard. 1653. *A Call Out of Egypt and Babylon.* London.

    1655a. *Antichrist's Man of War.* London.

    1655b. *The Pure Language of the Spirit of Truth.* London.

    1655c. *A Woman Forbidden to Speak in the Church.* London.

    1656. *The Priests' Ignorance and Contrary-Walkings to the Scriptures.* London.

    1663. *The Spirit of God Speaking in the Temple of God.* London.

Febvre, Lucien. 1973 [1938]. History and Psychology. In *A New Kind of History and Other Essays.* Peter Burke, ed. New York: Harper & Row.

Fell, Margaret. 1710. *A Brief Collection of Remarkable Passages and Occurrences.* London.

Ferguson, Charles. 1976. The Structure and Use of Politeness Formulas. *Language in Society* 5:137–151.

Fernandez, James. 1974. The Mission of Metaphor in Expressive Culture. *Current Anthropology* 15:119–145.

Finkenstaedt, Thomas. 1963. *You and Thou: Studien zur Anrede im Englischen.* Berlin: Walter de Gruyter.

Fisch, Harold. 1952. The Puritans and the Reform of Prose-Style. *ELH* 19:229–248.

Fisher, Samuel. 1660. *Rusticus Ad Academicos.* London.

    1679. *The Testimony of Truth Exalted.* London.

Foucault, Michel. 1972. The Discourse on Language. In *The Archaeology of Knowledge and the Discourse on Language.* New York: Harper & Row.

Fowler, Christopher, and Ford, Simon. 1656. *A Sober Answer to an Angry Epistle.* London.

Fowler, Edward. 1676. *A Friendly Conference Between a Minister and a Parishioner.* London.

1678. *A Vindication of the Friendly Conference Between a Minister and a Parishioner*. London.

Fox, George. 1657. *Concerning Good-Morrow and Good-Even* . . . London.

1664. *The Examination and Tryall of Margaret Fell and George Fox*. London.

1674a. Sermon preached at a General Meeting, 9th of the 4th month 1674. Headley MSS., pp. 247–260. Friends House, London.

1674b. Sermon preached at a General Meeting, 11th of the 4th month 1674. Headley MSS., pp. 262–283. Friends House, London.

1706. *Gospel-Truth Demonstrated*. London.

1831. *The Works of George Fox*. 8 vols. Philadelphia.

1952. *The Journal of George Fox*. Rev. ed. by John L. Nickalls. Cambridge: Cambridge University Press.

1972. *Narrative Papers of George Fox*. Henry J. Cadbury, ed. Richmond, Ind.: Friends United Press.

Fox, George, Stubbs, John, and Furly, Benjamin. 1660. *A Battle-Door for Teachers and Professors to Learn Singular and Plural*. London.

Fox-Genovese, Elizabeth, and Genovese, Eugene. 1976. The Political Crisis of Social History: A Marxian Perspective. *Journal of Social History* 10:205–220.

Fraser, Bruce. 1979. The Interpretation of Novel Metaphors. In *Metaphor and Thought*. Andrew Ortony, ed. Cambridge: Cambridge University Press.

Fraser, Russel. 1977. *The Language of Adam*. New York: Columbia University Press.

Furly, Benjamin. 1663. *The World's Honour Detected*. London.

Garfinkel, Harold. 1956. Conditions of Successful Degradation Ceremonies. *American Journal of Sociology* 61:420–424.

Geertz, Clifford. 1973. Ideology as a Cultural System. In *The Interpretation of Cultures*. New York: Basic Books.

1980. Blurred Genres: The Refiguration of Social Thought. *The American Scholar* 49:165–179.

Goffman, Erving. 1967. *Interaction Ritual: Essays on Face to Face Behavior*. Garden City, N.Y.: Doubleday (Anchor Books).

1974. *Frame Analysis*. New York: Harper & Row.

Goodman, Felicitas. 1972. *Speaking in Tongues: A Cross-Cultural Study of Glossolalia*. Chicago: University of Chicago Press.

Goody, Esther N. 1972. "Greeting," "Begging" and the Presentation of Respect. In *The Interpretation of Ritual*. J. S. La Fontaine, ed. London: Tavistock.

1978. Towards a Theory of Questions. In *Questions and Politeness*. Esther N. Goody, ed. Cambridge: Cambridge University Press.

Gratton, John. 1720. *Journal of the Life of . . . John Gratton*. London.

Graves, Michael P. 1972. The Rhetoric of the Inward Light: An Examination of Extant Sermons Delivered by Early Quakers 1671–1700. Ph.D. diss., University of Southern California.

Graves, Richard. 1969. *The Puritan Revolution and Educational Thought*. New Brunswick, N.J.: Rutgers University Press.

Gray, Bennison. 1971. Repetition in Oral Literature. *Journal of American Folklore* 84:289–303.

R. H. 1672a. *The Character of a Quaker in His Time and Proper Colours. The First Part*. London.

1672b. *Plus Ultra or the Second Part of the Character of a Quaker*. London.

Harvey, T. Edmund. 1923. *Silence and Worship: A Study in Quaker Experience*. London: Swarthmore Press.

1928. *Quaker Language*. London: Friends' Historical Society.

Hayes, Alice. 1723. *A Legacy or Widow's Mite*. London.

Hayes, T. Wilson. 1979. *Winstanley the Digger: A Literary Analysis of Radical Ideas in the English Revolution*. Cambridge, Mass.: Harvard University Press.

Herskovits, Melville J. 1963. *Cultural Anthropology*. New York: Knopf.

Higginson, Francis. 1653. *A Brief Relation of the Irreligion of the Northern Quakers*. London.

Hill, Christopher. 1964. *Society and Puritanism in Pre-Revolutionary England*. London: Secker & Warburg.

1975. *The World Turned Upside Down*. New York: Penguin.

Hill, Michael. 1973. *A Sociology of Religion*. London: Heinemann.

History Workshop. 1980. Editorial: Language and History. *History Workshop*, no. 10, pp. 1–5.

Howard, Luke. 1704. *Love and Truth in Plainness Manifested: Being a Collection of the . . . Writings . . . of . . . Luke Howard*. London.

Howgill, Francis. N.d. *A Copy of a Paper Sent to John Otway, Justice of the Peace Concerning Swearing*. N.p.

1676. *The Dawnings of the Gospel Day*. London.

Hymes, Dell. 1962. The Ethnography of Speaking. In *Anthropology and Human Behavior*. Thomas Gladwin and William C. Sturtevant, eds. Washington, D.C.: Anthropological Society of Washington.

1974a. *Foundations in Sociolinguistics*. Philadelphia: University of Pennsylvania Press.

1974b. Ways of Speaking. In *Explorations in the Ethnography of Speaking*. Richard Bauman and Joel Sherzer, eds. Cambridge: Cambridge University Press.

1977. Discovering Oral Performance and Measured Verse in American Indian Narrative. *New Literary History* 7:431–457.

Irvine, Judith T. 1979a. Communicative Behavior in Spirit Possession. Unpublished paper delivered at the annual meeting of the American Anthropological Association, Cincinnati, Ohio.

1979b. Formality and Informality in Communicative Events. *American Anthropologist* 81:733–790.

Jones, Richard F. 1951. *The Seventeenth Century*. Stanford: Stanford University Press.

1953. *The Triumph of the English Language*. Stanford: Stanford University Press.

Jones, Rufus M. 1921. *The Later Periods of Quakerism*. 2 vols. London: Macmillan.

1971 [1914]. *Spiritual Reformers in the 16th and 17th Centuries*. Gloucester, Mass.: Peter Smith.

Judt, Tony. 1979. A Clown in Regal Purple: Social History and the Historians. *History Workshop*, no. 7, pp. 66–94.

Keith, George. 1670. *The Benefit, Advantage and Glory of Silent Meetings*. London.

1687. *Concerning Prayer*. N.p.

Knowlson, James. 1975. *Universal Language Schemes in England and France, 1600–1800*. Toronto: University of Toronto Press.

Livingstone, Patrick. 1667. *Plain and Downright Dealing with Them That Were with Us and Are Gone Out from Us.* London.

Lloyd, Arnold. 1950. *Quaker Social History, 1669–1738.* London: Longmans.

Lombard, Emile. 1910. *De la Glossolalie chez les premiers chrétiens et des phénomènes similaires.* Lausanne: Bridel.

London Yearly Meeting. 1806. *A Collection of the Epistles from the Yearly Meeting of Friends in London . . . 1675–1805.* Baltimore.

Lord, Albert B. 1960. *The Singer of Tales.* Cambridge, Mass.: Harvard University Press.

E.M. 1658. *A Brief Answer Unto the Cambridge Model.* London.

Macfarlane, Alan. 1970. *The Family Life of Ralph Josselin, A Seventeenth-Century Clergyman.* New York: Norton.

MacRae, Donald G. 1977. The Body and Social Metaphor. In *The Body as a Medium of Expression.* Jonathan Benthall and Ted Polhemus, eds. New York: Dutton.

Malinowski, Bronislaw. 1923. The Problem of Meaning in Primitive Languages. In *The Meaning of Meaning.* C. K. Ogden and I. A. Richards, eds. New York: Harcourt, Brace & World.

    1965. *The Language of Magic and Gardening* (= vol. 2 of *Coral Gardens and Their Magic*, originally published 1935). Bloomington: Indiana University Press.

Marshall, Charles. 1677. *An Epistle to Friends Coming Forth in the Beginning of a Testimony.* N.p.

    1844. *The Journal of Charles Marshall.* London.

May, L. Carlyle. 1956. A Survey of Glossolalia and Related Phenomena in Non-Christian Religions. *American Anthropologist* 58:75–96.

Morris, Desmond. 1977. *Manwatching: A Field Guide to Human Behavior.* New York: Abrams.

Mortimer, Russell. 1971. *Minute Book of the Men's Meeting of the Society of Friends in Bristol, 1667–1686.* Vol. 26 of Bristol Record Society Publications. Bristol: Bristol Record Society.

Nayler, James. 1716. *A Collection of Sundry Books, Epistles and Papers Written by James Nayler.* London.

Nuttall, Geoffrey F. 1947. "Unity with the Creation": George Fox and the Hermetic Philosophy. *Friends' Quarterly* 1:139–143.

    1952. *Early Quaker Letters from the Swarthmore Mss. to 1660.* London: Friends House.

    1967. *The Puritan Spirit: Essays and Addresses.* London: Epworth Press.

Ong, Walter. 1967. *The Presence of the Word.* New York: Simon & Schuster.

Ormsby-Lennon, Hugh. 1977. *The Dialect of Those Fanatick Times: Language Communities and English Poetry from 1580 to 1660.* Ph.D. diss., University of Pennsylvania.

Ortner, Sherry. 1973. On Key Symbols. *American Anthropologist* 75:1338–1346.

Parnel, James. 1675. *A Collection of the Several Writings [of] James Parnel.* N.p.

Payne, John. 1655. *A Discovery of the Priests.* London.

Penington, Isaac. 1863. *The Works of Isaac Penington.* 4 vols. Philadelphia.

Penn, William. [1694]. *The Rise and Progress of the People Called Quakers.* Philadelphia: Friends Book Store.

1865. *No Cross, No Crown*. Philadelphia.

Penney, Norman. 1907. *First Publishers of Truth*. London: Friends Historical Society.

Reay, Barry. 1980a. Social Origins of Early Quakerism. *Journal of Interdisciplinary History* 11:55–72.

1980b. Popular Hostility Towards Quakers in Mid-Seventeenth-Century England. *Social History* 5:387–407.

1980c. Quaker Opposition to Tithes, 1652–1660. *Past and Present*, no. 86, pp. 98–120.

Richards, I. A. 1936. *The Philosophy of Rhetoric*. London: Oxford University Press.

Richardson, John. 1867. *An Account of the Life, Ministry and Travels of . . . John Richardson*. Philadelphia.

Rigge, Ambrose. 1678. *A Brief and Serious Warning*. London.

Roberts, John M., and Forman, Michael L. 1972. Riddles: Expressive Models of Interrogation. In *Directions in Sociolinguistics: The Ethnography of Communication*. John J. Gumperz and Dell Hymes, eds. New York: Holt, Rinehart & Winston.

Rosenberg, Bruce. 1970. *The Art of the Folk Preacher*. New York: Oxford University Press.

Sacks, Harvey; Schegloff, Emanuel; and Jefferson, Gail. 1974. A Simplest Systematics for the Organization of Turn-Taking for Conversation. *Language* 50:696–735.

Salmond, Anne. 1975. Mana Makes the Man: A Look at Maori Oratory and Politics. In *Political Language and Oratory in Traditional Society*. Maurice Bloch, ed. New York: Academic Press.

Samarin, William J. 1965. Language of Silence. *Practical Anthropology* 12:115–119.

1967. *Field Linguistics*. New York: Holt, Rinehart & Winston.

1972. *Tongues of Men and Angels*. New York: Macmillan.

ed. 1976. *Language in Religious Practice*. Rowley, Mass.: Newbury House.

Samuel, Raphael. 1980. On the Methods of History Workshop: A Reply. *History Workshop*, no. 9, pp. 162–176.

Sapir, J. David. 1977. The Anatomy of Metaphor. In *The Social Use of Metaphor*. J. David Sapir and J. Christopher Crocker, eds. Philadelphia: University of Pennsylvania Press.

Schegloff, Emanuel, and Sacks, Harvey. 1973. Opening up Closings. *Semiotica* 8:289–327.

Sebeok, Thomas A. 1976. Six Species of Signs: Some Propositions and Strictures. In *Contributions to the Doctrine of Signs*. Bloomington, Ind.: Research Center for Language and Semiotic Studies.

Sewel, William. 1867. *The History of the Rise, Increase, and Progress of the Christian People Called Quakers*. 2 vols. Philadelphia.

Sewell, William H. 1980. *Work and Revolution in France: The Language of Labor from the Old Regime to 1848*. Cambridge: Cambridge University Press.

Sherzer, Joel. 1977. The Ethnography of Speaking: A Critical Appraisal. In *Linguistics and Anthropology* (Georgetown University Round Table on Languages and Linguistics 1977). Muriel Saville-Troike, ed. Washington, D.C.: Georgetown University Press.

Sherzer, Joel, and Darnell, Regna. 1972. Outline Guide for the Ethnographic Study of Speech Use. In *Directions in Sociolinguistics: The Ethnography of Communication*. John Gumperz and Dell Hymes, eds. New York: Holt, Rinehart & Winston.

Shewen, William. 1830. *The True Christian's Faith and Experience*. Philadelphia.

Sinclair, J. McH., and Coulthard, R. M. 1975. *Towards an Analysis of Discourse*. London: Oxford University Press.

Smith, William. 1663. *The Work of God's Power in Man*. London.

Sontag, Susan. 1969. The Aesthetics of Silence. In *Styles of Radical Will*. New York: Farrar, Straus.

Speizman, Milton D., and Kronick, Jane C. 1975. A Seventeenth-Century Quaker Women's Declaration. *Signs* 1:231–245.

Spufford, Margaret. 1974. *Contrasting Communities*. Cambridge: Cambridge University Press.

Staves, Susan. 1979. *Players' Scepters: Fictions of Authority in the Restoration*. Lincoln: University of Nebraska Press.

Steiner, George. 1978. A Note on the Distribution of Discourse. *Semiotica* 22:185–209.

Stirredge, Elizabeth. 1810. *Strength in Weakness Manifest in the Life . . . of . . . Elizabeth Stirredge*. Philadelphia.

Stone, Lawrence. 1979. The Revival of Narrative: Reflections on a New Old History. *Past and Present*, no. 85, pp. 3–24.

Story, Christopher. 1829. *A Brief Account of the Life . . . of . . . Christopher Story*. London.

Strathern, Andrew. 1975. Veiled Speech in Mount Hagen. In *Political Language and Oratory in Traditional Society*. Maurice Bloch, ed. New York: Academic Press.

Swartz, Marc J.; Turner, Victor; and Tuden, Arthur. 1966. *Political Anthropology*. Chicago: Aldine.

Symonds, Thomas. 1656. *The Voyce of the Just Uttered*. N.p.

Taylor, Thomas. [166]. *A Faithful Warning to Outside Professors*. N.p.

Tedlock, Dennis. 1972. On the Translation of Style in Oral Narrative. In *Toward New Perspectives in Folklore*. Américo Paredes and Richard Bauman, eds. Austin: University of Texas Press.

Thomas, Keith. 1958. Women and the Civil War Sects. *Past and Present*, no. 13 (April), pp. 42–61.

⸻ 1971. *Religion and the Decline of Magic*. New York: Scribner.

Thompson, T. 1675. *The Quakers' Quibbles in Three Parts*. London.

Turner, Victor. 1974. *Dramas, Fields and Metaphors*. Ithaca, N.Y.: Cornell University Press.

⸻ 1975. Symbolic Studies. In *Annual Review of Anthropology*, vol. 4. Bernard J. Siegel, ed. Palo Alto, Calif.: Annual Reviews.

Tyler, Stephen A. 1969. *Cognitive Anthropology*. New York: Holt, Rinehart & Winston.

van Gennep, Arnold. 1960. *Rites of Passage*. Chicago: University of Chicago Press.

Vann, Richard T. 1969. *The Social Development of English Quakerism, 1655–1755*. Cambridge, Mass.: Harvard University Press.

Vipont, Elfrida. 1975. *George Fox and the Valiant Sixty*. London: Hamish Hamilton.

Walker, Harold E. 1952. The Conception of a Ministry in the Quaker Movement and a Survey of Its Development. Ph.D. diss., University of Edinburgh.

Watts, Michael. 1978. *The Dissenters*: vol. I, *From the Reformation to the French Revolution*. Oxford: Clarendon Press.

Webber, Joan. 1968. *The Eloquent "I": Style and Self in Seventeenth-Century Prose*. Madison: University of Wisconsin Press.

———. 1971. Stylistics: A Bridging of Life and Art in Seventeenth-Century Studies. *New Literary History* 2:283–296.

Weber, Max. 1946. The Protestant Sects and the Spirit of Capitalism. In *From Max Weber: Essays in Sociology*. H. H. Gerth and C. Wright Mills, eds. New York: Oxford University Press.

———. 1958. *The Protestant Ethic and the Spirit of Capitalism*. New York: Scribner.

———. 1978. *Economy and Society*. 2 vols. Guenther Roth and Claus Wittich, eds. Berkeley and Los Angeles: University of California Press.

Whitehead, George. 1832. *Memoirs of George Whitehead*. 2 vols. Philadelphia.

Whitehead, John. 1852. *The Life and Writings of John Whitehead*. London.

Wildeblood, Joan, and Brinson, Peter. 1965. *The Polite World: A Guide to English Manners and Deportment for the Thirteenth to the Nineteenth Century*. London: Oxford University Press.

Williams, Cyril G. 1981. *Tongues of the Spirit: A Study of Pentecostal Glossolalia and Related Phenomena*. Cardiff: University of Wales Press.

Williams, George H. 1962. *The Radical Reformation*. Philadelphia: Westminster Press.

Wilson, Bryan R. 1967. *Patterns of Sectarianism*. London: Heinemann.

———. 1970. *Religious Sects*. London: Weidenfeld & Nicolson.

Yinger, J. Milton. 1970. *The Scientific Study of Religion*. New York: Macmillan.

Zaretsky, Irving, and Leone, Mark P. 1974. *Religious Movements in Contemporary America*. Princeton: Princeton University Press.

INDEX